Wh[...]

This shadowy [...] [fi]gure who refuses to be interviewed or photographed . . . who—in a scene that might have come from one of his own books—was represented at the 1973 National Book Awards by a stand-up comedian . . . ?

Whoever Pynchon is, his three novels have been among the most widely discussed and acclaimed books of our time. Pynchon has been compared to James Joyce and to Vladimir Nabokov, to the Keystone Kops and to the Marx Brothers . . .

In *Thomas Pynchon,* Joseph W. Slade explores the incredible range and complexity of Pynchon's fiction and traces the development and continuity of his major themes.

Thomas Pynchon is the fifth volume in a series of critical appreciations called WRITERS FOR THE SEVENTIES.

WRITERS FOR THE SEVENTIES

Thomas Pynchon by Joseph W. Slade
Kurt Vonnegut, Jr. by Peter J. Reed
Richard Brautigan by Terence Malley
Hermann Hesse by Edwin F. Casebeer
J.R.R. Tolkien by Robley Evans

General Editor: Terence Malley,
Long Island University

Published by
WARNER PAPERBACK LIBRARY

Thomas Pynchon

by Joseph W. Slade

Long Island University

WARNER
PAPERBACK
LIBRARY

A Warner Communications Company

Acknowledgments

From "Entropy," "Low-lands," "The Secret Integration," "A Journey into the Mind of Watts," "Mortality and Mercy in Vienna" by Thomas Pynchon. Copyright © 1960, 1964, 1966 by Thomas Pynchon. Reprinted by permission of Candida Donadio & Associates, Inc.

From *The Crying of Lot 49* by Thomas Pynchon. Copyright © 1966, 1965 by Thomas Pynchon. Reprinted by permission of J. B. Lippincott Company.

From *V* by Thomas Pynchon. Copyright © 1961, 1963 by Thomas Pynchon. Reprinted by permission of J. B. Lippincott Company.

From *Gravity's Rainbow* by Thomas Pynchon. Copyright © 1973 by Thomas Pynchon. Reprinted by permission of The Viking Press, Inc.

From *Loss of the Self* by Wylie Sypher. Copyright © 1962 by Wylie Sypher. Reprinted by permission of Random House, Inc.

From *The Roots of Coincidence* by Arthur Koestler. Copyright © 1972 by Arthur Koestler. Reprinted by permission of Random House, Inc.

From *Duine Elegies* by Rainer Maria Rilke. Translation and Commentary by J. B. Leishman and Stephen Spender. Copyright 1939 by W. W. Norton & Company, Inc. Copyright renewed 1967 by Stephen Spender and J. B. Leishman. Reprinted by permission of W. W. Norton & Company, Inc.

From *Sonnets To Orpheus* by Rainer Maria Rilke. Translation by M. D. Herter Norton. Copyright 1942 by W. W. Norton & Company, Inc. Copyright renewed 1970 by M. D. Herter Norton. Reprinted by permission of W. W. Norton & Company, Inc.

From *Communication, The Social Matrix of Psychiatry* by Jurgen Ruesch, M.D., and Gregory Bateson. Copyright © 1968, 1951 by W. W. Norton & Company, Inc. Reprinted by permission of W. W. Norton & Company, Inc.

Lines from *The Waste Land* by T. S. Eliot. Reprinted by permission of Harcourt Brace Jovanovich, Inc.

From "The Mathematics of Communications" by Warren Weaver. Copyright © 1949 by Scientific American, Inc. All rights reserved. Reprinted by permission of *Scientific American*.

From *History of Science* by Sir William Dampier. Reprinted by permission of Cambridge University Press.

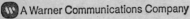

*For Cathy, of course—though she
never takes anything for granted*

CONTENTS

FOREWORD

Thomas Pynchon: A Writer for the Seventies

Thomas Pynchon, by Joseph W. Slade, is the fifth volume in a series of critical appreciations under the collective title, "Writers for the Seventies." Previous volumes in this series are *Kurt Vonnegut, Jr.,* by Peter J. Reed; *Richard Brautigan,* by Terence Malley; *Hermann Hesse,* by Edwin F. Casebeer; and *J.R.R. Tolkien,* by Robley Evans.

The intention of these studies is to provide clear and balanced discussions of the main themes and techniques of the authors in question. In each case, the critic has tried to avoid excessively technical, academic terminology. In general—though of course this varies from book to book—the critics have addressed their subjects directly or even personally, without the sort of detachment that makes so many critical studies seem remote. Hopefully, the volumes in the Writers for the Seventies series will serve as good introductions to the authors under discussion, for readers only slightly familiar with their books, while offering fresh insights for those who have already read the authors' major works.

Perhaps the most impressive thing about Thomas

Pynchon is the incredible breadth of his knowledge. It seems almost impossible that a writer still in his thirties could *know* so much. It is even more difficult to believe that any writer could assimilate so much in his fiction —and could treat it all with such authority, with such a sure sense of what Ernest Hemingway called "the way it was." Genocidal war in South West Africa or arcane global diplomacy in Alexandria; how it feels to sit waiting for a V-2 rocket to land or how it feels to learn that beneath the taken-for-granted business-as-usual America an organized counter culture of losers may be operating; from a sailors' bar in Norfolk in the 1950s to the Berkeley protest movement in the 1960s, from the bitterly determined German Left in the 1920s to a whacked-out South American anarchist movement in the 1940s—in reading Pynchon it often appears that he could make use of anything; indeed, it sometimes appears that he *has* made use of virtually everything.

Virtually everything, that is, affecting us in our sinister twentieth century, this period that Henry Miller has described as "the time of the assassins." Pynchon's three novels could be considered an extended meditation on the twentieth century. When did we go wrong? Where did we go wrong? Why did we go wrong? How did we get here and where do we go from here? In their different voices, these are the questions of Herbert Stencil, Oedipa Maas, and the brooding narrator of *Gravity's Rainbow*.

Although Pynchon's themes are directly and immediately relevant to our experience, his work presents formidable difficulties. More than any of the previous authors in the Writers for the Seventies series Pynchon requires explication. For one thing, the fantastically diverse elements of Pynchon's world are bewilderingly interconnected. A throwaway detail on an early page of one of Pynchon's novels is likely to grow into a central motif by the end of the book. Like Milton Gloaming— a very minor character in *Gravity's Rainbow*—Pynchon could be said to have a mind that is "always gathering correspondences. . . ."

Moreover, in common with such American contemporaries as Kurt Vonnegut, John Barth, and Donald

Barthelme, Pynchon is deeply interested in the effects of science and technology in our world. But, far more than any of these writers, Pynchon has made the discoveries of modern experimental psychology, physics, chemistry, and cybernetics crucial elements in his fiction. As I said before, Pynchon seems to know virtually everything, and one of the things he knows is what's been going on in the laboratories of the twentieth century.

Obviously, in order to write about Pynchon's work, one must know a lot too. In *Thomas Pynchon,* Joseph W. Slade explains lucidly the numerous scientific theories and technological practices referred to—sometimes obliquely—in Pynchon's work. In so doing, Professor Slade also shows Pynchon's profoundly ambivalent attitude toward modern science and technology. In addition, Slade elucidates Pynchon's complex view of history and his very extensive use of literary traditions.

At the same time, however, Slade does not lose Pynchon's zany, even lunatic humor. For, among so many other things, it must be said that Pynchon is one of the funniest writers America has produced. If Pynchon's highs take us into the abstruse realm of Einsteinian physics or into the mythic angelology of Rilke's *Duino Elegies,* his lows take us into a bizarre game of Strip Botticelli or hit us (quite literally) with a cream pie in the face. As with Melville or Joyce—or Shakespeare—there is nothing too corny, vulgar, goofy for Pynchon to try. Sometimes his characters even break into song; as Neal Cassady once said of Jack Kerouac, "what is too foolish to be said is sung." If at times in *Gravity's Rainbow* we seem to hear the celestial music of the spheres, we more often hear "a kazoo, playing a tune of astounding tastelessness."

This is a book for people who read *The Crying of Lot 49* and then wondered what the hell it was all about (a great deal, as Professor Slade brings out); for those who bogged down in the labyrinthine quest for V or who got lost in the Zone. Clearly and perceptively, Joseph Slade shows us what Pynchon's books are about, how they work, how he has developed as a writer.

This is also a book for anyone interested in contemporary American literature. Slade makes a convincing case for Pynchon as one of the major writers the United States has produced. A writer for the seventies, yes, but also for the eighties, the nineties . . . as many decades as you want to count.

Terence Malley
Long Island University
Brooklyn, New York

PREFACE

Very little is known about Thomas Pynchon, a factor of no small importance to readers enthralled by the mysteries which proliferate in his novels. In this respect he resembles B. Traven and J. D. Salinger, two other writers who have eschewed publicity. Only one photograph of Pynchon has ever been published; recently *New York Magazine* discovered a picture taken when Pynchon was a student at Cornell University. Anyone interested enough to look it up should be advised that it presents a callow, ordinary-looking youth of eighteen; Pynchon is now thirty-seven. Beyond that single journalistic coup, the information about the man is sketchy and not altogether reliable. The biographical details which follow have been pieced together from several sources.

Thomas Ruggles Pynchon was born May 8, 1937, in Glen Cove, on Long Island, the son of an industrial surveyor, Thomas R. Pynchon. At Cornell, which he attended on scholarship, he did exceptionally well academically. There he acquired the usual undergraduate habits of late hours and poor diet, and to judge from his frequent references to Cornell, he seems to have liked the place. An engineering major, he obviously read widely in the humanities as well. At some point he studied under Vladimir Nabokov, who, although an admirer of Pynchon's fiction, does not remember him as a student. Nabokov's wife does; she can recall Pynchon's distinctive handwriting from the papers she graded for her husband.[1] Pynchon took two years off for a hitch in the Navy, from which he drew much of the material for *V.*, his first novel; presumably he served on destroyers, whose fanciful names (the *John E. Badass,* for example) add humor to his narratives. When he returned to Ithaca, he graduated with the Class of 1959. In that year his first published story, "Mortality and Mercy in Vienna," appeared in *Epoch*, the Cornell literary magazine.

A year of bumming around Greenwich Village followed. During that time he wrote several short stories and began *V.* When he sold a section of the novel to *The Noble Savage,* a literary magazine, Lippincott took an option on the book. The following year he found a job in Seattle writing for the house magazine of Boeing Aircraft, which appears to be the model for the Yoyodyne Corporation of his fiction. From Seattle he moved to Mexico, where he finished *V.* This book won the William Faulkner First Novel Award for 1963 and established Pynchon's reputation as a coming author. It also generated interest in Pynchon personally, most of which he avoided by choosing his friends carefully.

One of these was a fellow student at Cornell, Richard Fariña, whose novel *Been Down So Long It Looks Like Up to Me* his friend would compare, in typically Pynchonian fashion, to "the Hallelujah Chorus done by 200 Kazoo players with perfect pitch."[2] To Fariña Pynchon would dedicate his third novel. When Fariña married Mimi Baez, sister of the famous folksinger, Pynchon came to Carmel, California, from Mexico City to be best man, dodging along the way photographers from *Life* magazine. In *Long Time Coming and a Long Time Gone,* published after his untimely death in a motorcycle accident in 1966, Fariña remembered tearing Pynchon away from a copy of *Scientific American* for a trip to the Monterey Fair. There Pynchon appears wearing an old red hunting-jacket and sunglasses, doting on Mexican food at a taco stand, and wincing at John Birchers who tried to pick a fight with Fariña on the midway.

California provided the setting, ambience, and inspiration for Pynchon's second novel, and—again by rumor—he has lived there or in Mexico ever since. *The Crying of Lot 49,* published in 1966, also won a prize, the Rosenthal Foundation Award of the National Institute of Arts and Letters, and clinched Pynchon's standing as a writer of skill and imagination, although hardly any of the critics understood the book. Then, except for an essay on Los Angeles in 1966, seven years of silence followed—broken in 1973 by the publication of the massive *Gravity's Rainbow. Gravity's Rainbow* shared (with I. B. Singer's *A Crown of Feathers and Other Stories)* the National Book Award for that year, but was denied the Pulitzer Prize on grounds of incomprehensibility and obscenity.[3] Numerous critics have called it a masterpiece. Whether one agrees with that assessment or not, *Gravity's Rainbow* has established Pynchon among the most important of American authors. And by any standard, *Gravity's Rainbow* represents the culmination of Pynchon's unique talents.

In future, the first sentence of *Gravity's Rainbow,* "A screaming comes across the sky," may become as famous as the "Call me Ishmael" which opens *Moby Dick.* Thomas Pynchon has been compared to Herman Melville—if only because both men produced a whale of a book—and for that matter to a host of writers, including William Burroughs, Nathanael West, S. J. Perelman, Joseph Heller, John Barth, Vladimir Nabokov, William Gaddis, John Dos Passos, Jorge Luis Borges, James Joyce and half a dozen lesser lights. From the point of view of a critic, the worst part of such comparisons is that none of them are strained, and having acknowledged them, I shall simply ignore most, for to explore them would make this book too lengthy. Doubtless Pynchon himself is amused by criticism which connects him with predecessors and contemporaries; the urge to perceive relationships is precisely his subject matter, and all of his works deal with a passion for design that is at once the glory and insanity of human beings. Besides, because his fictional backgrounds and methods are encyclopedic, the allusions to other writers are there in abundance in his

15

narratives; he is nothing if not a great synthesizer of what he has read.

In the course of this book I shall mention many of the authors and books whose ideas Pynchon has assimilated. I do not intend to say that a beginning reader can not read Pynchon without having first read so-and-so, because Pynchon's touch is so sure that he can captivate those who have not the faintest glimmering of his philosophical or literary framework. Nevertheless, a reader encountering him for the first time might wish to review some of these works: Joseph Conrad's *Heart of Darkness,* T. S. Eliot's *The Waste Land,* Henry Adams's *The Education of Henry Adams,* Max Weber's *The Protestant Ethic and the Spirit of Capitalism,* Machiavelli's *The Prince,* Robert Graves's *The White Goddess,* Goethe's *Faust,* Norbert Wiener's *The Human Use of Human Beings,* Rilke's *Duino Elegies* and *Sonnets to Orpheus,* Wagner's *Tannhäuser, Tristan and Isolde,* and *Ring* operas, and Alfred North Whitehead's *Process and Reality.* Also of benefit is a good history of science, with a bookmark for the pages on thermodynamics, field theory, and quantum theory; A. E. E. McKenzie's *The Major Achievements of Science* is excellent.

If that last reference seems odd, the reader will swiftly learn that Pynchon's enormous learning embraces both of the Two Cultures, and has earned reviews for *Gravity's Rainbow* in *Scientific American* as well as in *The New Yorker.* Those unfamiliar with Pynchon need not fear esoteric applications of science, however; he draws metaphors from classical physics such as another novelist might draw on classical mythology, and in each case the reference can be traced to the appropriate handbook. Whether scientific or humanistic, Pynchon handles the scholarship so evident in his work deftly rather than ponderously. The only warning I feel constrained to offer the beginning reader concerns Pynchon's comedy, which ranges from slapstick to black humor. He can be shameless in his pursuit of laughter, and will purvey the most ancient of chestnuts with a most obvious delight. The narrator of *V.* observes, "There is nothing like old jokes. It's a kind of stability about them: familiar ground." A high tolerance for low puns is also essential, as when the narrator of *Gravity's Rainbow* speaks of hipsters who tatto hexagrams from the *I Ching* on their toes only to find that they can not stay still because of their "I Ching feet." At their best, of course, Pynchon's jokes work wonderfully well, especially when tinged with the near-cosmic madness which is becoming his hallmark, and his occasional lapses can safely be regarded as aberrations of genius.

Since because of his great learning he seems to have sprung full-blown from the core of an IBM 360, it is perhaps absurd to speak of Pynchon as ever having been immature, but there is considerable distance—and even more development—between his early work and *Gravity's Rainbow*. The difference is not so much a matter of subject, although he does not repeat himself overmuch, as of shifted perspectives and altered awareness; ideas and characters are similar from work to work, but they meet each time on new ground. I will try to trace themes accordingly. Where possible, I will summarize plot. Because of their brevity, Pynchon's short pieces are easily recapitulated, and they should be, for they have not been widely reprinted and are not available to the general reader. The novels, however, present formidable difficulties, particularly *Gravity's Rainbow,* which weighs in at 760 pages. With *V.* and *Gravity's Rainbow* I will work in broad outline and fill in gaps as best I can. The longest single chapter goes to the shortest novel, *The Crying of Lot 49,* to illustrate the intricacy of plotting and design which is typical of all of Pynchon's fiction. Concentrating on theme and plot will unfortunately not leave much space for dealing with Pynchon's hyperdense metaphors, his felicities of style, or that humor I have mentioned, but this is only the first of many books I think sure to be written about a writer who surely will write others himself. In this one I use the paperback edition of the novels throughout, and in addition, where reference is made to secondary texts, have chosen the most readily accessible editions I could find.

My thanks to two of my students, Lawrence Doris and Jerold Millendorf, who besides chewing over Pynchon with me also did some of the legwork in tracking down material, and to Millicente Molyneaux, who in addition to typing the manuscript actually read it, more to my profit than hers, since she too made many suggestions. W. T. Lhamon of Florida State University furnished me with information and enthusiasm, and Edward Mendelson of Yale kindly sent me his excellent manuscript on *The Crying of Lot 49*. To them, thanks, and to Joseph Duchac of the Long Island University Library, who kept a stream of articles flowing across my desk.

CHAPTER ONE

Entropy and Other Calamities: Pynchon's Short Pieces

Although Pynchon's reputation thus far rests principally on his three novels, he has also published seven short stories in magazines. In chronological order they are "Mortality and Mercy in Vienna," in *Epoch* (1959); "Low-lands," *New World Writing* (1960); "Entropy," *The Kenyon Review* (1960); "Under the Rose," *The Noble Savage* (1961); "The Secret Integration," *The Saturday Evening Post* (1964); "The World (This One), The Flesh (Mrs. Oedipa Maas), and The Testament of Pierce Inverarity," *Esquire* (1965); and "The Shrink Flips," *Cavalier* (1966). In addition, he has written an essay entitled "A Journey into the Mind of Watts," *The New York Times Magazine* (1966). Of these shorter pieces three are slightly expanded versions of episodes in the novels: "Under the Rose" is taken from *V.*, while both "The World (This One), The Flesh (Mrs. Oedipa Maas), and the Testament of Pierce Inverarity" and "The Shrink Flips" are parts of *The Crying of Lot 49*. They will not be considered here. Those remaining are of interest because they are early examples of Pynchon's work, because they manifest themes—and characters—which appear later in his novels, or because they are significant in their own right. All three reasons justify a close look at Pynchon's first short story.

In "Mortality and Mercy in Vienna," the thirty-year-old protagonist, Cleanth Siegel, thinks of his mind as a memory bank fed by computer cards from which he can recall information to make cocktail party conversation. The metaphor suggests one of Pynchon's most persistent concerns: technology and its relationship to human activity. More important in terms of this story is the recall of the author himself, for Pynchon uses *his* erudition not to make idle chatter but to create the rich stuff of his literature. For example, he borrows the title from "Measure for Measure," one of Shakespeare's least pleasant comedies. In that play Duke Vincentio, aware that Vienna has become a lawless city, deputizes Angelo to clean it up, and gives him the authority to do so, including the power of life and death:

> In our remove be thou at full ourself;
> Mortality and mercy in Vienna
> Live in thy tongue and heart . . . (I, i).

In Pynchon's tale, Cleanth, who is supposed to find his girl friend at a party in Washington, D.C., inadvertently arrives early, meets his host, a Rumanian named David Lupescu, and discovers that they look very much alike. Lupescu too is startled by their Doppelgänger resemblance, and after installing Siegel as host, abandons the party to him, leaving behind a talismanic pig foetus (the first of several pigs in Pynchon's fiction) and these instructions: "As host you are a trinity: (a) receiver of guests"—ticking them off on his fingers—"(b) an enemy and (c) an outward manifestation, for *them*, of the divine body and blood." As an afterthought, as he flees "the jungle," Lupescu blurts, "Mistah Kurtz—he dead." The allusion is critical to understanding of the story. Pynchon is invoking Conrad's "Heart of Darkness," the literal and psychological jungle "where doubt itself is lost in an unexplored universe of incertitudes," to which Kurtz had hoped to bring civilization. Kurtz had been an agent of the International Society for the Suppression of Savage Customs. Siegel is a junior diplomat only recently returned from abroad to Washington, where he now serves on some unnamed commission. Washington, then, or more specifically, the area peopled by Lupescu's friends, would appear to be a "jungle," as in Conrad's tale, or a lawless place like Duke Vincentio's Vienna.

And it may be something else as well. "Mistah Kurtz —he dead" is also the epigraph of T. S. Eliot's "The Hollow Men." That Pynchon intends the double significance of the phrase is clear from additional references to Eliot in the story. Grossman, Siegel's roommate at Harvard, had read Eliot and Santayana as he degenerated from a healthy midwesterner into an effete Harvard type who now lives in Swampscott. Swampscott and Washington are part of an American waste land, Pynchon suggests, and the connection with Eliot's landscape is borne out by Siegel's thinking of himself as a prophet and a healer. By the time the party guests— "The Group"—arrive, singing a limerick about a man named Cheever and a beaver, Siegel in his Kurtz-role has developed "a light-headedness which he realized might be one of the first stages of hysteria but which he rather hoped was some vestige of the old nonchalance which had sustained him on the Continent for the past two years." In such a state he can even regard the limerick as profound.

Siegel is particularly susceptible to hysteria, it would appear, because of his background. He is the son of Catholic and Jewish parents, a genetic religious combination Pynchon will use later for Benny Profane in *V*. To Grossman, his roommate's Jesuitical side had prevented Siegel's being "kicked around or conscious of guilt or simply ineffective like so many of the other Jewish boys on campus." Yet, Grossman had said, "It is the seed of your destruction. . . . House divided against itself." Siegel's dual heritage has led to curious associations on his part. Instead of wanting to become a doctor, like the stereotypical Jewish son, Siegel equates healing with destruction; he remembers "sitting *shivah*" for a dead cousin while her husband cursed her doctor and the AMA.

In another allusion to Eliot, Lupescu designates Siegel a "Fisher of Souls." Siegel soon learns that he shares more than physical resemblance with the departed Rumanian. Something in their natures attracts the confidence of others; and in the past each has served as confidant and confessor for a "host of trodden-on and disaffected" people, the inhabitants of this modern waste land. Both the waste lands and the alienated characters will appear again and again in Pynchon's fiction, most notably in *The Crying of Lot 49*, and how the characters function in their sterile and sometimes hostile environment will become a major question. Siegel is not surprised when one by one the party guests tell him of his similarity to Lupescu and corner him in the Rumanian's "confessional," a bedroom decorated with crossed Browning Automatic Rifles hung on the wall. When Siegel prompts one penitent with a "Bless me father [for I have sinned]," she responds with "David said that too." This mock-priest hears confessions of decadent love affairs and emotional entanglements that increase his hysteria, "synopses and convolutions which should never have been exposed, revealing for Siegel the anatomy of a disease more serious than he had suspected. . . ." The waste land is blighted indeed.

Siegel finds one of the girls both enticing and repellent. A beautiful "sex machine," Debby Considine works for the State Department and has visited many countries, as she confesses to Siegel, there to pick up and later discard various males. Her latest prize and current escort is Irving Loon, an Ojibwa Indian she has acquired on a trip to Ontario. He stands now in a corner of the apartment like a "memento mori, withdrawn and melancholy." His melancholy triggers Siegel's memory banks. The resulting data come from a Harvard anthropology course taught by a professor for whom "all cultures were equally mad; it was only the form that differed, never the content." According to the professor, the Ojibwa live so perpetually on the brink of starvation and extinction that the Indian brave succumbs to paranoia, convinced that the forces of nature are directed against him. Debby Considine has responded to what she, for lack of understanding, refers to as Irving Loon's ability to "come closer to something which city dwellers never find all their lives." Siegel can agree, but he knows what Debby does not: that the paranoia of the Ojibwas culminates in a peculiar psychosis, a personal identification with the Windigo, a destructive, cannibalistic spirit. Once he believes himself to be the Windigo, the starvation-prone Ojibwa comes to regard even his own relatives as "fat juicy beavers," a "host" to be killed and eaten.

Irving has already mentioned the Windigo to Debby, who mindlessly attributes the term to the Indian's "poetic, religious quality." Such language, uttered casually, pushes the "healer and prophet" deeper into hysteria. As soon as Debby introduces her confessor to her lover, Siegel tests his thesis by whispering "Windigo." Irving reacts with weird affection towards Debby, calling her "my beautiful little beaver." The innocently lewd limerick, now sinister, is an early example of Pynchon's skillful manipulation of motifs. Everything connects in his fiction, sometimes with so audible a click that critics accuse him of too great a passion for unity and artificial linkages.

Of all the members of the party, only Siegel knows what to make of the taciturn Indian, and if Irving behaves as anticipated then Siegel in his hysteria believes he has the power "to bring them a very tangible salvation. A miracle involving a host, true, but like no holy eucharist." At this point the allusions to Eliot and Conrad began to swell. Eliot's waste land requires the imposition of a new mythology, a new religion, before it can be cleansed and healed of its sterility. Ironically, Siegel perceives in Irving Loon's primitive paranoia just the kind of healing the waste land needs. It will be a religion of retribution, of apocalypse. Conrad's Kurtz scrawls on his report to the International Society for the Suppression of Savage Customs the ominous words "Exterminate all the brutes." "The miracle *was* in his hands after all," Siegel's Jesuit side says to him: "It

23

was just unfortunate that Irving Loon would be the only one partaking of any body and blood, divine or otherwise." Spurred by Siegel and seen only by him, the Ojibwa takes a rifle down from the wall of Lupescu's bedroom and searches happily for ammunition. Siegel leaves the party without saying anything to the guests sprawled under the pig foetus, and hears the first reports of Irving Loon's celebration of the host from the street outside. By loosing the berserk Indian, he has acted as prophet and healer to the waste land; he has healed its sickness by annihilation.

Pynchon possesses the enviable ability to blend fact and fantasy in such a way that the facts seem less credible than the fantasies. The Windigo psychosis is well documented by anthropologists but appears more preposterous than Lupescu's leaving his party to a stranger or hanging BAR's on his walls. As Pynchon becomes more adept at incorporating his wide knowledge into his stories, the line separating the real and the ridiculous will grow thinner. Of continuing relevance also are several of the motifs of "Mortality and Mercy in Vienna." The weightiest is paranoia, which for Pynchon, as for novelists like Joseph Heller, Ken Kesey, William Burroughs, and Norman Mailer, is a means of perception, a way of restructuring the world. While Irving Loon is probably the most extreme of Pynchon's paranoids, other paranoids in his fiction seem almost reasonable. After all, in an insane world—call it waste land or whatever—paranoia represents an attempt to establish sanity, to create order out of chaos. To believe however erroneously that the world is hostile is to establish a basis for action. A second motif involves an assumed moral superiority of "primitive" cultures over the decadent, "civilized" type. Superseding the Objiwas in later stories will be Maltese and Africans, cultures which have been laid waste by colonialism, but which still retain some spark of vitality. A third motif is a human penchant for annihilation as an alternative to a blighted world. The desire grows out of the "irresistibly fascinating" whisper like that which Kurtz hears in *Heart of Darkness*. As Conrad's Marlowe says of Kurtz's whisper, "it echoed loudly within him because he was hollow at the core. . . ."¹¹ Cleanth Siegel suffers from a void within, and his whisper is amplified by the perception of a void without; Siegel and his successors in Pynchon's work can not tolerate such a vacuum.

While the mood of "Mortality and Mercy in Vienna" is somber, that of Pynchon's second story, "Lowlands," is deliberately funny, marking the advent of what is usually called his black humor, a label which Bruce Jay Friedman defines—very appropriately, since Pynchon's story concerns a sailor—as sailing "into darker waters somewhere out beyond satire."¹² The definition is doubly appropriate if one should regard T. S. Eliot's *The Waste Land* as satire, for "Low-lands" is almost a parody of that poem.

"Low-lands" differs from "Mortality and Mercy" in other respects also. Unlike Cleanth Siegel, Dennis Flange, the protagonist of "Low-lands," retreats into passivity. His stasis is one of the things that makes the story less than successful, but from it Pynchon will learn to use multiple plots to carry his themes. In some ways Dennis Flange anticipates Benny Profane; he has the earmarks of the schlemihl. Actually he is more the prototype for the disaffected husband who appears as Roony Winsome in *V.* and as Mucho Maas in *The Crying of Lot 49*. A lawyer in the firm of Wasp and that (presumably) same Winsome, Flange has been married—childlessly—for seven years to a respectability-seeking wife, Cindy. Over the years they have drifted apart, an impasse for which Flange blames Cindy, although he is aware of the ironies of his having been a communications officer in the Navy. The whole problem, he believes, is somehow Freudian, an interpretation promoted by Flange's mad psychiatrist, Geronimo Diaz—another prototype, this time for Dr. Hilarius of *The Crying of Lot 49* and the insane scientists and healers of "The White Visitation" in *Gravity's Rainbow*—who claims that he is Paganini and that he has made a pact with the devil which has cost him his genius with the violin. Diaz's sessions with Flange consist chiefly of his serving his patient endless martinis and reading from "random-number tables from the Ebbinghaus nonsense syllable lists, ignoring everything that Flange would be trying to tell him." Such practices, taken together with Flange's former occupation in the Navy, are early indications of Pynchon's preoccupation with communication and information theory. Diaz's madness, however, is of "no known model or pattern," and Flange finds that his visits are a necessary corrective to a life too conventional and too rational.

Flange perceives that since his hitch in the Navy the routines of his life have eroded the romantic image he once held of himself as a stalwart Officer of the Deck, "fortune's elf-child and disinherited darling, young and randy and more a Jolly Jack Tar than anyone human could possibly be." Gradually he has regressed into passivity, becoming more and more fetal. His house, which he calls his "womb with a view," perches on a cliff overlooking Long Island Sound. It is a curious structure rising out of a tumulus of earth; beneath it are secret subterranean passages built by rum-runners during Prohibition. House and honeycombed tunnels form an "almost organic mound" to which Flange feels joined as if by umbilical cord, a place where he can practice "molemanship." Throughout Pynchon's work, undergrounds both literal and metaphorical are recurrent motifs. Tunnels and sewers appear in his early efforts as psychological and metaphysical arcs, as negative parabolas which will have a positive counterpart in the parabola of the V-2 rocket in *Gravity's Rainbow*. While Flange has tried to think of the house as a bower, and himself and Cindy as happy birds in it, it has not worked out that way. Cindy is too cold, too logical; she likes paintings by Mondrian, whose angled landscapes contrasts markedly with the surfaces Flange encounters later in the story. Theirs has been a sterile marriage.

A second motif in "Low-lands" evolves more slowly and eventually gives the story its title. It is a complex and ambiguous motif borrowed from Eliot. Flange, his memory pitched at the 30° list of a heaving vessel, dreams of the sea. There his Doppelgänger strides the rolling deck. The sea, Geronimo Diaz fatuously tells him, is mother to us all, since it generated life and still in a sense flows through human veins. So strong is Flange's affinity for the ocean that he cannot even tell a sea story when his buddies do, believing that

> if you are Dennis Flange and if the sea's tides are the same that not only wash along your veins but also billow through your fantasies then it is all right to listen to but not tell stories about that sea, because you and the truth of a true lie were thrown sometime way back into a curious contiguity and as long as you are passive you can remain aware of the truth's extent but the minute you become active you are somehow, if not violating a truth outright, at least screwing up the perspective of things, much as anyone observing sub-atomic particles changes the works, data and odds, by the act of observing.

This invoking of the Heisenberg principle of physics, this refusal or inability to become involved—which is one of the things he admires about his psychiatrist—is the key to Flange's personality, as it is to those of many other characters in Pynchon's stories. Flange's attitude is an assertion of passivity, a willingness to take events as they happen, to withdraw from participation. An obvious symbol for such passivity is the womb, but to it Pynchon here somewhat clumsily links another, the sea. In one respect, the sea suggests the amniotic fluid in which the fetus floats and the security the womb offers. At the same time the sea is dangerous: It can drown victims. Still a third aspect affects Flange, however. In his irrational moments he thinks of the sea as a "low-lands," a term he remembers from a sea-chanty. Viewed at certain times, the ocean seems "a waste land which stretches away to the horizon," a plain or desert which requires but one human figure "for completeness." Flange has come to think of his life as a flat surface, with "an assurance of perfect, passionless uniformity"; what he fears most is a convexity, a bulging of the planet's curvature that would leave him exposed. This vision of a flat surface, of course, is of a sea without water—in short, Eliot's waste land, arid and sterile. Flange imagines himself walking across this flat, solid sea from city to city. His psychiatrist considers this fantasy "a bizarre variation on the messiah complex," but Diaz, as might be expected, is only partly correct. Flange is the traveler of the waste land, similar to the protagonist of Eliot's poem, the man who draws the Tarot card of the Phoenician Sailor.

On the day of the story Flange has stayed home from work to drink wine and listen to Vivaldi with Rocco Squarcione, the local garbageman. Offended, Cindy stomps around upstairs, but at least leaves them alone; Flange wonders how anyone can stand a house without a second story. Cindy hits the ceiling, however, when another old buddy arrives. This is Pig Bodine, one of the best and most ubiquitous of Pynchon's minor characters, the all-round pervert and good natured if slightly sinister slob that his name implies. Cindy despises him, for good reason; on her wedding night Bodine had inveigled Dennis into having a few beers, and she had not heard from them until two weeks later, when her husband wired her from Cedar Rapids, Iowa. Now, fed up with his friends and his habits, she throws them all out and tells Flange not to come back. He goes docilely. "Maybe if they had had kids . . .," he speculates only briefly.

In his garbage truck Rocco drives Bodine and Flange to the city dump, where the nightwatchman, a Negro named Bolingbroke, will put them up for the night. Pynchon borrows this name from Shakespeare to suggest mock royalty (Bolingbroke became Henry IV). Bolingbroke is a rootless former sailor of wide travel, having come into brief and comic contact with the absurdities of colonialism—another example of Pynchon's incipient interest in imperialism and injustice—before he retired to the dump. More to the point, Bolingbroke is king of the waste land; to Flange the dump is "an island or enclave in the dreary country around it, a discrete kingdom with Bolingbroke its uncontested ruler." Flange immediately perceives the predictable correspondence: The dump is a "low-lands." It is fifty feet below ground level but is inevitably rising as garbage fills it. This "fatedness" seizes and terrifies him, for it reminds him of his fear of convexity. He compares the gradual rise to a "maddeningly slow elevator . . . carrying you toward a known level to confer with some inevitable face on matters which had already been decided." By the time Pynchon writes *Gravity's Rainbow,* the accretion of debris or detritus will serve as his principal metaphor for the history of civilization. It is a frightening image: the waste land, in this case a literal one, sifting deeper and deeper in accumulated sterility.

Rocco leaves; Bolingbroke finds Pig and Dennis mattresses from a huge mountain of discarded household goods, the cast-off trash of a civilization, and then herds them into his ramshackle house with strange haste. Once inside, they begin the rather adolescent boozing which passes for camaraderie in so much of Pynchon's work. As they swap stories, Pynchon pulls out the stops in his eagerness to find amusing—if fuzzy —parallels for Eliot's *The Waste Land.* On his travels Bolingbroke has had an affair with a woman named Zenobia, a substitute for Eliot's Dido and Cleopatra. Allusions to Dante also echo Eliot's: Bolingbroke had once shipped on an Italian merchantman where he "shoveled coal as if into the fires of hell." For his part, in lieu of Eliot's Hanged Man, Dennis contributes a tale of a fraternity house escapade which ended with a stolen female cadaver hanging out of a window. When they have finished their muscatel, they turn in, but not before Bolingbroke warns the others not to pay attention to the gypsies who prowl the dump at night. His fear of them has caused him to put a strong lock on the door.

Some hours later Flange is awakened by a siren voice (Eliot: "voices singing out of empty cisterns and exhausted wells") calling to his Doppelgänger image of himself, as an "Anglo" with blond hair. Outside, before he can see who is calling, he trips one of Bolingbroke's booby-traps (laid for the gypsies), and disappears under a falling mountain of snow-tires. He is revived by a beautiful "angel," a girl only three and a half feet tall, who leads him to her home, a chamber deep underneath the dump reached by tunnels leading, ironically, from an abandoned GE refrigerator. The tunnel complex, complete with electricity stolen from the Long Island Lighting Company, she tells him, was built in the thirties by the Sons of the Red Apocalypse (the first of Pynchon's secret underground conspiracies) in preparation for revolution. When Federal agents arrested them all, the gypsies moved in.

The girl's name is Nerissa, which may also derive from Shakespeare (*The Merchant of Venice*), or Pynchon may be playing on "Nereids," the nymphs of the sea. Who she really is becomes apparent when she introduces Flange to her pet rat—the prototype of the rat Veronica in *V*. The rat's name is Hyacinth, and Nerissa is clearly the hyacinth girl of "The Burial of the Dead" section of *The Waste Land*. Nerissa wants Flange to be her husband; she had been told by a fortune teller named Violetta—Eliot's Madame Sosostris—that she would wed an Anglo like him. Flange considers. Noticing that Nerissa looks like a child, and the rat *her* child, he wonders again why he and Cindy never had children. He decides to stay:

> A child makes it all right. Let the world shrink to a *boccie* ball.
> So of course he knew.

What he knows is not entirely clear. In Eliot's poem, the protagonist encounters the hyacinth girl in this passage:

> "You gave me hyacinths first a year ago;
> They called me the hyacinth girl."
> —Yet when we came back, late, from the Hyacinth garden,
> Your arms full, and your hair wet, I could not
> Speak, and my eyes failed, I was neither
> Living nor dead, and I knew nothing,
> Looking into the heart of light, the silence.
> *Oed' und leer das meer* [Waste and empty the sea].

Pynchon's story ends with Nerissa holding the rat Hyacinth in her arms and with Flange visualizing her in terms of sea images: "White caps danced across her eyes; sea creatures, he knew, would be cruising about in the submarine green of her heart." Of possible relevance also is the passage immediately following the one just quoted from *The Waste Land*. There Madame Sosostris tells the fortune of Eliot's protagonist. When he draws the Tarot card of the Phoenician Sailor, she predicts death by drowning, as a sacrifice for the redemption of the Waste Land.

Probably by intention on Pynchon's part, several interpretations are possible. Eliot's waste land suffers from failures of communication and love. Similar failures afflict Flange, and the dump, Pynchon's waste land, symbolizes his life. The dump is not a particularly good paradigm, however. As Eliot himself would say, it is not an "objective correlative" for Flange's condition, if only because we know too little about him, but it does represent an amusing and imaginative attempt to unite the motifs of water and waste made so famous by Eliot's poem. At the conclusion of "Low-lands," Nerissa, who has much in common with the loving females Pynchon will develop later, offers Flange love, admiration for the image he has of himself, and the potentiality of fertility, although the rat, an indication of decay and disease in *The Waste Land,* is here at best a mocking promise. No real healing or redemption seems forthcoming, even if one assumes that Flange has symbolically died—drowned or buried by the falling snow tires—and risen; he is a miserable Messiah. Given his essential passivity, given his resemblance to other schlemihls in Pynchon's work, it is more likely that he has simply exchanged a "womb with a view" for a womb with no view at all, where, deep underneath the waste land, he is neither "living nor dead." He prefers withdrawal underground to the void, the emptiness above. Flange is inert—paralyzed by surfaces, surfaces Pynchon will convert into endless streets in his later fiction.

One of Pynchon's admirers, Richard Poirier, has observed that "the signal 'self-destruct' might be said to flash whenever a reader of Pynchon presses too confidently at the point where he thinks he's located the 'meaning.'" Although usually the ambiguity adds to appreciation, in "Low-lands" it seems merely the confusion of the author, the product of inexperience infatuated with cleverness of the type which, as Burton Feldman says, renders Black Humor frequently too academic.[5] Pynchon himself has Fausto Maijstral remark in *V.* that "Shakespeare and T. S. Eliot ruined us all." Although the story is pleasantly nutty, "Low-lands" is much less accomplished than "Mortality and Mercy in Vienna." In the latter, Pynchon's literary allusions bear the weight of his ambiguity without effort. In "Low-lands," because he too closely adapts Eliot's motifs, themselves very complex and ambiguous, the result is fuzziness. Moreover, the story is essentially static; at the end Flange returns full circle to a fetal state, and the plot does not advance. Nevertheless, elements of "Low-lands" presage motifs and incidents in Pynchon's later work: failures of communication, underground networks, oddballs who enjoy Vivaldi, loving females, images of history, midgets. Considered together, the first two stories exemplify the extremes of responses to the waste land of modern civilization: a desire for annihilation, for one's self or for others; and a desire for withdrawal, in order to protect one's self against the waste land's encroachment.

With "Entropy," Henry Adams displaces T. S. Eliot as Pynchon's principal literary creditor, although references to de Sade, Faulkner, and Djuna Barnes crop up as well. If "Low-lands" demonstrates that the saturation of one's work with allusions to the work of others is tricky business, "Entropy" reestablishes the method as a valid artistic approach. In a philosophical sense, Pynchon would say, we are all influenced by cultural history, so that what others have thought and written effects us in many ways. Pynchon differs from most similarly oriented writers in one important respect, however: He is just as insistent on the cultural value of the sciences as of the humanities, and in "Entropy" he makes far-reaching allusions to both. Willard Gibbs and Ludwig Boltzmann are juxtaposed brilliantly with Henry Adams and Henry Miller. From Miller, Pynchon borrows a metaphor; "Entropy" begins with an epigraph from *Tropic of Cancer* in which Miller speaks of this age's depressing cultural and metaphysical climate as inclement weather:

> There will be more calamities, more death, more despair.
> Not the slightest indication of a change anywhere. . . .
> We must get into step, a lockstep toward the prison of death. There is no escape. The weather will not change.

With this metaphor Pynchon associates a second, from *The Education of Henry Adams*: the concept of entropy as historical process. Adams in turn had developed the concept from the work of the American physicist Willard Gibbs. By updating Gibbs with references to Boltzmann and Rudolf Clausius, who with Gibbs contributed to theories of chemical and physical equilibrium, Pynchon can make use of entropy as a term denoting the unavailability of energy in thermodynamic processes.

The classic formulations of these processes are the three Laws of Thermodynamics. The first states that heat can be converted into work (and work into heat), that the amount of work is always equal to the amount of heat, that heat can always be expressed in terms of energy, and that the amount of heat in a closed system is always constant. The first law is commonly known as the Principle of the Conservation of Energy: Energy cannot be created or destroyed. The third law states that every substance has a definite availability of energy to do work that approaches zero as the temperature approaches absolute zero. As energy becomes unavailable, the entropy will increase. For the purposes of Adams and Pynchon, the second law is the most important; it states that when a free exchange of heat takes place between two bodies as a self-sustaining and continuous process, the heat must always be transferred from the hotter to the colder body. In other words, the entropy is irreversible; it will always increase until the two bodies are uniformly cold, and without any remaining energy.

From his study of thermodynamics Rudolf Clausius perceived an analogy between heat-systems and the universe itself, as Sir William Dampier explains in *A History of Science:*

> Mechanical work can only be obtained from heat when heat passes from a hot body to a cold one. This process tends to diminish the difference of temperature, which is also diminished by conduction of heat, friction, and other irreversible processes. The availability of energy in an irreversible system is always becoming less, and its converse—the quantity called by Clausius the entropy—is always tending to a maximum. Thus the energy of an isolated system, and therefore (it was assumed) of the Universe, is slowly passing into heat, uniformly distributed and therefore unavailable as a source of useful work. Eventually, it was thought, by this dissipation of energy the Universe must become motionless and dead.[6]

Clausius predicted that "heat-death" would occur when everything in the universe reached the same temperature, a prophecy Adams and Pynchon extend to human society, which is also a system. According to Adams, over history entropy increases; the world is running down. One manifestation of an increase in entropy is mounting chaos within the system as energy begins to disperse more and more randomly. Systems in good repair function in an orderly fashion, but as they succumb to entropy, order falls victim to chaos. Somewhat paradoxically, another manifestation of increasing energy, depending on the kind of system, is greater homogeneity among the system's parts. Healthy systems encompass diverse elements in relationship to one another, but as entropy increases, these elements lose their differentiation. Thus it is possible to speak of entropy as a measure of disorganization and unpredictability, and also as a measure of sameness and conformity.

But there are other kinds of systems and another kind of entropy. Complicating Pynchon's story is his introduction of communication theory. Within a communication system, many things can cause information to deteriorate; the effect of distortion and noise, say when two people are speaking on a telephone, can act like friction and conduction on energy within a thermodynamic system. In communication theory, entropy also represents the decay or loss of information, although the ramifications of the term grow complex. In *The Crying of Lot 49,* Pynchon explores the abstruse relationship between communication theory and thermodynamics; in "Entropy," the term entropy in communications serves merely as counterpoint to the term as applied to the running down of the universe and society.

"Entropy" is skillfully constructed around the interlocking metaphors of weather and entropy in its double sense. Its structure can be visualized—by an analogy Pynchon would appreciate—as parallel vectors pointing in opposite directions. The two tracks provide compression and tension for the narrative. On one floor of a Washington, D. C., apartment house Meatball Mulligan's lease-breaking party, now in its second day, has been disintegrating into chaos steadily augmented by newly-arriving guests. In this respect, the party as a system is not exactly closed, since people do enter and leave, but Pynchon may be suggesting that social systems are not entirely isolated; that would seem to be the point, that Meatball does not try to wall himself off from the outside. By contrast, on the floor above a man named Callisto has perfected an ordered existence in a hermetically-sealed, ecologically stable flat at cost of isolation from the world. In fact, Callisto's apartment is a small-scale jungle, a "hothouse" in which he lives with a girl named Aubade, of French and Annamese ancestry—by which Pynchon may be hinting at exploitation by a technological colonialism. They do not go out, since Callisto fears the outside. He worries about the "heat-death" of the universe, a fixation abetted at the time of the story by the weather. For three days the mercury has registered 37 degrees outside; the weather will not change. Paranoiacally Callisto seizes on the phenomenon as an omen of the end.

The significance of the story's title is amplified in Callisto's ruminations, which are interspersed with the events of the party below. Callisto has awakened holding a sick bird; he has been nestling the creature against himself for three days, trying to revive it with heat from his own body and forestall the heat-death that comes to all things. The bird's illness is a microcosmic event in Callisto's world, for he has ordered his life and his environment into "a tiny enclave of regularity in the city's chaos, alien to the vagaries of the weather, of national politics, of any civil disorder." He is resisting entropy with a kind of love. It is the first such linkage of love and power in Pynchon's fiction:

> Henry Adams, three generations before his own, had stared aghast at Power; Callisto found himself now in much the same state over Thermodynamics, the inner life of that power, realizing like his predecessor that the Virgin and the dynamo stand as much for love as for power; that the two are indeed identical; and that love not only makes the world go 'round but also makes the boccie ball spin, the nebula precess.

It is the "sidereal" aspect of power that bothers Callisto; he knows that energy decays and that entropy is on the rise.

To Aubade Callisto dictates his memoirs, in third person, like Henry Adams. In doing so he recalls a mnemonic device from his undergraduate days for memorizing the Laws of Thermodynamics: "You can't win, things are going to get worse before they get better, who says they're going to get better," which ties the narrative to the weather-epigraph from Henry Miller. Now in middle-age, Callisto is forced to consider the thermodynamic equations of Gibbs, Boltzmann, and Clausius. Until now Callisto has been a disciple of Machiavelli, whose *The Prince* assumed that human agency (*virtú*) and chance (*fortuna*) governed the human condition in approximately equal proportions, "but the equations now introduced a random factor which pushed the odds to some unutterable and indeterminate ratio which he found himself afraid to calculate." Outside, the world appears to have gone chaotic: Madison Avenue rules America through a "consumerism" which has reduced people and things from healthy "differentiation to sameness, from ordered individuality to a kind of chaos." For Callisto entropy is a metaphor for decadence in society, and he predicts "a heat-death for his culture in which ideas, like heat-energy, would no longer be transferred, since each point in it would ultimately have the same quantity of energy; and intellectual motion would, accordingly, cease."

While Callisto treads his mental paces, below stairs Meatball Mulligan's party rollicks on. Meatball's guests range from the weird to the aimless, most of them pseudo-intellectuals, phony would-be expatriates, polyglots from the State Department, girls from the National Security Agency (whose prime function is codebreaking)—most of them employed in some way by the government and engaged in some form of communications. Dominating the rest are the Duke di Angelis quartet, a spaced-out group of musicians sporting sunglasses and smoking marijuana, thoroughly decadent. At one point the four decide to have a session—*sans* instruments. They tap their feet and swing their bodies to the inaudible strains of "Love For Sale," which is only moderately successful: "at least we ended together," says one. For their second number they try a variation on Gerry (not Meatball) Mulligan; they will *think* the root chords. Unfortunately, one soundlessly plays "I'll Remember April" while the other three launch into "These Foolish Things," a highly appropriate title. No one hears a note, of course, but this absurd exercise is directly related to Pynchon's theme. By playing without instruments, the quartet try to avoid noise and distortion, to overcome entropy, to communicate on a purely mental level. If the attempt is fruitless, it is no worse than Callisto's experiment in divorcing himself from the world.

Only Meatball provides a viable approach to the pervasive problem of entropy in both communications and thermodynamics. After waking with a hangover, and after fixing a tequila sour for "restoring order to his nervous system," he listens sympathetically to his friend Saul, who has just split from his wife Miriam; the fight was over communication theory. Saul works for the government on a top-secret project called

37

MUFFET (Multi-unit Factorial Field Electronic Calculator), and Miriam has been angered by Saul's speaking of "human behavior like a program fed into an IBM machine." Meatball claims not to know anything about communication theory. "Who does?" asks Saul. Perhaps, offers Mulligan, there is a "language barrier." Saul will not buy that:

> "If it is anything it's a kind of leakage. Tell a girl: 'I love you.' No trouble with two-thirds of that, it's a closed circuit. Just you and she, but that nasty four-letter word in the middle, *that's* the one you have to look out for. Ambiguity. Redundance. Irrelevance, even. Leakage. All this is noise. Noise screws up your signal, makes for disorganization in the circuit."

Under Meatball's benign if inept influence, however, Saul finally admits that his friend's attitude is right. Nobody runs "at top efficiency," he concludes, and marriages are "sort of founded on compromises." By extrapolation, so is communication; one does the best one can to cope with entropy.

As the "system" of his party continues to decay, Mulligan does what he can to keep things functioning—not at top efficiency, but through compromise. Saul is dropping waterbags out the window, a girl is drowning in the bathtub, drunks are fighting, and horny sailors are gate-crashing in the belief they have found a whorehouse. Unlike Cleanth Siegel at a similar party, Meatball responds humanely. He has two choices: He can crawl in a closet and wait till everybody leaves, or he can "try to calm everybody down, one by one." The former option is tempting, and the latter involves hard work, but Pynchon is suggesting that hard work is the only legitimate means humans have to combat entropy in social systems and between ourselves. Hard as the job is, Meatball does "keep his lease-breaking party from deteriorating into total chaos"; he restores order among his different guests.

Contrapuntally, Aubade senses Callisto's rising terror with alarm. As one who comes from a colonialized country, Aubade is no stranger to compromise either.

38

Moreover, she apprehends the world through sound, as "music which emerged at intervals from a howling darkness of discordancy." Aubade hears Callisto's words mingled with car horns on the street outside and the wild music from the speakers in Meatball's flat:

> The architectonic purity of her world was constantly threatened by such hints of anarchy: gaps and excrescences and skew lines, and a shifting or tilting of planes to which she had continually to readjust lest the whole structure shiver into a disarray of discrete and meaningless signals. Callisto had described the process once as a kind of "feedback": she crawled into dreams each night with a sense of exhaustion, and a desperate resolve never to relax that vigilance.

Words like "signals" and "feedback" belong to communication theory. Aubade expends her energy balancing the "signal-to-noise ratio." Exhausted himself, Callisto has rejected all post-World War I music as decadent, but Aubade speaks in accents of pure melody. He can not forget that war, and is still living in its aftermath.

When the bird he is cradling begins to die, Callisto, "helpless in the past," is paralyzed. Like Meatball, Aubade must make a choice, but unlike him she elects to allow disorder to penetrate an ordered system—because either way the system will decay. With bleeding hands she smashes the windows of the hothouse, and turns to wait

> until the moment of equilibrium was reached, when 37 degrees Fahrenheit should prevail both outside and inside, and forever, and the hovering, curious dominant of their separate lives should resolve into a tonic of darkness and the final absence of all motion.

Death may be the consequence, but at least the hothouse has been opened to the life of the street. One must face the possibility of eventual annihilation, not try to arrest time. Aubade's act is an acknowledgment of the limited choices available. Callisto's love is not enough; love, like power, will decay. Mulligan shoulders responsibility for his life in time—and entropy is time's arrow. He merely retards the inevitable, but it is the only real choice he has. The choice, the polarity between hothouse and street, and the concept of entropy will structure Pynchon's novels.

"The Secret Integration," the first of Pynchon's stories to appear in a magazine of large circulation, is perhaps his least successful. Published after $V.$, it suffers from the very qualities that make the novel so engaging. $V.$ is discursive and loose, but its diffusion is appropriate to its global setting. Equally loose, "The Secret Integration" is set in Mingeborough, Massachusetts, the Berkshire Mountain hometown of Tyrone Slothrop, protagonist of *Gravity's Rainbow*, and the small community cannot contain the multiple motifs of the plot. Actually the story seems to have been lifted from *Gravity's Rainbow*, where it left a small hole in the larger narrative. While we are criticizing it, we should note that perhaps because the story was written for *The Saturday Evening Post*, it has an air of cuteness about it, as if Pynchon, having become a recluse like J. D. Salinger, felt constrained to write like him too.

Nevertheless, "The Secret Integration" has its moments, and more importantly, has elements of considerable relevance to Pynchon's other work. As one might expect, paranoia, technical terminology, and communication and its failures are given prominence. One of the protagonists is a Salinger-type prodigy named Grover Snodd, a young mathematical genius. A couple of days a week he attends a nearby college, having been forced out of his school by what he believes is a cabal of parents and teachers incensed at his helping other kids with their homework. Among Grover's several hobbies is a radio receiver he has built, on which he and his friends listen to police calls and other hams, "disembodied voices, sometimes even as far away as the sea," which fill their dreams of the world beyond the mountains. Their TV sets only pick up one channel.

Grover's friends are a mixed group. They include

Tim Santora, through whose eyes events are seen; Étienne Cherdlu (a play on Etaoin Shrdlu, the linotype operator's device), a boy who delights in practical jokes; Hogan Slothrop, brother to the Tyrone of *Gravity's Rainbow,* at nine the youngest member of Mingeborough's Alcoholics Anonymous, having renounced booze and gotten religion; Kim Dufay, a sixth-grader easily turned on by explosives, whose size 28A padded bra allows her to infiltrate PTA meetings; several minor characters like Nunzi Passarella, who has made his reputation by bringing a quarter-ton Poland China sow to school for Show-and-Tell; and Carl Barrington, a Negro boy new to the group. Actually, the story deals with how Carl came to be a member. Theirs is not so much a group as a conspiracy, a real one, led by Grover and directed against "the scaled-up world adults made, remade and lived in without" them, at "walls, at anything else solid that happened to be around," at "inertia and stubbornness."

With the exception of Étienne Cherdlu's father, a junk man who believes people should worry about automation rather than skin color, the parents of Mingeborough's children are all bigots, hysterical at the thought of a black family moving into town and at the prospect of integration in general. "What's integration mean?" Tim Santora asks Grover. The only kind the math whiz ever heard of is

"The opposite of differentiation," Grover said, drawing an x-axis, y-axis and curve on his greenboard. "Call this function of x. Consider values of the curve any little increments of x"—drawing straight lines from the curve down to the x-axis, like the bars of a jail cell—"you can have as many of these as you want, see, as close together as you want."

"Till it's all solid," Tim said.

"No, it never gets solid. If this was a jail cell, and those lines were bars, and whoever was behind it could make himself any size he wanted to be, he could always make himself skinny enough to get free. No matter how close together the bars were."

Grover has sketched the possibilities of human freedom in a highly "integrated" social system. Wiser than most of Pynchon's characters, Grover knows that the lines are artificial, mathematical conveniences, and he also knows that a paradox is involved: without integration there can be no differentiation in a healthy society. In a viable system disparate elements function in concert. Despite his wisdom, however, Grover will be defeated by the cell bars of society's functions, for this is a story of childhood loss of innocence. Grover has been training the other kids in a subversive organization he has named Operation Spartacus after the Kirk Douglas movie. Financed by contributions from school milk money and by the sale of building materials stolen from a new housing project into which a black family proposes to move, the Spartacists make sodium bombs to disrupt the school and sabotage the local paper mill by stirring up machinery-stalling silt in the river from which the mill draws its water.

Most of their sorties are abortive, partly because most of Grover's followers are too young to understand Grover's plans of attack, his passion for "symmetry" in strategy, and partly because the kids can be stopped by the lines of force the adults have drawn. In one raid on their school, the children are enthusiastic until they reach the playing field lines chalked around the perimeter; they cannot pass. Grover theorizes that "the line figure in the grass might have reminded the little kids of chalk lines on a greenboard." Grover tries to drill his troops by laying out lines on a practice field, but they lack adult authority, and Tim complains that the whole idea is unreal.

While the "Inner Junta" members of the group are not without sophistication, they are still fond of the trappings of adolescence. Their hideout is the mansion of "King Yrjö," an estate once owned, so legend has it, by a royal European pretender, and still inhabited by the ghost of the King's aide, a seven-foot-tall cavalry officer. It offers a suitable make-believe environment, and Grover and friends reach it in Huck Finn fashion, using an abandoned boat to cross the old canal system which surrounds the estate. Grover has almost given up

42

on Operation Spartacus when Hogan Slothrop gets a call from the local Alcoholics Anonymous to go to the town's hotel to sit with a transient trying to kick the habit.

The transient turns out to be a Negro, the first the children have ever seen, an indigent jazz musician who has just played at the Lenox music festival. None of the adult A.A. members will have anything to do with a Negro, so they have sent Hogan in answer to the man's call, as a joke. Of course Hogan takes the assignment quite seriously, persuades Tim Santora to accompany him, and bravely sets off to calm the alky's jitters. At first offended by what he knows to be an insult on the part of Mingeborough's adults, Mr. McAfee, the black, warms to the ingenuousness of the boys and soon unburdens himself. His tales of isolation both racial and personal elicit their sympathy; they remind Tim of "all those cops and merchant captains and barge tenders over the radio, all those voices bouncing off the invisible dome in the sky and down to Grover's antenna and into Tim's dreams." In McAfee's voice Tim recognizes other drifters, relatives who disappeared during the Depression, riders on buses and freight trains. So lonely is McAfee that Tim tries to telephone long distance to a girl the man can hardly remember, but whose number he has been carrying in his wallet for years. As the telephone circuits open

> Tim's foot felt the edge of a certain abyss which he had been walking close to—for who knows how long? —without knowing. . . . It was night here . . . one single night over the entire land, making people, already so tiny in it, invisible too in the dark; and how hard it would be, how hopeless, to really find a person you needed suddenly, unless you lived all your life in a house like he did, with a mother and father.

Before pathos can overwhelm the scene, it is relieved by the arrival of Grover and Étienne Cherdlu, the latter decked in his skin diver's suit from attempting to sabotage the paper mill, both afraid the police are after them. Cherdlu's panic and McAfee's need for a drink soon do bring the cops, who arrest the Negro for vagrancy and run him out of town. The boys never see McAfee again, but his treatment by the adults has two consequences for the kids. The first is a retaliatory caper which momentarily rejuvenates Operation Spartacus; it is also an attempt "to resurrect a friend," McAfee. The kids rig up green flood lights along the railroad tracks, dress up in costumes and masks, and stage a night attack that terrifies a trainload of passengers. It is an affirmation of color, says Grover: "I feel different now and better for having been green, even sickly green, even for a minute."

The second consequence concerns Carl Barrington. The racism in Mingeborough reaches a head when the townspeople learn that blacks have actually moved into the new housing project. Tim and the other boys overhear their parents making hate-telephone calls to the newcomers, the Barringtons. The Inner Junta compensates by accepting Carl without reservation; it is a "secret integration." The point of the story, revealed at the end, is that the Barringtons have no children. Carl is imaginary, "put together out of phrases, images, possibilities that grownups had somehow turned away from, repudiated, left out at the edges of towns, as if they were auto parts in Étienne's father's junkyard." Carl will not survive an adult counterattack, however. From a day of planning strategy at King Yrjö's mansion the group of rebels returns to find the Barrington lawn completely covered with garbage. As the kids try to clear it away, they discover garbage from their own homes. It is too much. Carl decides he will go to live at King Yrjö's estate permanently: "he was entirely theirs, their friend and robot, to cherish, buy undrunk sodas for, or send into danger, or even, as now, to banish from their sight." Carl is being discarded, consigned to the junkheap of childish fantasies. And so is youthful rebellion. Each child leaves for "his own house, hot shower, dry towel, before-bed television, good night kiss, and dreams that could never again be entirely safe."

Indeed, those dreams will never be safe. Tim Santora has already discovered that his dreams are full of "struggle down the long, inexhaustible network of some

44

arithmetic problem where each step led to a dozen new ones." For Pynchon, networks are reality, and humans stumble through them.

Pynchon's fascination with junkheaps furnishes a focus for "A Journey Into the Mind of Watts," his 1966 study of the slums of Los Angeles. The essay is a skillful piece of journalism in which Pynchon traces the ironies and absurdities of black life in a prosperous white city. It is an excellent tonic for the reader daunted by the surrealistic difficulty of some of Pynchon's fiction. Although as journalism it is unremarkable, from the standpoint of continuity within Pynchon's work it is important, for it offers a sober and concise view of the Los Angeles he treats comically in *The Crying of Lot 49*. Pynchon constructs his essay around a real junkheap, a landmark in Watts erected by an Italian immigrant named Simon Rodia, who for thirty years gathered scrap and waste into "his own dream of how things should have been: A fantasy of fountains, boats, tall openwork spires, encrusted with a dazzling mosaic of Watts debris." Rodia's heap becomes a metaphor for the wasted lives in the black ghetto.

Between that ghetto and the white metropolis are sharp divisions, says Pynchon; "Watts is country which lies, psychologically, uncounted miles further than most whites seem at present willing to travel." Los Angeles and its subculture are different states of mind, and Watts is quite simply paranoiac. That condition obtains in part because Los Angeles itself is "a little unreal, a little less than substantial. For Los Angeles, more than any other city, belongs to the mass media." Watts lies "impacted in the heart of this white fantasy," and as a consequence suffers from aberration aggravated by the prevalence of the unreal. Paranoia assists the blacks in knowing who they are. For a time they had accepted the white version of what blacks should be, but the acquiescence has faded as the civil rights movement has flagged. Nevertheless, "assorted members of the humanitarian establishment" continue in their efforts to mold the denizens of Watts in the image of whites. Pynchon singles out the Economic and Youth Opportunity Agency, a "bizarre, confused, ever in flux, strangely ineffectual" organization characterized by internecine liberal bickering and bureaucratic bungling. E.Y.O.A. begins the molding process with the young; its counselors tell black girls to trim their afros and dress conservatively and advise black boys to cultivate "Niceguymanship," to look and act as white as possible. Strengthened by the rebellious spirit of the times, the young blacks resent and resist efforts to change them. Nothing, however, can fend off the fantasies of the mass media; television signals come into Watts, continually reshaping reality.

Paranoia flourishes in Watts for a second reason: *real* violence. The violence in August 1965 turned Watts into "Raceriotland," a literal battlefield strewn with the rubble of rage, the remnants of a community that was never much to begin with. Pynchon's eye instinctively picks out absurd details as he surveys the terrain. For instance, when a storekeeper decides to rebuild his destroyed business instead of fleeing the area, he breaks ground ceremoniously "in the true Watts spirit" by having his wife smash a bottle of champagne over a rock. Since this is a study after the fact, Pynchon does not advance causes for the riots. He does review events afterwards to suggest patterns to the violence and to emphasize the possibility of recurrence.

He begins "A Journey Into the Mind of Watts" with an account of a recent police killing of a black man, and observes that the ever-present gun in the hand of the ever-present white cop ensures continual racial confrontation. Past experience and fear make the roles of white and black inevitable, make "it impossible for the cop to come on any different, or for [the black] to hate him any less." Both cop and hassled black are caught up in a system which traps the two of them; neither wants the confrontation. Thus, when it comes, the violence follows the laws of physics; "for every action there is an equal and opposite reaction." Violence may also "be an attempt to communicate," since without it whites take no notice of the black individual beyond the role which the white system has assigned him.

46

The point Pynchon is making is not that the whites are necessarily wrong in pushing their values and standards, particularly since many whites genuinely want to give the blacks a place in the system. Nor is he saying that the police are necessarily wrong for enforcing the laws; he notes the "earnestness" of many cops. If we borrow the math language of "The Secret Integration," the problem is that the whites attempt to force integration without allowing for differentiation, a mistake which rebounds, since it guarantees that the blacks will prize their differences. The more the blacks assert differentiation, the less regard whites have for it. The blacks thus become effectively isolated, part and no part of the system. Beyond that, the law the cop enforces is a reflection of the faulty system; the blacks get annoyance instead of justice. They receive no rewards even when they join the system and cooperate with the law. Whites are driven by the carrot, blacks by the stick. The citizens of Watts have been disinherited of America's bounty and disabused of their humanity. As Pynchon walks the streets he always finds so revelatory, he sees the poverty, the hopelessness, the blankness of Watts. Most of all he notices the absence of "surprise" to black life: "Watts is full of street corners where people stand, as they have been, some of them, for 20 or 30 years, without Surprise One ever having come along." Without surprise, life has little to offer.

Pynchon will return to the absence of surprise and the necessity of its possibility in his second and third novels. The blacks in Watts, he thinks, may be preparing their own surprise, however. Pynchon ends his essay on an apocalyptic note, with an example of black Watts art, found objects plunked from the junkheap of the ghetto. It is a smashed TV set; inside the cavity that once held the picture tube, generator of white fantasy, is a skull; the title of the piece is "The Late Late Late Show." It is an arresting image and a terrific conclusion.

CHAPTER TWO

The Track of the Energy:
History in V.

Dualism structures Pynchon's first novel, *V.*, a multifaceted work stretched between two picaresque plots. The first plot involves Benny Profane, a self-proclaimed schlemihl who traces his ancestry back to Job but who otherwise has no sense of the past. Profane wanders the "streets" of the present—a period of several months in 1955 and 1956. His motion, aimless if perhaps not entirely random, since his peregrinations are called "yoyoing," frames the other episodes in the novel. Profane's travels intersect those of Herbert Stencil, who, like Callisto of "Entropy," moves within the "hothouse" of the past, specifically the past of the twentieth century, and seizes on every hint of the apocalyptic. In contrast to Profane's, Stencil's movements have purpose: He is searching for manifestations of a mysterious female called V., who he believes has appeared at various social and political junctures since the turn of the century. Because Stencil's burrowings into the past furnish the greater part of the novel's considerable length, we shall deal with them in this chapter, and reserve Benny Profane for the next.

Stencil has inherited the object of his quest from his

father, Sidney Stencil, a British Foreign Officer dead since 1919. Stencil *père,* who appears in several episodes that his son recreates in his search, is a "Machiavelli on the rack, less concerned with immediacy than idea," "a spy who has risen above the political turmoil of his time" (451).[1] As a British spy, the elder Stencil tries to believe in cause and effect, the rules of the game, in Machiavellian power and virtú. On his various assignments, however, he discovers a ubiquitous factor in Situations—his word—of apocalyptic magnitude, and makes brief, cryptic reference to it in his journal. "There is more behind and inside V. than any of us had suspected. Not who, but what: what is she. God grant that I may never be called upon to write the answer, either here or in any official report" (43).

When Stencil *fils* first appears in the story, he has been hunting V. since 1945, a date on which Pynchon need not elaborate; it is the date of the unleashing of the massive destructive energy of the atomic bomb. Stencil's fitness for his task is accidental. Born in 1901, the year Queen Victoria's death closed one era, he is the "child" of the new century, and appropriately for that office, he seems permanently displaced and deracinated. Stencil himself knows little of the circumstances of his birth; his father has told him nothing about his mother. It is conceivable that V., whatever else she may be, is Stencil's mother, although Stencil tries to dismiss that possibility. His quest has galvanized him from "inertness to—if not vitality—then at least activity . . . for no other reason than that V. was there to track down" (44). Inertness and vitality, or inanimateness and life, are two of the principal dualisms of the book. From other of his earmarks, it is obvious that Stencil is a Henry Adams. Like Adams, to whom Pynchon refers explicitly (and, again, like Callisto of "Entropy"), Stencil speaks of himself in the third person. This manner of speaking helps Stencil "appear as only one among a repertoire of identities" (51), as a multiplicity of selves which equip him for an Adamsian perspective on history.

In *The Education of Henry Adams,* Adams writes that the child born around the turn of the century

49

would "be born into a new world which would not be a unity but a multiple" (457).[2] According to the historian, new forces had so altered the world by that time that alterations of mind were necessary also:

As far as one ventured to interpret actual science, the mind had thus far adjusted itself by an infinite series of infinitely delicate adjustments forced on it by the infinite motion of an infinite chaos of motion; dragged at one moment into the unknowable and unthinkable, then trying to scramble back within its senses and to bar the chaos out, but always assimilating bits of it, until at last, in 1900, a new avalanche of unknown forces had fallen on it, which required new mental powers to control. If this view was correct, the mind could gain nothing by flight or by fight; it must merge in its supersensual multiverse, or succumb to it (460-461).

Stencil does in a sense merge into a multiverse; he becomes "He who looks for V." through a series of historical events. For Pynchon's readers, Adams also offers the most reliable clue as to who—or what—V. is. Until 1900, Adams believes, history could be apprehended, although with difficulty, as a continuous process. Laws of causality seemed to hold true. After 1900, energies did not function so predictably; nature's energies became destructive and random. Entropy disrupted the world, which seemed almost to be running down. In "The Dynamo and the Virgin" chapter in *The Education,* Adams speaks at length of his two symbols as they have operated in history:

Yet in mechanics, whatever the mechanicians might think, both energies acted as interchangeable forces on man, and by action on man all known force may be measured. Indeed, few men of science measured force in any other way. After once admitting that a straight line was the shortest distance between two points, no serious mathematician cared to deny anything that suited his convenience, and rejected no symbol, unproved or unprovable, that helped him to accomplish work. The symbol was force, as a compass needle or a

50

triangle was force, as the mechanist might prove by losing it, and nothing could be gained by ignoring their value. Symbol or energy, the Virgin had acted as the greatest force the Western world ever felt, and had drawn man's activities to herself more strongly than any other power, natural or supernatural, had ever done; the historian's business was to follow the track of the energy; to find where it came from and where it went to; its complex source and shifting channels; its values, equivalents, conversions. It could scarcely be more complex than radium; it could hardly be deflected, diverted, polarized, absorbed more perplexingly than any other radiant matter. Adams knew nothing about any of them, but as a mathematical problem of influence on human process, though all were occult, all reacted on his mind, and he rather inclined to think the Virgin easiest to handle (388-389).

Adams goes on to comment on his own quest through "labyrinths" on the track of the energy.

Again like Adams, Herbert Stencil finds the Virgin "easiest to handle"; he will personify force as a woman. The phrase "to follow the track of the energy" describes Stencil's course exactly; he will follow it into quite literal labyrinths, some of them darkly comic. Where Adams's Virgin symbolizes the energy he seeks to fathom with reasonable precision, Stencil's V. is hopelessly vague, for a reason with which Adams would surely sympathize: The energy Stencil tracks is more complex than Adams thought. To poor muddled Stencil, V. is any proper noun beginning with that initial. He is a parody of Henry Adams, and engaging as it is in itself, this comic distortion is crucial to an assessment of Pynchon's purpose.

Critical opinion on this adaptation of Adams is divided between those who think Pynchon succeeds brilliantly by creating a "Virgin who has become a dynamo"[3] and those who believe the author has "been raped by Henry Adams," an experience which leads him to employ the tiresome "all purpose quest."[4] While to the unfriendly critic one might concede that the quest does at times become tedious in the novel, it is also essential to note that Pynchon is deliberately mocking Adams. Adams's approach to history is rational and sophisticated; Stencil's is instinctual and bumbling. Stencil conceives of history much as would a Rosicrucian or a mad Mason, and indeed, he resembles Tolstoy's Pierre Bezúkhov, who, having joined the Masonic Order, clutches at manifestations of the apocalyptic Beast 666.

Moreover, Pynchon laughs not only at historians who would discover a key to history, but also at the tradition of Western letters from which such historians derive—and at the same time makes use of the tradition to inform his book. For example, Stencil's quest, although less noble than Faust's, has something in common with the quest of Goethe's character, if only that both are endless, and that both are meaningful to the degree that they remain uncompleted. To make sure that the reader does not miss this similarity, Pynchon names another of his characters Fausto, has him speak also in Adamsian third person, and links him to Stencil by suggestive circumstance: Fausto Maijstral is Stencil's figurative brother, for reasons we shall discuss later.

The quester-historians of *V.*, then, are actually two. Fausto Maijstral occupies a room on Malta, a hothouse like Callisto's, which shuts out the present so that its occupant can "deal with the past." Fausto also is a multiplicity of selves, which he names Fausto I, II, III, IV. In fact, he reflects on little else than the self and its preservation and alterations over the course of time. As a Maltese, Maijstral can decide that "perhaps British colonialism has produced a new sort of being, a dual man, aimed two ways at once: towards peace and simplicity on the one hand, towards an exhausted intellectual searching on the other" (289). Herbert Stencil is the second half of this dichotomy, too humorous a figure to qualify as a Faust. Occasionally the indefatigable Stencil dreams that he is lost in a dream, that his is "a scholarly quest after all, an adventure of the mind, in the tradition of *The Golden Bough* or *The White Goddess*" (50). These allusions add dimensions to the ob-

52

ject of Stencil's quest, even as Pynchon comically undercuts them at every opportunity.

Sir James George Frazer's *The Golden Bough* and Robert Graves's *The White Goddess* are classic studies of the anthropological, mythical, and historical origins of Western civilization. Of the two, Graves's is the more important for Pynchon, because it focuses on what that writer believes is the principal archetype of our culture. Known by many names, including Venus, The White Goddess is an ambivalent deity, at once creative and destructive, loving and cruel, beneficent and implacable.[5] According to Graves, the worship of the principles she embodies determined the contours of Western man's progress in morality, philosophy, art—the humanist tradition. The converse of that thesis is that his culture has generally declined with Western man's loss of faith in that great symbol. Since he believes that pagan and soulless science has robbed the goddess of the reverence due her, Graves calls for a reestablished mythology to reverse degeneracy and sterility—to refresh the waste land of modern Western Culture. With Adams's Virgin, Pynchon entwines Graves's symbol—with an ironic twist. The Virgin or Venus in *V.* has been almost wholly perverted.

Whether V. be the eternal feminine of Goethe or the great goddess of Graves, symptom or cause of the chaos of the twentieth century, blighter or ghastly redeemer of the waste land, Western civilization, as Pynchon sees it, is caught in a dying fall. Randomly dispersed natural energies, creeping inanimateness, rampant colonialism and racism, expiring romanticism, perverted sexuality, degenerate politics, and holocaustic wars have turned the Western world into a waste land. Somehow, Herbert Stencil feels, V. explains what has been happening, how "the avalanche of unknown forces" started, and he traces her spoor across three continents, a small figure on an enormous global landscape chasing what may be a will-o'-the-wisp.

Pynchon sharpens the point of Stencil's quest with allusions to still another literary source, one almost as important as Adams in the novel. This is Niccolo Machiavelli's *The Prince,* which postulates the motive forces of history as virtú, or skillful human agency, and fortune, or chance. The goddess Fortuna whom Machiavelli invokes is a Renaissance conception of accident. She is commonly represented in the literature of the Renaissance as controlling large-order events, and she is usually associated with the wheel, her symbol. Images of the wheel occur everywhere in *V.*; two of the principal examples are Benny Profane's circular "yoyoing" and Malta, "the hub" of a wheel, on which lives Fausto Maijstral, Stencil's "brother." The tension between Adams and Machiavelli, between V. and Fortuna, drives Pynchon's novel.

Literary or mythical as this dichotomy may seem, it functions on a different level as well. Pynchon begins with the Adamsian notion that entropy has overtaken the systems of the world. The question then becomes one of how man regards the phenomenon. Is entropy—disorder—simply chance, as in the caprice of fortune, or is it the result of some malignant purpose? In an extended discussion of entropy in *The Human Use of Human Beings,* Norbert Wiener remarks on man's tendency to characterize it as evil. This view Wiener designates as the Manichean, as opposed to the Augustinian, a more scientific attitude toward entropy. According to the Augustinian, disorder in the universe is merely the absence of order, a matter of chance, part of the aleatoric aspect of nature. The Manichean attributes evil intent to disorder, a position which can verge on paranoia.

Just as there are two historians in the novel, so are there two ways of regarding "the avalanche of unknown forces," and so are there two goddesses, Fortuna and V. Herbert Stencil, of course, is a Manichean—or perhaps only a paranoid. For him, V. is colophon and cabal of the twentieth century; he must

affirm that his quarry fitted in with The Big One, the century's master cabal. . . . If she was a historical fact then she continued active today and at the moment, because the ultimate Plot Which Has No Name was as yet unrealized, though V. might be no more a she than a sailing vessel or a nation (210).

In *War and Peace,* using an equally broad landscape, Tolstoy outlined a theory of history devoted to disproving the illusion that humans effect the movements of history. Pynchon leaves the question open. Stencil may be pursuing illusion, may perceive design and conspiracy in V.'s appearances where no such order obtains. Stencil weaves tales from evidence he has acquired by scholarship and also by accident, and there is the rub: Stencil was present at none of the events he recounts. His information comes at second-hand, and he may be "stencilizing" the events to suit his purpose. Complicating his embellishments and embroideries are the various narrative voices involved in specific episodes. In short, the novel reflects Stencil's confusion. The historical events are jumbled in *V.,* as if to suggest the haphazard design he attributes to them. We shall review them in their chronological sequence rather than in the order Stencil and the other narrators relate them.

The first avatar of V. steps into Stencil's canvas in 1898, in Alexandria and Cairo. Alexandria, "temporarily occupied" by the British since 1882, is a city of intrigue. Britain, France, and Germany have each been pressing territorial claims in Africa. Britain's colonialism has been especially provocative; for the better part of the nineteenth century that country has followed a policy of "splendid isolation" by avoiding alliances with other nations and intervening unilaterally just about everywhere to create or preserve a balance of power. Since both Britain and France are attempting to take over Africa, matters come to a head quickly, with Germany trying to exploit the hostility to her advantage. While British forces have been pushing south along the Nile, French expeditions have been moving east across the continent. A British contingent under Kitchener and a French under Marchand meet at Fashoda, in the Sudan, in July 1898. When Kitchener threatens to drive out the French, the clash precipitates the Fashoda crisis. Hasty diplomacy averts war; both Britain and France realize that antagonism will be to Germany's advantage.

To the espionage services of the various countries involved, the crisis is of major proportions, almost apocalyptic. "The balloon is going up," the British dryly predict, and that phrase recurs throughout the novel each time events mount. As Pynchon views the Fashoda crisis, it is the first of several near-apocalypses that dominate the climate of the new century, and in "Under the Rose," the short story which became Chapter 3 of *V.*, he emphasized Armageddon. The "game" of espionage, Pynchon said in the story, is "an irresistible vector aimed toward 1900," and the spies are "comrade Machiavellians, still playing the games of Renaissance Italian politics in a world that had outgrown them." Both the short story and the chapter deal with a plot to assassinate a public figure to hasten war, its failure, and the death of Porpentine, friend and colleague of Sidney Stencil, at the hands of Bongo-Shaftesbury, a spy working for the Germans. In revising the short story for inclusion in *V.*, Pynchon added extra characters and fragmented the narrative into multiple points of view, so that Arab natives become the filters for the action. The multiple points of view permit the events to be seen from different angles, although all of them vector eventually into the blankness of the desert which is Egypt.

One of Pynchon's principal themes in *V.* is that Western culture has exhausted itself in an absurd and deadly colonialism. Seen through the eyes of Aïeul the cafe owner, Yusef the anarchist factotum, Waldetar the train conductor, Gebrail the farmer, and Girgis the mountebank, the machinations of the espionage services seem a game played out against the backdrop of an "inert" city which is "only the desert in disguise" (71). Europeans circulate about the city, tourists who, like the spies, expect that the travel game has rules that must be adhered to. Here Pynchon introduces a metaphor for human motion, particularly as regards colonialism, tourists in "Baedeker land" on tours arranged by the Cook agency, which protects imperialist sightseers from contact with any but "inanimate" natives, "automata: waiters, porters, cabmen, clerks. Taken for granted" (59). Waldetar the conductor, one of those features of the topography for the tourists, reflects on his passengers: "There's no organized effort about it but there remains a grand joke on all visitors to Baedeker's world: the permanent residents are actually humans in disguise" (66). Waldetar *is* human; he loves his wife and children in a way, Pynchon implies, that makes him superior to the tourists.

One of these tourists at first seems an exception to the sterile type. She is Victoria Wren, named after her Queen, daughter of a member of Parliament. An eighteen-year-old Catholic, she speaks frequently of her religion, had indeed yearned to be a nun until she considered "the competition" of a "harem" of nuns for God's attention, and transferred her affections instead to a dashing colonialist uncle who fired her adolescent imagination: "So it came about that God wore a wide-awake hat and fought skirmishes with an aboriginal Satan out at the antipodes of the firmament, in the name and for the safekeeping of any Victoria" (61). She still clings to the symbols of the Church, however, the candles, the statuary, the black robes, which Pynchon suggests are signs of decadence. Victoria is England gone degenerate, a secular goddess who develops a taste for the apocalyptic. From this point forward, assuming Herbert Stencil's reconstruction of her movements to be correct, she will turn up like a bad penny wherever there is crisis and decline in the world. For Victoria, the world becomes increasingly inanimate, as she herself becomes inanimate; she is a moribund deity playing with "a colonial doll's world" (61). In the Egyptian episode, she is seduced by Porpentine's partner, Goodfellow, and having learned from her lover of the plots afoot, she indirectly causes Porpentine's death.

Porpentine's weakness is that of Stencil's father, an inherent and (under the circumstances) anachronistic humanity that expresses itself in compassion. By contrast, his spy opponent, Bongo-Shaftesbury, has literally turned himself into a mechanical doll, one of the toys Victoria will in future find so attractive. During a surrealistic sequence Bongo-Shaftesbury terrifies Victoria's sister by showing her a switch embedded in his arm with wires leading to his brain. Porpentine demands that he stop: "One doesn't frighten a child, sir." To which Bongo-Shaftesbury replies:

"Hurrah. General principles again." Corpse fingers jabbed in the air. "But someday, Porpentine, I, or another, will catch you off guard. Loving, hating, even showing some absent-minded sympathy. I'll watch you. The moment you forget yourself enough to admit another's humanity, see him as a person and not a symbol—then perhaps—"
"What is humanity?"
"You ask the obvious, ha, ha. Humanity is something to destroy" (69).

Porpentine's sympathy betrays him into acting humanly, and Bongo-Shaftesbury kills him. Beyond this personal tragedy looms apocalypse. The Europeans wait on revelation. The native colonials see none forthcoming. Waldetar, the kindhearted Jew, knows that events depend on Fortune but knows also that people prefer to believe otherwise: "Men, he felt, even perhaps Sephardim, are at the mercy of the earth and its seas. Whether a cataclysm is accident or design, they need a God to keep them from harm"(66). Waldetar's assessment points up the larger concern of the novel: the necessity to believe in some historical pattern, call it deity or Zeitgeist. Gebrail the farmer, from long acquaintance with the desert, takes a cynical view. Watching his horse's ass, he laughingly wonders if that is the revelation of Fashoda and concludes: "The desert was prophecy enough of the Last Day. . . . Nothing was coming. Nothing was already here" (72-73). Gebrail stares at the waste land with a courage others can not muster.

Yet, surely, some sort of revelation is at hand. Hanne, the barmaid at a German *bierhalle* in Cairo, develops a triangular stain—a V—on her arm. Soon she sees it dancing above the crowd at the *bierhalle*, "like a tongue on Pentecost" (74). V. has made her (or its) first appearance. Her domain is nothing, the waste land, her office the dispersal of energy toward equilibrium and inanimateness.

But V.'s sinister nature is some time in manifesting itself. A year later, in 1899, Victoria pops up in Florence, where Sidney Stencil encounters her. Of this episode the spy's son admits his knowledge is sketchy (it is not even clear who recounts the tale, Stencil or the narrator), but he is certain that in Florence V. had "been connected, though perhaps only tangentially, with one of those grand conspiracies or foretastes of Armageddon which seemed to have captivated all diplomatic sensibilities in the years preceding the Great War" (141). Again the diplomats and spies are Machiavellians who apply outdated political methods unsuitable for an apocalyptic century. Clearly Pynchon regards Machiavelli as unjustly condemned for cynicism and puts in the mouth of the Gaucho a defense of the Italian political theorist:

> He was an apostle of freedom for all men. Who can read the last chapter of *Il Principe* and doubt his desire for a republican and united Italy? . . . His morality was as simple and honest as my own and my comrades' in South America (148).

The Gaucho is arguing with Signor Mantissa, an aging, inept, small-time Italian operator who has learned little from his career of intrigue but who also feels an affinity for the author of *The Prince*: "like Machiavelli, he was in exile, and visited by shadows of rhythm and decay" (145). For Mantissa,

> all men were corrupt: history would continue to recapitulate the same patterns. . . . He belonged to that inner circle of deracinated seers . . . for whom the continent of Europe was like a gallery one is familiar with but long weary of, useful now only as shelter from the rain, or some obscure pestilence (145-146).

If the colonial regions of the world are galleries for

jaded tourists, Europe is a gallery for decadent aestheticians and politicians.

The Gaucho accuses Mantissa of extracting only deviousness from Machiavelli's handbook of statecraft: "You once heard him speak of the lion and the fox and now your devious brain can see only the fox. What has happened to the strength, the aggressiveness, the natural nobility of the lion?" (147) The Gaucho fancies himself just such a lion. He has come to Florence to organize a Venezuelan colony into a small army he calls the Figli di Machiavelli, which will riot before the Venezuelan Consulate to further revolution in Caracas itself. Just why he should have taken this task upon himself is unclear, since as a gaucho he is presumably from Argentina. But, as a Venezuelan official remarks, Argentina is on "the same continent, is it not?" (161) This cavalier explanation resembles Stencil's grasping at circumstances to discover conspiracy where none may exist.

If this scheme seems hare-brained, the Gaucho's alliance with Mantissa is predicated on one still more loony, a plot to steal Botticelli's *Birth of Venus* (which hangs on "the western wall" of a literal gallery, the Uffizi), conceal it in a hollow Judas tree, and escape over the Ponte Vecchio. V's—as in Venezuela, Venus, and Vecchio—multiply comically. Still another is introduced by Captain Hugh Godolphin, colonial army officer, explorer, veteran of the force sent to relieve General Gordon at Khartoum, who is tormented by his memories of Vheissu, a country to which, fifteen years previously, he had led an expedition, and from which only he returned.

The dominant features of Vheissu, Godolphin tells Victoria Wren, are "random" colors, constantly changing, as if one "lived within a madman's kaleidoscope" (155). It is a savage land, with "barbarity, insurrection, internecine feud" and "music, poetry, laws and ceremonies" (155), none of which explain it, for they are superficial attributes, like skin. Hunting for metaphor, Godolphin decides Vheissu is like "a dark woman tattooed from head to toe," a dusky native the imperialist seizes for his mistress:

But soon that skin, the gaudy godawful riot of pattern and color, would begin to get between you and whatever it was in her that you thought you loved. And soon, in perhaps only a matter of days, it would get so bad that you would begin praying to whatever god you knew of to send some leprosy to her. To flay that tattooing to a heap of red, purple and green debris, leave the veins and ligaments raw and quivering and open at last to your eyes and your touch (156).

It is almost as if Godolphin had borrowed his metaphor from the Marquis de Sade, whose legacy is a reminder that whatever one does to another, love him or hate him, torture or kill him, one can never break through another's self—or one's own. It is the same with Vheissu, a country or a state of mind equally impenetrable, whose "skin" resists efforts to unite with it, perhaps by merely reflecting the yearning of the aggressor. Godolphin's is a sexual metaphor of sado-masochistic dimensions; it will recur thoughtout *V*.

Godolphin's original expedition had taken place just after Khartoum, when the Mahdi had destroyed General Gordon and crucified some of his troops. The perception of annihilation had contributed to Godolphin's reaction to Vheissu. Since then, he has explored other places, driven by a need to fathom reality, to get beneath the skin. He tries to explain to his old friend Signor Mantissa just why he has quested:

"... it is the opposite of what sends English reeling all over the globe in the mad dances called Cook's tours. They want only the skin of a place, the explorer wants its heart. It is perhaps a little like being in love. I had never penetrated to the heart of any of those wild places, Raf. Until Vheissu. It was not till the Southern Expedition last year that I saw what was beneath his skin" (188).

On his Southern Expedition, Godolphin tells Mantissa, he actually reached the South Pole, the Ultima Thule of explorers, but did not publicize the triumph because of what he found there. Beneath the skin of the ice he saw "a dream of annihilation": "Nothing."

Perhaps it was only the radiance of aleatoric colors, yet it hardly matters to him whether he has really seen nothing: "It is what I thought. What truth I came to" (190). That truth is the final product of the phenomenon of colonialism, of which Godolphin represents the other aspect, in which the imperialist seeks to possess what he has conquered, only to end by being debased by the slave's submissiveness. On this rich metaphor Pynchon will ring changes in the course of his novel, for it is the key to the process by which human beings reify themselves into states of inanimation. To a degree, Godolphin is redeemed by his horror at his loss of self as it is subsumed by nothing, as he is annihilated by _his_ need to penetrate "skin." But V. will attempt to perfect herself by transcending her personality through degradation, through objectification; she will attempt to achieve dehumanization, to become nothing.

Enter V., in the person of Victoria Wren, veteran of three profitable affairs since her seduction by Goodfellow. She has acquired freedom from her family (having been "ruined"), incipient fascist political convictions, a promiscuous sexual hunger heightened by perverse innocence and religiosity—and a curious comb. The latter she picked up at a bazaar; the comb is carved in the shape of five crucified British soldiers, a commemorative relic of the Mahdi's brutality toward Gordon's army. At this point Pynchon's motifs begin to give off sparks. Robert Graves has identified a comb as an essential accessory of the White Goddess, and asserts that "Botticelli's _Birth of Venus_ is an exact icon of her cult."[6] Despite the ominous implications of her comb, if Victoria is the goddess, her aspect is still benign. For one thing, she succors and perhaps seduces the raving, semi-senile Godolphin, and falls in love with Godolphin's romantic son, Evan, who has come to Florence in answer to his father's call. The old man is convinced that Vheissu has launched a plot, and that apocalypse is imminent.

Victoria helps because she is also a Machiavellian—albeit a perverse one—herself, because "she felt that skill or any virtú was a desirable and lovely thing purely for its own sake; and it became more effective the

62

further divorced it was from moral intention" (182-183). Like the Gaucho and Signor Mantissa

> She would act, when occasion arose, on the strength of a unique and private gloss on *The Prince*. She overrated virtú, individual agency, in much the same way Signor Mantissa overrated the fox. Perhaps one day one of them might ask: what was the tag-end of an age if not that sort of imbalance, that tilt toward the more devious, the less forceful? (183)

For V., Machiavelli is the father of political technology, the theorist who dissociated morality from action. Thanks in part to the Italian, ethical considerations no longer check the excesses of political and social engineering. Although that was not Machiavelli's intention, as the Gaucho has said, his writings have fostered ideology for its own sake, and method without humanity. Machiavelli theorized within a tradition that did not take into account disruptive energies and entropic processes. At this point V. still accepts Machiavelli's program for action, but she will soon realize that his analysis is outdated. Her discovery will be akin to Callisto's, who also believed with Machiavelli that Fortune and virtú governed man's history in equal proportion until he began to notice the factor of randomness or some sinister determination. The irony of V's discovery is that she herself may be that evil factor.

Old Godolphin's apprehensions infect the espionage community of Florence. Rumors soon associate Vheissu with a gigantic plot by barbarians to attack Florence through a network of underground tunnels running from Antarctica and exiting through the volcano Vesuvius (another V.). Another balloon seems about to go up. Since they thrive on crisis, the diplomats and spies believe that Armageddon is possible, and among them all only Sidney Stencil remains calm. He has evolved a theory on the Situation:

> . . . no Situation has any objective reality: it only existed in the minds of those who happened to be in on it at any specific moment. Since those several

minds tended to form a sum total or complex more mongrel than homogeneous, The Situation must necessarily appear to a single observer much like a diagram in four dimensions to an eye conditioned to seeing its world in only three (174).

Hence Sidney Stencil advocates teamwork, or, to put it another way, common cause or brotherhood.

Evan Godolphin has a complementary theory. He tells the Gaucho that the diplomats and the spies are all human and frightened:

> "Their anxiety is the same as my father's, what is coming to be my own, and perhaps in a few weeks what will be the anxiety of everyone living in a world none of us wants to see let into holocaust. Call it a kind of communion, surviving somehow on a mucked-up planet which God knows none of us like very much. But it is our planet and we live on it anyway" (178).

The energy which fuels events seems to be running down, decaying like "radium" over the ages. The reference recalls the "radiance" of Vheissu, and also the radium and the radiance Adams mentions in the passage from *The Education* cited earlier. The track of the energy runs through Florence in her decadence.

The crisis has its own zany momentum. The Gaucho leads his soldiers against the Venezuelan Embassy. Mantissa makes it to the Uffizi Gallery, reaches his objective, and poises his knife to cut *The Birth of Venus* from its frame. At that moment the painting shimmers in the colors Godolphin has described. The Venus Mantissa adores suddenly seems "a gaudy dream, a dream of annihilation" (193). Mantissa abandons the attempt, gathers up Hugh and Evan Godolphin, commandeers a barge, and sails away from Florence. The "streets" of the city are now full of rioters and troops. The Gaucho, his Machiavellianism gone sour, muses on the futility of human action: "Perhaps it is all a mockery, and the only condition we can ever bring to men a mockery of liberty, of dignity" (194). But Victoria

Wren, transfixed, watches the streets erupt, feeling herself a part of the violence and carnage. She has found her element:

> It was as if she saw herself embodying a feminine principle, acting as complement to all this bursting, explosive male energy. Inviolate and calm, she watched the spasms of wounded bodies, the fair of violent death, framed and staged, it seemed, for her alone in that tiny square. From her hair the heads of five crucified also looked on, no more expressive than she (192-193).

The significance of V. is enlarged in the next historical event, the first of two set in South West Africa, a German colony from 1890 until after World War I. This was a huge region, most of it desert, a literal waste land. Indeed, the coastal Namib desert, prized only for its diamonds, was known as the "skeleton coast" or the "coast of death," and further inland the Kalahari was scarcely less arid. Only the highlands contained good farming land, and there, before the Germans took over, Hottentots and Hereros (Bantus) made a prosperous living. In 1904, the same year the British and the French signed the accord which laid to rest the bickering generated at Fashoda, the Hereros revolted against the Germans. The German general Lothar von Trotha issued a *Vernichtungs Befehl*," or "annihilation order," and in the name of this "V." exterminated about 80 per cent of the rebels, or about 60,000 people. As Stencil says, "This is only 1 per cent of six million, but still pretty good" (227). The reference is of course to the six million Jews exterminated by the Germans during World War II; von Trotha's atrocities anticipate the accelerating destruction that reaches its peak later in the century.

The tale of von Trotha is actually interpolated into an episode of 1922, with which it has similarities, and is focused on an anonymous German soldier in von Trotha's army identified only as the rider of a horse named Firelilly. In fact, the episode is a surrealistic dream of Kurt Mondaugen, a character influenced by

Vera Meroving, another incarnation of the goddess V. When that dream is in turn retold by Herbert Stencil, the reason for the soldier's anonymity becomes apparent. Anonymity is something to be achieved.

It is a "dream of annihilation," apocalyptic in a classic psychological sense. In *The Pornography of Power*, Lionel Rubinoff has explained the phenomenon:

> Racism is an apocalyptic phenomenon which proceeds from the exhausted imagination of a defeated culture, a culture that has lost faith in its basic values.
> Racism is a passion which provides a source of security for the individual who embraces it by releasing him from the anguish of being human . . . *in order* to negate one's own humanity, as a flight from freedom and responsibility. . . .[7]

Because the racist soldier can ascribe nonhumanity to the Hereros, he becomes "free" in an irresponsible sense; he is no longer required to be a human in their presence. As Rubinoff says, he has "obliterated their individuality in order to negate [his] own individuality."[8] In treating the Herero as a mere object, something to be shot or hung, the soldier reifies himself. By reducing the Herero to nonhuman status, the soldier makes him subject to a racism of collective German origin, and the soldier becomes merely part of an anonymous mob. The soldier has no name in Pynchon's novel because he is part of that collective impulse toward the inanimate which is the principal theme of the book.

Under von Trotha's tutelage, the soldier learns to escape guilt, "not to be ashamed" (239) when he disembowels a Herero or rapes a girl in front of his fellow soldiers: "It had only to do with the destroyer and the destroyed, and the act which united them . . ." (245). On the coast, at Lüderitzbucht (Bay of Corpses), where the strand wolf or hyena picks the skeletons, the German troops inflict sexual perversions on the black slave laborers. Firelilly's rider seizes a concubine named

66

Sarah from a work crew building a jetty out into the sea. Because of the terms in which Pynchon describes the jetty, as a path for the Hereros, "as if the sea were pavement for them, as for our Redeemer" (252), the incident recalls a motif from "Low-lands," in which the passive Dennis Flange imagines himself traversing the ocean as a savior.

Sarah's body is scarred ("tattooed") with the marks of many whippings; she is Hugh Godolphin's metaphor for Vheissu made flesh. The soldier tries to possess Sarah utterly and exclusively, but can not prevail against his comrades who desire her also. On that sterile coast, the anonymous soldier thinks, "community may have been the only salvation possible against such an assertion of the Inanimate" (253), yet it is a ghastly kind of sharing to oppose to a waste land. After Sarah has been raped repeatedly by the Germans, she drowns herself. The dead girl becomes for the anonymous soldier one of "the dearest canvases in his soul's gallery" (254), a vision of absolute nothingness, and he becomes a citizen of the twentieth century, walking through a gallery of inanimate objects.

Inanimateness continues to increase, hastened by sexual perversion. The next episode involves a woman the narrator specifically identifies as V. At about this point the anonymous omniscient narrator of *V.* has more or less taken over. Actually, Pynchon has had that narrator intrude at various junctures of the book; he is part of a complex web of diverse narrative styles, including interior monologue, diary narration, and multiple character points of view, most of which are further embroidered by Herbert Stencil. In tone the narrator's voice is mocking; one of his functions is to suggest that Stencil's quest for conspiracy is delusion, that randomness alone governs the motion of the twentieth century, that the successions of V.'s Stencil discovers are unrelated to each other, are merely coincidental occurrences of a common initial. On the other hand the narrator is a conscious artificer who serves to filigree the significance of events beyond Stencil's capacity to extract meaning from them. The device of the omniscient narrator thus allows Pynchon to have his cake and eat it too; there may be no pattern at all, but at the same time the seeming pattern is elaborately worked out.

The ambiguity is humorous and central to the book, since it heightens the epistemological dilemma every historian faces: Does he extrapolate significance from accurately perceived events or does he impose that significance on history out of sheer human desire for symmetry? Having the narrator gloss parts of the story guarantees that the reader will not miss the flashes of déja vu, or, as James Joyce called the recognition of recurrent motifs in *Finnegans Wake,* "the Herewearea-gain Gaieties." Pynchon's method is in some ways similar to Joyce's in that book; in it the protagonist, Humphrey Chimpden Earwicker, is also known as H.C.E., or Here Comes Everybody, a character who is all things to all men. A more pertinent comparison might be Thomas Mann's *Joseph and His Brothers,* in which Joseph consciously invokes archetypes to give meaning to his history and experience, and does so to the amusement of the novel's narrator. Like Mann, Pynchon thus laughs at himself and his own artistry. The novelist too makes use of a willed recurrence or correspondence to structure the lives of his characters, the persistence of themes, and the continuity of his book. By permitting the narrator cheerfully to abet Stencil's search for correspondences and then to pull the rug out from under the quester, Pynchon implies that his own function is suspect, which adds a disarming sense of contrivance to the architecture of *V.*

Considering the trompe l'oeil aspects of the next scene, it is appropriately set in Paris in 1913, during one of that city's most romantically decadent phases, which Pynchon emphasizes by allusions to Black Masses, inversions of Catholicism on which V. dotes. In Paris V. conducts a lesbian affair with Mélanie L'Heuremaudit ("the cursed hour"), a fifteen-year-old dancer who has previously committed incest with her father. Mélanie has come to the city to dance the lead in *The Rape of the Chinese Virgins,* a ballet by Vladimir Porcépic, a thoroughly decadent composer, at the Théâtre de Vincent Castor. This fictional debut Pynchon has based on the scandalous initial production of Igor Stravinsky's ballet *The Rite of Spring* at the Théâtre des Champs-Elysées in Paris in 1913.

Besides "barbaric" music similar to Stravinsky's, Porcépic's ballet boasts another innovation, the use of German automata, androids which will dance as Mélanie's handmaidens. Mélanie herself dreams that she is a mechanical doll with a winding key imbedded between her shoulder blades. Her principal fetish, however, is her narcissism; Mélanie adores her image in a mirror. As a narcissist, she personifies a mirror-metaphor Pynchon introduces at various points in the novel. Juxtaposed in *V.* are "mirror-worlds," in which events happen in "mirror-time." There are several of these pairs, and each pair asserts the polarity of inanimateness and life, the principal duality of the novel. The mirror provides a reflection of the creeping inanimateness overtaking the characters. Time and energy run down even faster in the anti-worlds, and gradually, over the course of the century, the inanimate realms coincide with animate worlds. Although the anti-worlds are ill-defined and overlap too easily, the general outlines are clear.

One such anti-world is Baedeker land, the country of tourism which has evolved into "a parallel society" within the "real" world. That other society is artificial and sterile, warranted to keep tourists from contact with life. More than anything else it resembles a puppet-show, in which tourists and those who serve them are automata, or dolls like Mélanie, capable only of stylized motion and stiff attitudes. In countries which the stultifying decadence of Western civilization has not completely infected, the natives can retain a primitive, vital spontaneity behind a Baedeker facade. Generally, however, tourism represents the tendency of Western man to extend his dominion over primitive healthy cultures, to "order" and control those cultures with his technology and social and political engineering to the point where decay becomes inevitable and irreversible. The anti-world of tourism thus threatens to displace the "real" world, to lay it waste. Ironically, the tourists believe that they have achieved a kind of community by robbing the world of healthy diversity, that homogeneity of culture makes for communication and understanding, when in actuality it leads to inanimateness and death. Guidebooks in hand, money at the ready, the tourists isolate themselves from normal human intercourse in the anti-world:

> Its landscape is one of inanimate monuments and buildings; near-inanimate barmen, taxi-drivers, bellhops, guides: there to do any bidding, to various degrees of efficiency, on receipt of the recommanded baksheesh, pourboire, mancia, tip. More than this it is two-dimensional, as in the street, as are the pages and maps of those little red handbooks. . . . Tourism thus is supranational, like the Catholic Church, and perhaps the most absolute communion we know on earth: they share the same landscapes, suffer the same inconveniences, live by the same pellucid time-scale. They are the street's own (384).

Like the rituals of the Catholic Church, and the rituals of tourism, the rituals of normal human behavior have lost meaning. Yet those exhausted rituals are the only defense humans have against assertions of the inanimate. V. and some of the other characters in the novel are endowed with awareness that the inanimate is overtaking them, and they try to distill what meaning they can from rituals and relationships that have become banal. In the Montmartre cafes, while orchestras play the tango ("a dance for automata"), Porcépic and his friends talk of decadence, a key fixture of which is awareness of itself:

> "A decadence," Itague put in, "is a falling-away from what is human, and the further we fall the less human we become. Because we are less human, we foist off the humanity we have lost on inanimate objects and abstract theories" (380).

And another decadent, Kholsky, links the process with V.:

"It is a bleak world we live in, M. Itague; atoms collide, brain cells fatigue, economies collapse and others rise to succeed them, all in accord with the basic rhythms of History. Perhaps she [History] is a woman; women are a mystery to me" (380-381).

When V. makes her appearance, she is not yet the doyenne of decadents she will become. She is still— apparently—Victoria Wren, in process of decline but still human, as the narrator observes:

If she were Victoria Wren, even Stencil couldn't remain all unstirred by the ironic failure her life was moving toward, too rapidly by that prewar August ever to be reversed. The Florentine spring, the young entrepreneuse with all spring's hope in her virtú, with her girl's faith that Fortune (if only her skill, her timing held true) could be brought under control; that Victoria was being gradually replaced by V.; something entirely different, for which the young century had as yet no name (385-386).

Nevertheless, V. already possesses many trappings of decadence. In Paris she runs a dress shop, dresses flamboyantly, smokes black cigarettes held in a bizarre holder, lives in an apartment decorated in primitive African and lush Oriental styles, and moves in a circle of acquaintances "inclined toward sadism, sacrilege, endogamy and homosexuality" (382). Under V.'s spell Mélanie dresses as a transvestite, which Parisians consider unusual because V. would seem to be the dominant lesbian, and that role should belong to her. Porcépic amuses a group of decadents by adding up the dominant-submissive sexual and social role combinations between V. and her lover; it works out to 64.

Sexual perversions, if performed ritualistically, are attempts to extract meaning from the sexual act, but the perversions can become reductive, especially if the impulse which gave them birth has less and less meaning itself. Again, as in "Entropy," Pynchon appears to be leaning on the works of the Marquis de Sade, those catalogues of exhaustion and decadence. Lesbianism, the narrator of the episode says, "stems from self-love projected on to some other human object. If a girl gets to feeling narcissist, she will also sooner or later come upon the idea that women, the class she belongs to, are not so bad either" (382). Actually the intercourse between the two women takes place with "minimum friction"; it is almost all voyeurism, with V. watching Mélanie watch herself in a mirror. Pynchon is working with Doppelgängers again: "With the addition of this other—multiplied also, perhaps, by mirrors—comes consummation: for the other is also her double" (385). For Mélanie, the images provide gratification. For V., the affair is more profound, and for Pynchon as well:

As for V., she recognized—perhaps aware of her own progression toward inanimateness—the fetish of Mélanie and the fetish of herself to be one. As all inanimate objects, to one victimized by them, are alike. It was a variation on the Porpentine theme, the Tristan-and-Iseult theme, indeed, according to some, the single melody, banal and exasperating, of all Romanticism since the Middle Ages: "the act of love and the act of death are one" (385).[9]

The Tristan-Iseult theme, which equates love and death, is central to Pynchon's work. Motivating many of the characters of *V.* is a sexual love of death or inanimateness; caught in the decadence of an expiring romanticism, they succumb to exhaustion. V., in falling in "love" with Mélanie, begins her career as a full-fledged decadent, and for this reason the Paris episode is the most important in the novel, since it more than any other marks her transformation into a goddess of death, a symbol of moribund Western culture. The lesbian affair, says the narrator, is a species of tourism, because it represents an infiltration of inanimate fetishism into human relationship. The narrator wonders whether V. realizes the full implications of her declining curve:

The smallest realization—at any step: Cairo, Florence, Paris—that she fitted into a larger scheme leading eventually to her personal destruction and she might have shied off, come to establish so many controls over herself that she became—to Freudian, behaviorist, man of religion, no matter—a purely determined organism, an automaton, constructed, only quaintly, of human flesh. Or, by contrast, might have reacted against the above, which we have come to call Puritan, by journeying even deeper into a fetish-country until she became entirely and in reality—not merely as a love-game with any Mélanie—an inanimate object of desire (386).

Henceforward V. will incorporate bits and pieces of inanimate matter into her body. Stencil visualizes his goddess as a living machine with glass eyes and metal feet, and alloys and plastics at anatomical points in between, including a cunningly designed artificial vagina. The more inanimate material V. assimilates, the more reified she becomes. A mirror arrests Mélanie's image; machinery arrests V. herself—she is turning into a dynamo. Obviously to a decadent the inanimate offers something that life does not—the extinction of individuality, the perfection of death, the peace of annihilation, "the artifice of eternity," as Stanley Edgar Hyman has called V.'s goal.[20] Even objectified humans feel the need to commune with others, however, and V.'s love for Mélanie is an attempt to reach another person. Pynchon seems to be saying that humans in our era may be able to communicate only as objects, and the frustration at their limitations may impel them to perverse forms of sexuality. If one cannot recognize the humanity in another, if the normal channels by which a person contacts another are blocked, then he adopts what method he can, even if it is a method doomed to failure. V. accepts Mélanie's fetish.

Mélanie's narcissism is a measure of her longing for the inanimate; her look into the mirror is a look into the void of the self. Because a death-wish is at the root of Mélanie's attempts to freeze her image in a mirror, Freud's psychoanalytic version of the theory of entropy is in force here. Wylie Sypher has discussed this aspect of Freud in *Loss of the Self in Modern Literature and Art:*

> If, [Freud] says, the tendency of instinct is toward repeating or restating an earlier condition, then the desire to return to the inorganic is irresistible, and our instinct is to obliterate the disturbance we call consciousness. "The organism is resolved to die in its own way," and the path of our life is simply our own way of choosing our progress toward death. The ultimate pleasure is an untroubled security of not-being; therefore the drag toward inertia [Thanatos] is constantly behind that self-assertion we call living. "The inanimate was there before the animate"—a wisdom graven ineffaceably, though illegibly, within the unconscious self. Like Schopenhauer or Nietzsche, Freud assumes that the root of all our troubles is our individuality, which we would extinguish.[11]

Like the anonymous soldier of von Trotha's army, Mélanie desires to extinguish her self. She has a foot in each of the mirror-worlds. She is also a redeemer doomed to failure, like Porpentine the spy and Sarah the concubine, another sacrificial victim to V., the goddess of the waste land. Paris in 1913 *is* a waste land; the landscape has changed, but not its essential deadness. While earlier settings edged on actual desert, Paris suffers from lack of rain, an observation repeated several times. The climate is oppressive, an atmosphere of unpleasant expectancy, and Mélanie has "rainy" eyes (388). Her eyes, however, are her only animate attributes. Predicting that she will become the toast of the city, Porcépic tells Mélanie that she is "not real but an object of pleasure. . . . doll-like. You will drive Paris mad. Women and men alike" (379).

As might be expected, Mélanie's "cursed hour" arrives in the midst of riot, which has become V.'s element. Turmoil erupts at the Théâtre Vincent Castor on the night of Porcépic's ballet when the audience splits into pro- and anti-Porcépic factions. Backstage all is chaos increased by catcalls, the savage music, and the running amok of the German automata. In the confusion Mélanie either deliberately refuses or forgets to prepare for the climax of her dance, in which she is to be impaled at the crotch (the V of spread thighs) on a lance and raised high above the stage. She is supposed to wear a device to protect her from injury, but "she might have become confused in this fetish-world and neglected to add to herself the one inanimate object that would save her" (389). The curtain falls on a ghastly scene, a bleeding, once-living marionette crucified on a lance, a mockery of redemption for the waste land of Paris. Nearly hysterical, V. flees the city with a proto-fascist Italian.

Pynchon does not try to grapple directly with the chaos of World War I, although he views it as an even larger theater for V. Obliquely, however, two characters focus attention on that holocaust. The first is Evan Godolphin, whose face is destroyed when his plane crashes in the battle of Meuse-Argonne. Plastic surgeons reconstruct his face using inanimate materials: paraffin, celluloid, silver, and ivory. His tissue eventually rejects the inert foreign matter, which results in permanent disfigurement. Young Godolphin's tragedy inspires one Schoenmaker to become a plastic surgeon who can work with bone and skin, but Schoenmaker properly belong to the present, and will be considered in the next chapter.

The second character is Sidney Stencil, Herbert's father, who learns that the evils of the World War have shattered even his flexible theory of the Situation:

> Ten million dead. Gas. Passchendaele. Let that be now a large figure, now a chemical formula, now an historical account. But dear Lord, not the Nameless Horror, the sudden prodigy sprung on a world unaware (431).

These reflections are part of the final section of the book, an epilogue spoken by the narrator, which deals with events apparently not known by Herbert Stencil. The episode is set in 1919, on Malta, to which the elder Stencil has come to cope with a revolutionary nationalist movement against the British, who hold the island.

In spite of the chaos of the war, or because of it, Stencil *père* is still searching for logical explanations for lethal historical motion. He would like to believe in "they"—that some conspiracy is responsible for the evil that dogs him on his assignments, but he is still too much the Machiavellian to surrender wholly to paranoia. Enroute to Malta on an ancient Levantine xebec, Stencil has been tutored by the captain of the ship, Mehemet, who claims to be from the past, from 1300, to be exact—the parameter of Henry Adams's survey of history—when the Virgin reigned supreme. Mehemet is familiar with the avatars of the older goddess of Western culture: his ship is named *Astarte,* "goddess of sexual love" (429), and he tells Stencil tales of Mara, the fertility goddess of Malta, who was by turns loving and cruel, but always comprehensible. Having sailed his ship through a time-warp, Mehemet bridges past and present; he is wise. He places his trust in still another goddess, or at least, in the aspect of deity that a Machiavellian can appreciate. "Fortune," he reminds his passenger, is "an inconstant goddess" (430), and to her, not to some evil plot, he attributes the cause of events. Moreover, Mehemet understands the Second Law of Thermodynamics: "Both the world and we, M. Stencil, began to die from the moment of birth" (432). The time-traveller even has a metaphor for man's life. He once saw a sailor, the last man on board an abandoned ship, painting the sides of the vessel as it sank.

On Malta Stencil *père* encounters Veronica Manganese, who wears to their meeting a comb in the shape of five crucified soldiers, by which he recognizes her as his (presumed) former love, Victoria Wren. She is much changed; she has a clock for an eye, a star sapphire for a navel, and a fixation on the void: "How pleasant to watch nothing" (459), she tells Sidney. Almost wholly perverted, she is evil, if only because she has turned almost into a machine. Appropriately enough, Sidney Stencil fears machines; automobiles terrify him, for instance. Veronica Manganese came to

Malta in 1914, and has since become friendly with D'Annunzio and Mussolini. Apparently independently wealthy, she lives on Malta at a villa where Evan Godolphin—grotesquely disfigured—is caretaker. Aware that V. seems to act as catalyst for crisis, Stencil hopes that these coincidences are merely chance, the working of the goddess Fortuna, and not an evil plot of which V. is a part, "not a signal for the reactivation of those same chaotic and situational forces at work in Florence twenty years ago" (442). If a balloon is going up, Stencil can expect "chaos in the streets" (443), in which various factions run riot, subsumed within the anonymous collective crowd; "mob violence, like tourism, is a kind of communion. By its special magic a large number of lonely souls, however heterogeneous, can share the common property of opposition to what is" (443).

Stencil is in a pensive mood. "If there is any political moral to be found in this world," he writes in his journal

> it is that we carry on the business of this century with an intolerable double vision. Right and left; the hothouse and the street. The Right can only live and work hermetically, in the hothouse of the past, while outside the Left prosecute their affairs in the streets by manipulated mob violence. And can not live but in the dreamscape of the future.
>
> What of the real present, the men-of-no-politics, the once-respectable Golden Mean? Obsolete; in any case, lost sight of. In a West of such extremes we can expect, at the very least, a highly "alienated" populace within not many more years (440).

It is a black but of course accurate prophecy, and requires no elaboration.

Stencil also waxes apocalyptic, in a passage which unites various themes in the novel. Perhaps this time crisis will bring revelation:

> The matter of a Paraclete's coming, the comforter, the dove; the tongues of flame, the gift of tongues:

77

Pentecost. Third Person of the Trinity. None of it was implausible to Stencil. The Father had come and gone. In political terms, the Father was the Prince; the single leader, the dynamic figure whose virtú used to be a determinant of history. This had degenerated to the Son, genius of the liberal love-feast which had produced 1848 and lately the overthrow of the Czars. What next? What Apocalypse?

Especially on Malta, a matriarchal island. Would the Paraclete be also a mother? Comforter, true. But what gift of communication could ever come from a woman . . . (444).

Machiavelli's strength and virtue have given way to an effeminate Christianity, degenerate in a Nietzschean sense, and now some new deity seems immanent and imminent on Malta. Will she be Machiavelli's Goddess Fortuna, or will she be the evil V.? Circumstances hint at the latter. Stencil shadows Veronica Manganese in and out of churches. He also establishes contact with Father Fairing, a Jesuit priest with a penchant for spying, who is motivated by antipathy to chaos, which he considers Anti-Christian. Fairing will discover his own Paraclete some years later.

Among Stencil's other clandestine contacts is a Maltese named Maijstral, a double agent working both for the British and for Veronica Manganese. Maijstral's wife, pregnant with the child who will become Fausto, fears for her husband's life, appeals to Stencil for help, and threatens to commit suicide if that assistance is not forthcoming. Stencil does help, averts the suicide, and thus, in a sense, becomes Fausto's "father," who will succeed his sire as a man of the Golden Mean and produce a child of the present.

In spite of V.'s efforts to incite rebellion by ordering atrocities—which include sexual mutilation—the crisis evaporates, and Sidney Stencil sails from Malta once again on the *Astarte*. A day's sail out, the ship is sunk by a waterspout, apparently a chance phenomenon, although Veronica Manganese has watched him leave the quay at Malta. Perhaps V., at the head of a conspiracy Stencil suspects exists, has destroyed him. More likely, the Goddess Fortune has come at last to the good Machiavellian.

The next episode involving the woman V. occurs in 1922, once again in South West Africa, now under the mandate of the Union of South Africa. The circumstances are another native uprising and its colonial repression. The Bondels (Bondelswaartz or Bondelswarts) rebel, and when they refuse to surrender one of their leaders, the authorities overreact.[12] Herbert Stencil learns this story from Kurt Mondaugen, a German engineer working for Yoyodyne, Inc., a Long Island defense firm headed by one Bloody Chiclitz. When Mondaugen casually mentions having worked at Peenemunde on the V-1 and V-2 rockets, a bulb lights above Stencil's head: "The magic initial!" (211). The quester pumps the German for information, and in retelling it, "stencilizes" it. In the twenties, Mondaugen is engaged in research in South West Africa on atmospheric radio disturbances, or sferics. He has a complicated system of antennas and receivers to pick up mysterious noises presumed to emanate from the earth's magnetic field. During the rebellion Mondaugen takes refuge with other white colonials in the fortified villa of a German named Foppl, a veteran of von Trotha's genocidal army, who is overjoyed that history seems about to repeat itself. Mondaugen tries to continue his experiments at the villa, with difficulty, for Foppl turns the gathering into a siege party. Representatives of various colonial nations are thus thrown together, "all creating the appearance of a tiny European Conclave or League of Nations, assembled here while political chaos howled outside" (217).

Apocalypse stalks the fortified ramparts; inside the party rapidly degenerates into a macabre orgy reminiscent of that in E. A. Poe's "The Masque of the Red Death." Here Mondaugen meets the elderly, tottering Hugh Godolphin, who tells him of an expedition to the South Pole; Lieutenant Weissmann, an army officer from Munich, who believes Mondaugen is a spy and his listening equipment coding devices; Vera Meroving, a sinister woman also from Munich, whose most interesting feature is an artificial eye containing a tiny clock in the iris; and Hedwig Vogelsang, a sort of Mélanie l'Heuremaudit, who will not sleep with the infatuated Mondaugen until after he contracts scurvy during the siege. If Hedwig, the Doppelgänger V., is sexually aroused only by disease, the other V., Vera Meroving, is no less perverse; she plays sado-masochistic games with the transvestite Weissman. Both Vera Meroving and Weissmann are early followers of Hitler. Decadence now borders on madness. Foppl dreams of the atrocities of 1904. As he brutalizes his own black servants the German tells them of von Trotha's imminent Second Coming: "like Jesus returning to earth, von Trotha is coming to deliver you" (222). Still driven by Vheissu, old Godolphin whips a prisoner to death to the tune of "Down by the Summertime Sea." Hedwig Vogelsang dances with the planet Venus in Foppl's basement planetarium.

Vera Meroving overshadows the other guests at the Siege Party. She is, of course, another avatar of V., and she holds long talks with her old friend Godolphin. They speak of Vheissu. 1904, says Vera, is her Vheissu, and the current siege is also Vheissu. Godolphin chides her: Vheissu is "a luxury, an indulgence" the two of them can no longer afford. Vheissu had been for them a private dream of annihilation, but now it has spread to the whole twentieth century. Godolphin's prophecy is worse than Sidney Stencil's. The Siege Party itself typifies the century; the festivities are an apex of "a constantly rising curve, taking human depravity as an ordinate" (225).

Cultural desolation leads to moral atrophy. Pynchon's indictment of Western civilization becomes freighted with complexities which we should perhaps pause to sort out. Pynchon has levelled his attack against diverse aspects of Western culture: politics, religion, art, sexuality—all of which have been blighted by decadence. Decadence is simply an exhaustion of tradition, a decay of values, which leads to inertness and to death; it is the cultural equivalent of entropy. Those affected by decadence clutch at what vitality remains. In the political realm, only crisis, a sense of apocalypse provides the necessary *frisson*; in religion, the Black Mass; in art, the barbaric, the novel; in sexuality, perversion and cruelty. Spontaneity has given way to febrile, diseased imagination. Decadence results, Pynchon believes, from the romantic consciousness which animated the last century and which might be said to extend from de Sade to Sartre in our time. That consciousness rested chiefly on a conception of the self. It was assumed by the romantic that man had a real essence, a real personality that was obscured by the roles society compelled him to play. That real self could be recaptured or renewed in one of two ways. First, he might seek to reverse his dissociation from nature, to refresh himself, and thereby counter his alienation. In Pynchon's world, that path is closed, for nature herself has been altered irrevocably, either by man's own corruption of nature, as in the tourism Western civilization has extended over the world, or by entropy inherent in nature itself, which has had the similar effect of turning the landscape into a waste land. Without that option, man can merely explore the identities open to him. That is what V. has done, but as she exhausts her identities, she comes closer to death.

The second route open to the romantic is to revolt against society itself, to define himself in opposition to the collective. Rejecting tourism, which has ordered and controlled nature, Godolphin has struck off on his own, hoping to be able to penetrate reality. He finds a vision of nothing, nihilism, a dream of annihilation. But, he discovers, he has no private claim to his nihilism; the mob has coopted it. Nihilism provides the collective with its sense of fraudulent communion; it is the source of mob violence, since it frees the individual from any responsibility for his actions, as with the soldiers in von Trotha's army. Identities merge into homogeneity and anonymity; everyone dreams of annihilation. Only one alternative, perhaps, is left to the man who would stave off the inanimate: a choice of the hothouse, with its private, limited consciousness, over the street, with its chaos and violence. These are irreconcilable opposites. The hothouse is a realm of the past, of introspection, the street of the spurious present, of anonymity. Sidney Stencil thinks that V. herself has bridged the two, but only, as Robert Golden has suggested in his article on *V.*, because "her brand of politics, vaguely associated with fascism, is a mixture of right-wing nostalgia and mob violence and because she represents that *nada* which underlies everything in *V.*"[13] In any case, V. has betrayed her humanity. She is a symbol of modern man in his collective mass, striving for community by denying that which makes him human.

Outside Foppl's villa is the waste land, literally the Kalahari, figuratively the geography of our century. While chaos roars, the members of the Siege Party inside strive for what communion they can achieve, and it is an awful communion, an attempt to stave off the inanimate by methods that can only accelerate it. Parallels with other episodes are abundant. In Mondaugen's mind, Foppl and Godolphin, bent on achieving inanimateness, both determined to penetrate the "skin" of reality to its interior nothingness, begin to merge. Vera Meroving seems to induce Mondaugen's dream of the anonymous soldier, the rider of the horse Firelily. When the engineer awakes, Hedwig Vogelsang rides into his room on the back of a Bondel prisoner she calls Firelilly. Surveying the diseased imaginations around him, Mondaugen decides that decadence has produced "a soul-depression which must surely infest Europe as it infested this house" (258).

Finally, Lieutenant Weissmann succeeds in "decoding" a sferic message. It reads: "Die Welt Ist Alles Was Der Fall Ist" or "The world is all that the case is," which is Proposition One of Ludwig Wittgenstein's *Tractatus Logico-Philosophicus*. Beginning with that position, Wittgenstein goes on to say that whatever sense the world has lies outside the world, that there is no causality we can perceive as inherent in the world, that any values we attribute to the workings of the world are accidental. In the context in which Pynchon has been working, the allusion is another assertion of the unpredictable nature of the motion of history and reinforces the possibility that entropy is simply random disorder. Put another way, Wittgenstein merely echoes Sidney Stencil's assertion that no Situation has "any objective reality." If there is no design in nature, there is no meaning, and having confronted this vision of nothing, Mondaugen flees the villa into the Kalahari.

The next fifteen years or so are lacunae in Stencil's narrative, although they will be filled in to a certain extent when the quester meets Profane. In the present Stencil also encounters Paola Maijstral, who gives him her father's journal, "The Confessions of Fausto Maijstral," containing an account of the seige of Malta in World War II. This extended narrative is the center of Pynchon's novel, and while all the motifs and themes of the book come together in it, it is confusing and to a degree unconvincing, the product of Fausto Maijstral's hyperactive literary imagination, which sees the world not in a grain of sand but in an island of rock in the Mediterranean. Fausto can resist metaphors no more than Stencil can resist clues. Malta, "where all history seemed simultaneously present, where all streets were strait with ghosts" (452), is a fault line between various dualities, or, to use a term Pynchon comes increasingly to prefer, an interface. Past and present, or hothouse and street, form one such duality, and Fausto is a sojourner in each realm. Animation and decadence are a second; "real" life and tourism a third; and the street and "below the street," which figure more prominently in the Profane half of the story, a fourth. The sequence also presents what may be the apotheosis of the woman V.

It occurs amid a conjunction of V.'s. Malta herself is a stronghold of the White Goddess; it is, as Sidney Stencil has observed, a matriarchal island. World War II has brought chaos. German planes bomb the island's capital, Valetta. Those planes fly over in "plots," Maijstral's word for the formations, picked up by the "scatter" of the searchlights, another word suggestive of V., since the narrator will laconically observe that the object of Stencil's search is "a remarkably scattered concept" (364). Beneath the planes Malta waits, "an immemorial woman. . . . spread [as in V] to the explosive orgasms" (298) of destruction. Sex and death once again conjoin, this time in an ultimate decadence.

According to Maijstral, decadence has even before

the war come to Malta, which is a colonial possession, and which is, after all, inanimate rock. And yet, at moments, even in the course of war, life still springs, borne by the wind that is Maijstral's namesake, a "resurgence of humanity in the automaton, health in the decadent" (316). Fausto has devoted himself to a study of decadence, defined as "a clear movement toward death or, preferably, non-humanity" (301), and has perceived its progress in himself. He has divided his life into segments; each represents a personality he calls Fausto I, II, III, and IV. Herbert Stencil resolves his multiple selves into He Who Looks for V., which may or may not put him in the category of contemporary man in search of an identity. But Stencil never examines his identity; his quest negates introspection, since it ultimately turns on a paranoia which directs his vision outward, away from the self. He spends his days "at a certain vegetation" (209), fitting together the pieces of the conspiracy.

By contrast, Fausto pores over his personalities in Adamsian third person. In some ways the succession of his selves resembles the stages of the woman V.'s decline, since she too changes identities, although his takes place over a shorter period and proves to be a reversible process, where hers is not. Now a "man of letters," a poet-historian, Fausto IV, writing in 1956, recalls Fausto I, himself in the years before the war. Like Victoria Wren a Catholic, Fausto I had wanted to take Holy Orders, and had even studied for the priesthood. In those days he was ambitious, a believer in virtú. Two of his friends, a future politician and a future engineer, with Fausto as a future priest, formed a semi-political "Movement"; all three wanted to become the nucleus of a school of Anglo-Maltese Poetry, the Generation of '37. Steeped in T. S. Eliot, they fancied themselves able to synthesize their "simple" Maltese heritage and their colonial English intellectualism into a literature of hardy aesthetic and religious affirmation. They find it difficult. Desire to be "builders" as they might, Maltese affinites strain against English, and the stress is too powerful:

84

> ... we are torn, our grand "Generation of '37." To be merely Maltese: endure almost mindless, without sense of time? Or to think—continuously—in English, to be too aware of war, of time, of all the greys and shadows of love? (289)

Moreover, Fausto I loses his faith in God, not in dramatic steps, but through "an accumulation of small accidents: examples of general injustice, misfortune falling upon the godly, prayers of one's own unanswered" (309). Accident becomes an important factor in Fausto's life.

Loss of faith, the beginning of the war, which turns history into a "freak show" (287), and the arrival of his daughter result in Fausto II. He has fallen "in love" with his wife, Elena, but that love is mixed up with his nationalism and his poetry. The English side of him interferes with his natural ability to love. At one point, on an outing, Elena and Fausto pretend to be English tourists, and as they sit in a cafe they grip each other's arms and press their nails into each other's flesh. Frustration at being objects to one another makes them try to reach out, to penetrate the "skin" of the other, just as other characters in the novel have done. Elena and Fausto are luckier than those others, however, because their not wholly attenuated affection (their Maltese side) permits them to accept their limitations. Moreover, they produce a child. Still, Fausto takes this mild cruelty as a sign of decadence which the war aggravates. It is harder now to feel on a personal level, since one is too caught up in the larger conflict. Some "communion" is possible here; Fausto can "build," or rebuild, the island's airfields nightly bombed by the Germans. He and his comrades achieve a communion by "expiating sins they are unaware of" (295), by resisting the onslaught of death and the inanimate. Each day their work is destroyed, and yet they prevail against disorder. Fausto II and his family take refuge in the sewers and tunnels which honeycomb Malta. "Below the street," they survive. Characteristically, Fausto seizes on the situation for metaphor:

But in dream there are two worlds: the street and under the street. One of the kingdom of death and one of life. And how can a poet live without exploring the other kingdom, even if only as a kind of tourist? A poet feeds on dream (304).

Fausto regards the underground much as does Dennis Flange of "Low-lands," as a source of life. Penchant for metaphor also keeps Fausto and his friend writing poetry, usually in a heroic vein, although as the war continues they come closer to despair. Without dream, metaphor, poetry, how can one survive, Fausto asks.

Fausto III, who takes "on much of the non-humanity of the debris, crushed stone, broken masonry, destroyed churches and auberges" (286) of Valletta, is born on the Day of the 13 Raids in which two people die: Elena Maijstral and the Bad Priest. Several years before, a mysterious priest had appeared, ostensibly Catholic, clothed in the usual black robes and cowl, but with a message diametrically opposed to that of Valletta's orthodox Father Avalanche. The Bad Priest proselytizes for the inanimate, especially among the island's children. Appearing suddenly from nowhere, the Bad Priest preaches chastity for girls, and tells boys

that the object of male existence was to be like a crystal: beautiful and soulless. "God is soulless?" speculated Father Avalanche. "Having created souls, He himself has none? So that to be like God we must allow to be eroded the soul in ourselves. Seek mineral symmetry, for here is eternal life: the immortality of rock. Plausible. But apostasy."

The children were not, of course, having any. Knowing full well that if every girl became a sister there would be no more Maltese: and that rock, however fine as an object of contemplation, does no work: labours not and thus displeases God, who is favorably disposed towards human labour (319).

Although hardly a full-fledged Machiavellian, Fausto is endorsing virtú, the agency of human labor. The other half of Machiavelli's equation the poet-historian apprehends gradually. The Bad Priest advises Maijstral's wife to abort the child she is carrying. She is ready to do so, but she meets Father Avalanche, the legitimate priest, "by accident" (320), and he convinces her to give birth. Accident causes the death of Fausto's wife in a bombing raid, and also causes the apparent death of the Bad Priest. The Goddess Fortuna reigns.

The Bad Priest is V., sexually inverted, only vestigially human, a virtual machine. Once a would-be nun, she has come full-circle to transvestite priest. Worse, her body is much as Herbert Stencil has visualized it, composed of metals and plastics, jewels and springs; her decadence has led her to near-total inanimateness. The same bombing raid that kills Fausto's wife leaves the doll-like figure helplessly pinned under a fallen timber, where the children, presumably including Fausto's own Paola, literally disassemble it. His humanity arrested by the shock of his wife's death, Fausto only watches as the children rip off V.'s metal limbs and gouge the star sapphire from the navel and the clock eye from its socket. Her attackers, Fausto IV can later theorize, have "a certain fondness for the Manichean common to all children" (317). In the midst of chaos, the children rely on metaphor; they play war games in imitation of the real battles around them, and call one side good and one side evil. Because of their immaturity, these metaphors are "poetry in a vacuum" (311), not much different from Fausto's own early poetry—which he will disavow in subsequent palinodes.

By trying to so easily discover good and evil, the children make the same mistake as Herbert Stencil; they misunderstand fortune:

Here the combination of a siege, a Roman Catholic upbringing, and an unconscious identification of one's own mother with the Virgin all sent simple dualism into strange patterns indeed. . . . But if their idea of the struggle could be described graphically it would not be as two equal-sized vectors head-to-head—their heads making an X of unknown quantity; rather as a point, dimensionless—good—surrounded by—any number of radial arrows—vectors of evil—pointing inward. Good, i.e., at bay. The Virgin assailed. The wingéd mother protective. The woman passive. Malta in siege.

A wheel, this diagram: Fortune's wheel. Spin as it might the basic arrangement was constant. Stroboscopic effects could change the apparent number of spokes; direction could change; but the hub still held the spokes in place and the meeting-place of the spokes still defined the hub. The old cyclic idea of history had taught only the rim, to which princes and serfs alike were lashed; that wheel was oriented vertical; one rose and fell. But the children's wheel was dead-level, its own rim only that of the sea's horizon —so sensuous, so "visual" a race are we Maltese (317).

Not knowing any better, the children think it is a game: The "priest" is the bad guy, and a machine is something to be taken apart. For months they have kept the Bad Priest under "surveillance," and Fausto himself as he watches feels "like a spy," as if he and the children were like Sidney Stencil's unsavory colleagues, or like V. herself, who can regard life as a game, as action divorced from ethical considerations. To his credit, Fausto is horrified at his inaction. Whatever else she may be, V. is still human and suffering. Fausto gives her Extreme Unction, or what he can remember of the sacrament, but can not hear her confession, for the children have taken her teeth. He detects contrition in her weeping, however, as he prays for her. Fausto never sees her again after he reels away from the scene, but he assumes that she is dead.

His guilt precipitates Fausto IV, inheritor of "a physically and spiritually broken world. No single event produced him. Fausto III had merely passed a certain level in his slow return to consciousness or humanity. That curve is still rising" (286). On his guilt Fausto erects a philosophy, almost a religion, of fortune. That is not to say that Fortuna reigns supreme. God can "suspend the laws of chance" (309), but at the same time "there is more accident to [life] than a man can ever admit to and stay sane" (300). Within that framework, the war itself would seem to be a species of accident. Fausto goes further: life itself is accident, embodied within woman herself:

> Their babies always seem to come by happenstance; a random conjunction of events. . . . They do not understand what is going on inside them; that it is a mechanical and alien growth which at some point acquires a soul. . . . Or: the same forces which dictate the bomb's trajectory, the deaths of stars, the wind and the waterspout have focussed somewhere inside the pelvic frontiers without their consent, to generate one more mighty accident (301).

Fausto decides that "to have humanism we must first be convinced of our humanity" (302), but also concedes that man needs a "Great Lie" (305) in order to exist. That lie is the illusion of meaning, which can only come through metaphor and artifice. Endorsing Wittgenstein's and Sidney Stencil's appraisal of the universe, he also endorses Herbert Stencil's. If Stencil Jr. must have his great symbol, Fausto must have his endlessly ramifying metaphors, and at one point Fausto comes close to accepting the metaphor of V. herself. The impulse to survive, Fausto writes,

> the same motives which cause us to populate a dream-street also cause us to apply to a rock human qualities like "invincibility," "tenacity," perseverance," etc. More than metaphor, it is delusion. But on the strength of this delusion Malta survived (305).

Herbert Stencil will not be able to accept the possibility of V.'s death, and will continue to search for her. Nor will Fausto be able to halt his metaphors, for if they do not invest life with significance, they at least act as a drag on meaninglessness. While there is a measure of futility to their endeavors, it is perhaps not their place to make any final statement. Women dominate the story, and it is to them that Pynchon turns in the present.

CHAPTER THREE

The Street of the Twentieth Century: Schlemihlhood in V.

In addition to being the rock at the hub of Fortune's wheel, Malta is "a clenched fist around a yo-yo string" (418), which draws the yo-yoing Benny Profane—along with Herbert Stencil and Paola Maijstral—eventually to the Mediterranean. Pynchon transforms this child's toy into a metaphor of broad application to the modern human condition, since the yo-yo suggests a spinning in place, or inertia in motion. In contrast to Herbert Stencil's quest, which has a zany but definable direction, the yo-yoing of Benny Profane and others—for Profane has no monopoly on the metaphor—represents motion without meaning, or decadence, a condition Pynchon implies is vitality persisting around a core of stillness. A principal symptom of decadence is its affinity for the mechanical, and to strengthen the appropriateness of his metaphor Pynchon associates the yo-yo with a second child's toy, the gyroscope. The entrepreneur Bloody Chiclitz is content to manufacture such mechanical playthings until he discovers that gyroscopes are more valuable in missile guidance systems. Converting his toy factory to a "defense" plant, Chiclitz names the new corporation Yoyodyne: the dyne (a unit of force) is put to mindless and lethal use. Envisioned another way, the yo-yo parodies the random spin of the Wheel of Fortune; its motion is accidental and therefore unpredictable. And finally, yo-yoing is a form of tourism on a less global scale, because it mandates a similar superficiality of contact among people, and because it usually takes place on the street, although Profane and his fellows can yo-yo on subways under the street as well.

Herbert Stencil trots the globe; Benny Profane walks —or yo-yos—the street which Fausto Maijstral identifies as

the street of the 20th century, at whose far end or turning—we hope—is some sense of home or safety. But no guarantees. A street we are put at the wrong end of, for reasons best known to the agents who put us there. If there are agents. But a street we must walk (303).

For Profane, streets offer no safety and have no turnings; he feels menaced by them because they seem to go on forever. The longer he sojourns, the less comfortable he feels, and the less he seems to understand the street:

Road work had done nothing to improve the outward Profane, or the inward one either. Though the street had claimed a big fraction of Profane's age, it and he remained strangers in every way. Streets (roads, circles, squares, places, prospects) had taught him nothing: he couldn't work a transit, crane, payloader, couldn't lay bricks, stretch a tape right, hold an elevation rod still, hadn't even learned to drive a car (27).

Profane is a schlemihl, a vocation he chooses deliberately; incompetence is merely one of its attributes. He is a victim, dispossessed and alienated, an object of mercy—or so he hopes. Profane is quite content to be an object to other people, content especially to be a victim, since his condition permits him to "take" from other people without giving of himself. Schlemihlhood is a method of preserving the self—of defining it—by reaching a kind of accommodation with a world always trying to violate that self. On the few occasions that Profane reaches out to others, his overtures are attempts to leave his mark on the street:

> It was a desire he got, off and on, to be cruel and feel at the same time sorrow so big it filled him, leaked out his eyes and the holes in his shoes to make one big pool of human sorrow on the street, which had everything spilled on it from beer to blood, but very little compassion (128).

Generally, however, Profane prefers to leave no trace of himself, by escaping all but the most minimal contact with others. A romantic trying to hold on to what illusions he permits himself, he does not rebel against society; he merely declines the "communion" with others that he senses leads to the homogeneity of the mob and the decadence of the age. He is not entirely successful, if only because his unwillingness to be vulnerable frustrates others and renews their claims upon him, but the attitude makes it possible for him to survive in the midst of chaos and advancing inanimateness. For Profane, yo-yoing is a fetish, as much a defense against the inanimate as is his schlemihlhood. Essentially passive, he spins through the present protected by his refusal to become involved with anybody —and anything. It is as if he hopes to stave off inertia by coopting that psychological state before it can overtake him. Yet being an object has its perils. In Fausto's words, Profane is not "convinced of his own humanity"; he worries about becoming a machine, and worries about his own disassembly. Among his nightmares is the chestnut about the man born with a golden screw in his navel, who tries desperately to remove it and who finally succeeds, only to have his ass fall off.

Profane has a fair-sized ass at stake; he is fat and "amoebalike," with close-cropped hair and pig eyes. In Pynchon's fiction, such characteristics usually insure a man's attractiveness to women, and Profane's are no exception: "women had always happened to Profane the schlemihl like accidents: broken shoelaces, dropped dishes, pins in new shirts" (121). The narrator's observation establishes Profane's antecedents and his role. If Herbert Stencil may be the literal child of V., Profane is the figurative child of Fortune. His career is a series of accidents, just as his characteristic motion is a version of Fortune's wheel. At the same time, Profane, like everybody else in the present, has inherited the world of V., he perhaps a legatee more than others, since he was born during the Depression, in 1932, in an American Hooverville. Profane is the proletarian of the novel, the Sancho Panza to Stencil's Don Quixote, the citizen of the secular world that his name indicates. Herbert Stencil searches for his goddess, but only up to a point. Were he actually to find V., he would lapse back into inertia himself. To sustain animation, Stencil has to hunt; "but if he should find her, where else would there be to go but back into half-consciousness? He tried not to think, therefore, about any end to the search. Approach and avoid" (44).

A similar ambivalence toward women afflicts Profane. Women: (a) make Profane horny, so much so that he possesses a near-constant erection. Had he been the type to evolve theories of history, the narrator remarks, Profane

> might have said all political events: wars, governments and uprisings, have the desire to get laid at their roots; because history unfolds according to economic forces and the only reason anybody wants to get rich is so he can get laid steadily, with whomever he chooses (198).

Women: (b) frighten Profane by reminding him of the inanimate, a fear he has in common with Stencil *père* and *fils* and with Fausto Maijstral, who has referred to female biological processes as "mechanical and alien" (301). One can become lost in the V which is the void of woman. Women: (c) repel Profane by seeking to become dependent on him. He can not respond when a woman treats him "like he was a human being. Why couldn't he be just an object of mercy?" (123). Although women continually offer Profane "grace," he can not rise above his profane level. His schlemihlhood is sterile.

That sterility is particularly ironic, since Pynchon intends Profane to be something more than a denizen of the street, if only because there is more than one street. The "sea's highway" (393) leads to Malta, and Profane travels that road too. When Herbert Stencil asks Profane if he will accompany Paola and himself to Malta, the schlemihl's response is, "I have always wanted to be buried at sea," an answer that disturbs the quester:

> Had Stencil seen the coupling in that associative train he would have gathered heart of grace, surely. But Paola and he had never spoken of Profane. Who, after all, was Profane? (358)

He is, of course, "a schlemihl Redeemer" (427).

Reviewing Pynchon's short stories provides more clues. For example, Dennis Flange of "Low-lands" is an ex-sailor; so is Benny Profane. In *V.* sailors are presented as children and creatures of emotion, although Pynchon can be coy about this latter quality, and has the narrator remark that sailors are, "under frequently sentimental and swinish exteriors, sentimental swine" (400). As Hugh Godolphin has discovered, surface qualities are all there is to reality. Like Dennis Flange, Profane fears "land or seascapes . . . where nothing else lived but himself. It seemed he was always walking into one . . ." (12). As a result, Profane shares Flange's affinity for undergrounds, and like his predecessor will descend into tunnels, there to consort with rats. The Hyacinth Girl offers Flange love, sexual communion, and spiritual communication; several women proffer Profane these gifts, and he can not respond. In short, Profane is an updated version of Flange, who in turn is a parody of the Phoenician Sailor in Eliot's *Waste Land,* a potential savior and redeemer doomed to failure by his lack of courage and his inability to heed what communication is offered.

Profane also resembles Cleanth Siegel of "Mortality

and Mercy in Vienna" in that people single him out as a priest-confessor and endow him "with all manner of healing and sympathetic talents he didn't really possess" (9). A second similarity with Siegel occurs when Profane toys with the idea of bringing retribution to the waste land. When he is drunk, he wishes to piss on the sun "to put it out for good and all, this being somehow important for him" (17). Drunk again, this time up a mast high above a shipboard party the Shore Patrol is breaking up, the schlemihl tries mentally to "zap" the enemy:

> "Suppose," said Profane to the seagull, who was looking at him, "suppose I was God." He inched on to the platform and lay on his stomach, with nose, eyes and cowboy hat staring over the edge, like a horizontal Kilroy (22).

The ubiquitous graffito of soldiers and sailors, Kilroy, an image of the schlemihl, will reappear in the novel, and here suggests that Profane is a weak deity, as he decides himself before passing out, drunk: "Maybe, Profane thought, God is supposed to be more positive, instead of throwing thunderbolts all the time" (22). Cleanth Siegel and Benny Profane have one more aspect in common: both are half-Jewish, half-Catholic. Given the perversions V. works on Catholicism, and statements like Catholicism is "fashionable during a Decadence" (331), the implication of Profane's heritage is that his Jewish schlemihlhood can rejuvenate the sterile rituals of the Catholic faith, and somehow turn them into viable values.

Profane's willingness to play victim does not result in his sacrifice for redemption of the waste land, however, because his schlemihlhood proves impervious. The tension between Profane's desire to be an object of mercy and his fear of becoming inanimate produces just enough vibration to keep him moving, but not enough to let him bestow any salvation. In the words of another character, Profane manages to keep "cool," but he does not "care." His emotional invulnerability keeps him out of the category of other "Redeemers" in the novel like Porpentine, Sarah the concubine, and Mélanie l'Heuremaudit. Even Profane's relationship with his Jewish-Catholic parents is remote; so far as he is concerned, they simply fill the refrigerator. A man of large appetites, he thinks of himself as afoot in "the aisles of a bright, gigantic supermarket, his only function to want" (27), but those wants, even were he able to verbalize them, are rarely satisfied, for their purchase requires more of himself than he will give.

V. opens in a flurry of motifs with Profane in Norfolk, Virginia, where, "with its usual lack of warning, East Main was on him" (2). As he stands on it, the street seems to fade off "in an asymmetric V to the east where it's dark and there are no more bars" (2). This first appearance of a V. in the novel is followed almost immediately by a mechanical parody of femininity called "Suck Hour" in a bar known as the Sailor's Grave. During "Suck Hour" the sailors are treated to free beer, which they must suck from taps disguised as foam rubber breasts. Bars—and beer—furnish the undemanding camaraderie Profane prefers, and before the sailors fighting to get at the taps turn the bar into the usual chaos, Pynchon introduces several minor characters and gets in a couple of yarns.

Now a PFC, for "Pore Forlorn Civilian," Profane has yo-yoed into Norfolk to reencounter his buddies in Destroyer Division 22. Most of them have improbable names, one of which, Dewey Gland, is supposed to have sent Vladimir Nabokov into fits of laughter.[1] Another is Pig Bodine in all his soiled and salacious glory. His old shipmates fill Profane in on their last tour of duty; the most humorous event involves Ploy, the engineman on a minesweeper, who, having had his teeth replaced by false plates, tried to commit suicide. A giant Negro named Dahoud talked him out of it:

"Don't you know," said Dahoud, "that life is the most precious possession you have?"

"Ho, ho," said Ploy through his tears. "Why?"

"Because," said Dahoud, "without it, you'd be dead."

"Oh," said Ploy (4).

96

Dahoud's witticism resonates throughout the novel, and might be designated the Great Joke that goes along with Fausto Maijstral's Great Lie. For that matter, false teeth, a means by which the inanimate achieves a beachhead in the human body, become a wildly-ramifying metaphor in later episodes in the novel. By filing his new teeth to sharp points, Ploy himself compensates for the invasion of the inanimate; he bites everyone who comes within reach, including the waitresses of the Sailor's Grave.

Through a quirk of the Italian owner of the bar all the waitresses are called Beatrice, an evocation of Dante's *Divine Comedy*, in which figure both Fortune and Beatrice, who guides the pilgrim Dante to grace. One of these Beatrices is Paola Maijstral, now married to Pappy Hod, another old shipmate of Profane. Paola has left her husband for reasons never made clear; she says only that he was not "good" to her. She attaches herself to Profane. Vacillating between eager lust and rejection of her dependency, and having reached an apocheir (Pynchon's playful term for a yo-yo's apogee) in his latest yo-yo swing, Profane takes Paola to New York more to keep her from the advances of Pig Bodine than out of any real sense of responsibility toward the fetching eighteen-year-old. Paola may indeed be a Beatrice, i.e., an intercessor for tourists in the hell of the waste land, for she could be almost "any age" and "any nationality" (6). Besides, as Paola explains later, "nobody knows what a Maltese is. The Maltese think they're Semitic, Hamitic, crossbred with North Africans, Turks and God knows what all" (328). Whatever she is, Paola is a strong candidate for revitalized goddess of the waste land. The very fact that her colonial heritage has not been labelled by Western civilization is in her favor.

Paola is but one of several women who seem to promise potential redemption for Profane. Heading the list is Rachel Owlglass, whom Profane met when he worked at a Catskills resort where she was a guest. There they formed "a relationship," although Profane is grateful that she has never called it that, consisting of maternalism on her part, bewilderment on his. Pro-

fane's confusion and diffidence stem from his secretly
observing Rachel's fondness for inanimate objects. For
instance, she not only drives her prized MG at break-
neck speed, but also croons to it and strokes it in sexual passion. Recoiling from this revelation, Profane in
disgust thumbtacks condoms he has won in a card
game to the doors of the resort's cabins, feeling like
"the Angel of Death" (20). The episode recalls the
Bad Priest's sermon on chastity.

Because of her penchant for the inanimate, Rachel
seems tainted, an impression heightened by her acquaintance with a group of decadents in New York
called the Whole Sick Crew. R. W. B. Lewis has sur-
mised that Pynchon modified the name from "the sinful
crew," a term in Michael Wigglesworth's *The Day of
Doom,* a long Puritan apocalyptic poem written in
1662. Since one of the characters in *V.* is called Brenda
Wigglesworth, it would appear likely.[2] In this connection, it is worth noting that the most sympathetic members of the Whole Sick Crew, those with some sense of
what they have lost, appear to derive from the Puritan
tradition. For example, Roony Winsome's real Christian name is Gouverneur, and Rachel's father is Stuy-
vesant Owlglass. By any name, Whole Sick Crew or
otherwise, the decadents serve Pynchon's purpose.
Against the tapestry of historical decadence Herbert
Stencil paints, the activities of the Crew almost pale,
although they are enlivened by ribaldry. Naturally V.
and her sinister colleagues have the edge; evil such as
theirs is almost always attractive. Moreover, V.'s pas-
sions are intense, even when directed toward the inanimate, and the Crew's are bloodless by comparison, almost harmless in their ineptitude and adolescent in their
lack of imagination. Decadent or not, V. had one great
virtue: as Victoria Wren, Victoria Manganese, or whoever, she pursues experience to exhaustion, while the
members of the Whole Sick Crew have already suc-
cumbed to lassitude.

Of course, that is the point of Pynchon's historical
survey, that the energies have run down, that the values
have fallen into desuetude, that the whole culture has
become sick, and that evil itself has become banal.

Nevertheless, the events in Profane's sphere are informed and explained by those in Stencil's, and vice versa. The manipulation of a continuous parallel between present and past is a way of giving shape and form to the panorama of anarchy in the contemporary era. At times Stencil seizes on similarities between America in the 1950s and Africa in the early years of the century; he thinks the Crew's hijinks recapitulate Foppl's Siege Party. Considering the horrendous deviations of the latter, the comparison seems strained, far more "metaphorical" than "real," but that too is deliberate, since such design-seeking is inherent in Stencil's character.

The Whole Sick Crew includes a motley range of screwballs. At one extreme is Fergus Mixolydian,[3] an "Irish-Armenian Jew and universal man," the "laziest living being in Nueva York" (45). Mixolydian's collaboration with the inanimate has led him to wire himself to a TV set which flicks on whenever he falls asleep; he thus becomes "an extension of the TV set" (45). At the other extreme is Slab, whose decadence manifests itself more energetically, although the result is lethargic. A painter, Slab belongs to the self-titled school of Catatonic Expressionism, "the ultimate in non-communication" (45), and litters his studio with Warhol-type canvases of Cheese Danishes, symbols Slab declares will replace the Cross in Western Civilization. In its very inanity the Danish does hint at the exhaustion of the waste land:

> The subject of Cheese Danish #35 occupied only a small area, to the lower left of center, where it was pictured impaled on one of the metal steps of a telephone pole. The landscape was an empty street, dramatically foreshortened, the only living things in it a tree in the middle distance, on which perched an ornate bird, busily textured with a great many swirls, flourishes and bright-colored patches (263).

Between Fergus and Slab are artists and theorists of exhaustion and slowly expiring sensibilities, "bohemian, creative, arty" in pattern, says the narrator, except that it was even further removed from reality, Romanticism in its furthest decadence being only an exhausted impersonation of poverty, rebellion and artistic "soul." For it was the unhappy fact that most of them worked for a living and obtained the substance of their conversation from the pages of *Time* magazine and like publications (46).

They survive "at the mercy of Fortune" (46).

None of them are very different from the fraternity boy who hovers on the edges of the Crew, knowing full well that he will always be a fraternity boy type but convinced that he is missing something:

> If he is going into management, he writes. If he is an engineer or architect why he paints or sculpts. He will straddle the line, aware up to the point of knowing he is getting the worst of both worlds, but never stopping to wonder why there should ever have been a line, or even if there is a line at all. He will learn how to be a twinned man and will go on at the game, straddling until he splits up the crotch and in half from the prolonged tension, and then he will be destroyed (47).

At one time or another most of the Crew sleep in the apartment of Roony Winsome, all-around voyeur and hip recording executive of Outlandish Records. His great dream is to record Tchaikovsky's 1812 Overture using Strategic Air Command bombers instead of the usual cannons. In spite of such absurdities, Winsome is a likeable sort, bright enough to perceive that the Crew is sick indeed. He is searching for the affection denied him by his wife Mafia, who writes novels expounding her Theory of Heroic Love.[4] Because it combines worship of sexual gymnastics with a crude racial bigotry, the Theory adds cachet to the term "fucking Fascist" (327), as her husband refers to her. In her novels Mafia exalts primitive sex between well-proportioned Aryans; in practice she plays a game called Musical Blankets with the Crew members Charisma and Fu, and if her selection of enervated lovers were not

100

enough to undermine her Theory, Mafia also wears an inflatable brassiere. Amoral and promiscuous, although she is careful to practice birth control, a fact which makes her more unnatural, Mafia is the most frightening woman Profane meets. Other males are not so intimidated, however: Pig Bodine is easily her match, as is Charisma, who sings with Mafia a love-duet based on Wittgenstein's *Tractatus,* in the usual manner of Pynchon's characters, who break into song at every opportunity. According to the narrator, this propensity to vocalize is almost a national characteristic: Where the English see "history," the Yanks see "novelty and an excuse for musical comedy" (412).

When they are not sleeping with Mafia or sponging off Roony, the Crew members congregate at the Rusty Spoon or the V-Note Bar (neither Stencil nor the narrator says Aha!, but the reader will) to discuss art and life in "proper nouns," as the narrator calls their slick labels for ideas they scarcely grasp. The Crew and their assorted hangers-on are merely play-acting, choosing their roles from the storehouse of romanticism, combining old values and old stereotypes, and adding only the most superficial novelty; originality is dead, since art and lifestyles have declined to a demotic level. Hugh Godolphin's fears have been realized; private vision has become the property of the mob. But if the humans and their values can no longer renew themselves, they are at least still alive. Anemic the Crew may be, vitiated even of a quality of desperation that would be a saving grace; dead they are not. So reasons at least Dudley Eigenvalue (the name is a negative mathematical term), D.D.S., a "soul-dentist" who wishes to be a Patron of the Arts. Eigenvalue knows that the Crew will never produce original art or thought. The artists copy what has already been done, and the thinkers merely rearrange ideas in various ways:

"Mathematically, boy," he told himself, "if nobody else original comes along, they're bound to run out of arrangements someday. What then?" What indeed. This sort of arranging and rearranging was Decadence, but the exhaustion of all possible permutations and combinations was death (277).

Eigenvalue is echoing Vladimir Porcépic, who catalogued permutations also.

In addition to his patronage, which takes the form of reduced dental rates, Eigenvalue offers the Whole Sick Crew his services as an analyst. According to *V.*'s narrator, who seems at moments as nutty as Herbert Stencil, dentistry in the 1950s has usurped the throne of psychoanalysis. Behind this notion is Pynchon's vision of the inanimate and the unnatural invading the human and the living. Into the mouth go fillings and plates, so that the head, the seat of the brain itself, contains alien substances. One need not even go that far, for in a sense even natural teeth have inanimate qualities:

> The pulp is soft and laced with little blood vessels and nerves. The enamel, mostly calcium, is inanimate. These were the it and I psychodontia had to deal with. The hard, lifeless I covered up the warm, pulsing it; protecting and sheltering (139).

Psychodontia develops its own terminology: "you called neurosis 'malocclusion,' oral, anal and genital stages 'deciduous dentition,' id 'pulp' and superego 'enamel'" (138-139). If the human head is partly foreign matter, psychoanalysis simply will not suffice. It is an imaginative and amusing but somewhat limited conceit, and Pynchon does not push it.

He does use Eigenvalue as a sounding-board for Herbert Stencil, however, and has him comment on the quester's obsessions:

> Cavities in the teeth occur for good reasons, Eigenvalue reflected. But even if there are several per tooth, there's no conscious organization there against the life of the pulp, no conspiracy. Yet we have men like Stencil, who must go about grouping the world's random caries into cabals (139).

For his part, because the dentist deals in the inanimate,

Stencil suspects that Eigenvalue, Bloody Chiclitz, and a plastic surgeon named Shale Schoenmaker are part of an inner "Circle" connected with The Plot That Has No Name, i.e., linked somehow to V. It is hinted several times that Stencil's paranoia blooms in the same hothouse which produced Henry Ford's demented notion that thirteen Jews rule the world. His possible participation in a cabal is only one of two reasons Eigenvalue interests Stencil, however. The other is that the dentist owns a set of false dentures, each tooth of which is fashioned from a different precious metal. Stencil visualizes these teeth in the mouth of his dynamo-goddess.

Stencil has come to New York, naturally, on the trail of his quarry. In the city he inadvertently becomes involved in the story of Esther Harvitz, an important subplot in Benny Profane's half of the novel. Esther is as 1950s Mélanie l'Heuremaudit. She is a neurotic Jewish girl obsessed by her large nose, for which she compensates by sleeping with any interested male. Because she is a perennial victim—without Profane's defenses —Rachel Owlglass adopts her, pays her bills, and generally tries to keep tabs on her. Herbert Stencil begins "a father-daughter" (89) affair with Esther which recalls Mélanie's incest and to alleviate her unhappiness introduces her to the plastic surgeon Shale (as in rock) Schoenmaker (beauty maker). Schoenmaker had become an artist in skin after seeing his friend Evan Godolphin disfigured in World War I. At first his motives were pure: "if alignment with the inanimate is the mark of a Bad Guy, Schoenmaker at least made a sympathetic beginning" (88):

... Schoenmaker's dedication was toward repairing the havoc wrought by agencies outside his own sphere of responsibility. Others—politicians and machines— carried on wars; others—perhaps human machines— condemned his patients to the ravages of acquired syphilis; others—on the highways, in the factories— undid the work of nature with automobiles, milling machines, other instruments of civilian disfigurement (89).

From battling the ravages of the inanimate he has gradually moved to a lazy acceptance, allowed his idealism to deteriorate into pragmatism; he has come to "care" less and less just what justifies his work, until he is, at last, in league with the inanimate. Schoenmaker's virtú—for there is no question of the excellence of his skill—has been divorced from moral considerations. While he may claim that his alterations of faces are governed by aesthetic concern and by sympathy for human suffering, like V. Schoenmaker wishes to perfect nature by freezing it into eternal form, and like her also he takes sexual pleasure in doing so. Moreover, the excessive prices he charges have further corrupted the spirit of his original idealism. To Rachel Owlglass, who despises him, Schoenmaker defends his expensive cosmetology by asking how he has mutated evolution:

"Am I altering that grand unbroken chain, no. I am not going against nature, I am not selling out any Jews. Individuals do what they want, but the chain goes on and small forces like me will never prevail against it. All that can is something which will change the germ plasm, nuclear radiation, maybe" (37).

Given such massive forces as nuclear radiation, he argues, his scalpel can do little harm. Rachel replies that he sets up "another chain" when he fixes noses for unhappy Jewish girls:

"Changing them inside sets up another chain which has nothing to do with germ plasm. You can transmit characteristics outside, too. You can pass along an attitude . . ." (38).

Schoenmaker protests that his surgery changes only the skin, the "outside" of the self, not the "inside." But Rachel instinctively knows that outside is inside, that beneath the skin may be nothing, so that the exchange meshes with other episodes in the novel. Schoenmaker has already tatooed hundreds of freckles on the face of his nurse, a woman called Irving. Irving resembles the sexually inverted V. and Mélanie, and also the tattooed woman of Hugh Godolphin and Sarah, the concubine of Firelily's rider. Skin is all.

Several critics believe that Pynchon has been influenced by *Tristram Shandy,* a novel in which prominent noses are prominent metaphors. If so, Pynchon stands Laurence Sterne on his nose: Schoenmaker transforms Esther Harvitz's Jewish proboscis into an Irish retroussé in what surely is the most faithfully described and harrowing such operation in literature. The tools, instruments, and gadgets the surgeon uses are symptomatic of decadence, as is the purpose of the operation, to give Esther's nose "cultural harmony," to make it WASP-like, to recreate it "identical with an ideal of nasal beauty established by movies, advertisements, magazine illustrations" (91). Afterwards Esther describes her sensations to friends in a passage that might have come from Fausto Maijstral's "Confessions":

"It was almost a mystic experience. What religion is it—one of the Eastern ones—where the highest condition we can attain is that of an object—a rock. It was like that; I felt myself drifting down, this delicious loss of Estherhood, becoming more and more a blob, with no worries, traumas, nothing: only Being . . ." (93).

The incisions and penetrations into Esther's nasal cavity ("a cavity is a cavity") are couched in sexual terms; Schoenmaker's assistant chants "Stick it in . . . pull it out . . ." (92). The scalpel is a miniature of the lance that penetrates Mélanie l'Heuremaudit. The effect is not lost on Esther, who after the operation becomes Schoenmaker's mistress. For their first assignation Esther dabs Shalimar on her gauze-covered nose, and takes a bus across the waste land of Central Park ("reserved as if by covenant for cops, delinquents and all manner of deviates" [847]) while the bus driver's radio plays Tchaikovsky's "Romeo and Juliet Overture," that variation on the Tristram-Iseult theme. Predictable consequences conclude the affair. Schoenmaker can not resist trying to persuade Esther to let

him make further "improvements" on her: more pro-
tuberant pelvic bones and larger breasts, for example.
Worse, she becomes pregnant.

Esther turns to Slab, the Catatonic Expressionist, for
help. He convinces her to fly to Cuba for an abortion,
and raises money for the trip by passing the hat at a
party for the Whole Sick Crew. The Crew call Slab a
great humanitarian, and from their stock of proper
nouns multiply the plaudits,

> crediting him with being (a) a neo-Wobbly and re-
> incarnation of Joe Hill, (b) the world's leading paci-
> fist, (c) a rebel with taproots in the American Tradi-
> tion, (d) in militant opposition to Fascism, private
> capital, the Republican administration and Westbrook
> Pegler (332).

Rachel Owlglass, on the side of life, does not see it
that way at all, and the issue of the abortion causes her
to break with the Whole Sick Crew. To abort an em-
bryo is to alter by technology what has happened by
accident. It is as if Rachel grasps what Fausto Maijstral
had learned so painfully, that Fortune *is* nature—which
puts V. in the category of the unnatural—and that
Fortuna is a mighty goddess, but also that human
agency counts for something too. A world ruled by
chance is a world not wholly determined, or, if we accept Fausto's doubts, a world which we can not afford
to believe is wholly determined, and therefore a world
in which free will still operates. Virtú entails responsibility, and if humans act without considering the consequences, they simply increase the chaos of a world
already prone to disorder. Obviously, virtú is one of the
principal elements in the concept "V." Virtú occurs in
the novel more frequently than any other word beginning with the magic initial, although always in lower-
case, so that it does not seem a "proper noun" and thus
goes almost unnoticed. If nature's energies are running
down, humans have been and are contributing to the
process, by introducing greater indeterminacy into the
world, through technology, through mindless love of
objects, and through armored virtú.

Even Slab, with whom Rachel has had an affair, admits that she is a "good woman, member of a vanishing race" (40). Put simply, she is good because she "cares" about other people. As she matures, Rachel discards her fondness for the inanimate MG in favor of involvement that is painful but necessary if humans are to survive. She reflects on the perils: "If you did take the trouble, even any first step, it meant stacking income against output; and who knows what embarrassments, exposés of self that might drag you into?" (334). Enlisting Profane's help—unwisely, as things turn out—Rachel tries to prevent Esther from boarding the plane for Havana. She fails. Free of the Crew's inertia, determined to live in an animate world, Rachel pins her hopes on Profane, but runs up against his usual ambivalence.

Actually Profane has avoided Rachel until this point. When he and Paola had arrived in New York from Virginia, he had sent the Maltese to Rachel, since he was unwilling to accept the girl as a dependent. Before she left him, Paola, slightly smitten with Benny herself, had asked if he and Rachel are "in love." "The word doesn't mean anything" (26), he replied, and had gone off on his own. Paola, as Rachel's second roommate—the other being the hapless Esther—had instantly riveted the attention of the Whole Sick Crew. Pig Bodine, who wanders into town in search of Profane, and Roony Winsome, alienated from his wife, are Paola's most persistent suitors. Winsome tries to define her appeal in Mélanie-like terms:

> The girl had the passive look of an object of sadism, something to be attired in various inanimate costumes and fetishes, tortured, subjected to the weird indignities of Pig's catalogue, have her smooth and of course virginal-looking limbs twisted into attitudes to inflame a decadent taste (205).

Paola has much in common with Profane in her passivity and her inability to speak in "proper nouns," i.e., decadent ideas. By contrast, Pig Bodine fits into the Crew easily, and picks up the nouns quickly. "What do

you think of Sartre's thesis that we are all imperson-
ating an identity?" (118), Pig asks Rachel, who fears
for Paola in his presence.

But Paola has resources of her own. She disappears
from Rachel's apartment for days at a time. Only gradually does the reader learn of her relationship with
McClintic Sphere,[5] a black alto saxophone player at
the V-Note bar. His decadent fans regard Sphere as
the reincarnation of Charlie "Bird" Parker, and attribute to him "soul and the anti-intellectual and the rising rhythms of African nationalism" (49). Being
weighted with such mystique does not prove fatal to
Sphere, however, for he has "never gone along all the
way with the 'cool' outlook that developed in the post-
war years" (272). More important is his interest in
stochastic music, which puts him under the aegis of
Fortune. He is fascinated by "a two-triode circuit
called a flip-flop" (273), which causes a computer to
run through the probability distribution on a set of
notes to produce sound. Sphere does not understand
the concept very well, but he does see that the flip and
flop have something to do with the pulse of life itself,
with dualities and their relationship. He makes up a little song about set-and-reset and flip and flop.

To relax, Sphere from time to time flees the V-Note
on the Bowery to go to Harlem, another world within
the city. There he patronizes a whorehouse run by one
Matilda Winthrop, whose Puritan name suggests her
essential integrity. He falls in love with a black whore
called Ruby. She does not understand his music, but
she does understand Sphere's frustration at having to
live and function in a white and black world. Depressed
terribly one day, Sphere suggests to Roony Winsome,
who is weary from life with Mafia and with desire for
Paola, that they drive to Lenox, Massachusetts. He will
take Ruby and Winsome can take whomever he wants.
Winsome agrees, because "it would be a fresh thing,
clean, a beginning" (328). To his shock, however,
Ruby turns out to be Paola in black-face; she has
darkened her already swarthy skin with burnt cork.
Winsome does not tell Sphere of his discovery, but,

unhinged by it, declines the trip and enters a suicidal phase which culminates in his leaving Mafia and the Whole Sick Crew. Ruby-Paola and Sphere go alone to "where things you expect to happen do happen" (327), that is, to the as yet unspoiled Puritan countryside. Walden Pond is already a chaos of beer-drinking parents and urinating kids, says the now—cynical Winsome. Perhaps there is no more nature where fortune's wake is strewn with gentle, flower-like accidents of life.

This lightly-sounded chord notwithstanding, Pynchon does not harp on agrarian myths. Although it offers peace, nature refreshes but little. Driving through the countryside with Ruby-Paola, McClintic Sphere formulates a philosophy that his companion implicitly acknowledges:

> The only way clear of the cool/crazy flip/flop was obviously slow, frustrating and hard work. Love with your mouth shut, help without breaking your ass or publicizing it: keep cool, but care. . . . "Nobody is going to step down from heaven and square away Roony and his woman, or Alabama, or South Africa or us and Russia. There's no magic words. Not even I love you is magic enough. . . . Keep cool but care . . ." (343).

What accommodation with the world is available is also limited, but if there is any hopeful note in *V.* it is the musician's—and Paola's. The pastoral sequence validates the credentials of Paola as a goddess for the waste land. She is not the prostitute with the heart of gold, nor a reincarnation of the Earth-Mother; she is a new and fragile Venus, not so much an archetype as a wholly human figure. She is the Redeemer, if Redeemer there be. Profane has the requisite coolness but cannot care. Rachel Owlglass cares too much; she craves dependents. Her very maternalism—considering the fear of mothers shared by Fausto and Sidney Stencil—lessens her fitness for Paola's office. For all her good qualities, Rachel resembles the quintessential Jewish mother. Her desire to succor cripples and decadents had originally made her Den-Mother to the Whole Sick Crew. She has cast the Crew off, but she is ready for more dependents.

Besides, Paola has already been set apart by another of Pynchon's metaphors, the clock. One such clock is in Shale Schoenmaker's office, where Rachel sees it, a "turn-of-the-century" mechanism driven by a disc escapement on which "two imps or demons, wrought in gold, posed in fantastic attitudes" (35). Rachets, levers, springs, and demons perform a dance reflected in a mirror. Their images correspond to the mirror-time images which pop up in Stencil's part of the novel. Next to Paola's bed in Rachel's apartment is another clock, electric:

> Its minute hand could not be seen to move. But soon the hand passed twelve and began its course down the other side of the face; as if it had passed through the surface of a mirror, and had now to repeat in mirror-time what it had done on the side of real-time (41).

Like Mehemet the time-traveller, who teaches Sidney Stencil, Paola moves in dual worlds. It is significant, of course, that she is Maltese, half-British and half-whatever mysterious race the Maltese are. On her and McClintic Sphere, another dual person, a black in a white-dominated world, rests the future. Accustomed to balancing the claims of one world against another, they can also juxtapose their integrity with concern for others. In a world so far gone, Pynchon seems to be saying, few other options are possible.

While Paola gets the crown—or more accurately, the comb, as we shall see—Rachel gets most of the character; Rachel is one of Pynchon's most fully-realized figures. When first Herbert Stencil sees her,

> smoke seemed to be in her voice, in her movements; making her all the more substantial, more there, as if words, glances, small lewdnesses could only become baffled and brought to rest like smoke in her long hair; remain there useless till she released them, accidentally and unknowingly, with a toss of her head (41).

110

Rachel is also bright, level-headed, and aware of her weaknesses. Having learned a good deal from the unpleasant scene with Schoenmaker, she too has formulated a theory, by borrowing the surgeon's "chain" metaphor. Rachel reflects on "daisy chains" (one of Pynchon's favorite terms) of "freeloaders and victims," or "screwers and screwees" (38), and concludes that New York stands on the foundation of this system "from the bottom of the lowest sewer bed right up through the streets to the tip of the TV antenna on top of the Empire State Building" (40).

In the meantime Benny Profane has been exploring the world of the screwee from street to sewer. After foisting Paola off on Rachel, Profane for a time yo-yos on the subways, where he feels comfortable. On one car he identifies with a bum who has been shuttling around for days under the city and under the rivers, a Bolingbroke of the transit system, for "if under the street and under the sea are the same then he was king of both" (199). Among the other riders are beggars, nomads, migrant farmers, the ethnic poor, yo-yos like Profane, the screwees and schlemihls of the city. The Whole Sick Crew members occasionally yo-yo on the subways too, but only as a drunken lark. Taken together, the Crew, as caricatures of alienation, and Profane's fellow victims, as very real examples of disaffection, make up the "highly alienated populace" Sidney Stencil had prophesied in 1919. On the advice of Slab, Sidney's son takes up yo-yoing, but unfortunately makes his debut at rush hour, when the riders look like "vertical corpses" jostled into a "Dance of Death" Herbert associates with Foppl's Siege Party. That undergrounds are symbolic graves becomes steadily more obvious as Profane moves even deeper under the street.

On one of his subway revolutions Profane is taken in hand by several young Puerto Ricans, who promise to find him a job and provide him with a place to stay. Soon he is sleeping in a bathtub in the home of the Mendoza family, one of whom, Angel, enlists Profane in the Alligator Patrol. Here Pynchon takes advantage of a myth popular a decade ago, when baby alligators from Florida became a fad in Manhattan. Somehow the story started that children flushed the creatures down toilets into the sewer system, where they grew into full-sized beasts. Pynchon has Profane join the crews which hunt down the alligators with shotguns and flashlights. Most of the men are down-and-outers, bums like Profane, or kids like Angel Mendoza and his friend Geronimo, for whom better jobs are hard to find. Profane gravitates toward these people because he identifies them with the human flotsam of the American Depression, an era he has made his own. But no real sense of the past possesses him. Rather it is a "great temporal homesickness for the decade" (134) of his birth, a sketchy nostalgia which is essentially narcissistic. "In every no-name drifter, mooch, square's tenant" (335) he meets, Rachel later tells Profane, he sees himself reflected. Freight trains, men with picks and shovels, and songs of the 1930s move him to artificial sentiment. Like the frauds among the Whole Sick Crew, although from different motives, Profane copies a romantic role from the past.

Profane thus represents the exhaustion of that liberal tradition which exalted the proletarian in America. Nostalgic references to the thirties in *V.* are numerous, and are usually sabotaged by humor, so that Pynchon can evoke the nostalgia without catering to modern anarchic sympathy for the underprivileged. Profane is the proletarian hero manqué, having adopted the stance not as protest but as goal. He is capable of hard work only when he cultivates the image of the drifter, the Okie, the dispossessed; he sentimentalizes his own exploitation, by which he justifies his scrounging, adds clumsiness, which he persuades himself is his fate, and enjoys his own insincere guilt, which he rationalizes by continuously apologizing for the authentic emotion he allows to seep out. The perfect schlemihl is also T. S. Eliot's "hollow man." Intent on coolness, i.e., non-involvement, he can not care. Profane has been arrested by the circumstances of his birth, just as Herbert Stencil—assuming that he is either V.'s child or merely the "child of the century," a century of multiplicities rather than unity—has been arrested by his. There is only one thing worse than fragmenting the self into multiplicities, as does Stencil, and that is clinging to a hollow unity in an era which demands at least the recognition of multiplicities, as does Profane. Listening to Stencil spin his tales of conspiracy, Dudley Eigenvalue decides that Stencil's problem can be diagnosed à la Henry Adams, as a loss of a sense of continuity, and the dentist-analyst's reflections apply to Benny Profane as well:

> Perhaps history this century . . . is rippled with gathers in its fabric such that if we are situated, as Stencil seemed to be, at the bottom of a fold, it's impossible to determine warp, woof or pattern anywhere else. By virtue, however, of existing in one gather it is assumed there are others, compartmented off into sinuous cycles each of which come to assume greater importance than the weave itself and destroy any continuity. Thus it is that we are charmed by the funny-looking automobiles of the 30's, the curious fashions of the '20's, the peculiar moral habits of our grandparents. We produce and attend musical comedies about them and are conned into a false memory, a phony nostalgia about what they were. We are accordingly lost to any sense of continuous tradition. Perhaps if we lived on a crest, things would be different. We could at least see (141).

As Stencil's dossier has revealed, V. and her colleagues moved largely toward the Right. While Profane stands on the Left, he is no closer to the Golden Mean Sidney Stencil prized. Neither position offers a comprehensive view, because the partisans of both extremes are almost equally alienated from a nature herself denatured and from their fellow humans. Had they some sense of continuity, perhaps they could see where things began to go wrong. Herbert Stencil is trying, but his paranoia is irrational, and colored by a fanaticism which amounts to religiosity. Between him and Profane stands Fausto Maijstral, a self-styled "ex-priest," who gets as close to Stencil *père*'s "man of no politics" as anybody. Profane's nature is wholly secular. Even so, if we take Goethe's word for the reason people convert to

Catholicism during Romantic periods, because Protestantism "has given the individual too much to carry,"[6] it is ironic that Profane favors the Jewish schlemihl side of his heritage for a similar reason, to escape the burden of individuality—very like the Catholic V.

Profane's nostalgia for the past is too shallow to place him in the hothouse, although insofar as he is in search for identity he has that in common with Stencil and Fausto. As César Graña has pointed out, "the search for identity is really an act of conjuration, the effort to give life to a metaphor."[7] Schlemihlhood is Profane's metaphor, but probably because the state is so little removed from the inanimate, he needs the mirror—it can hardly be called "communion," mob or otherwise—of other schlemihls in the street. A would-be victim, he wears his suffering on the outside; it is his identity, visible, he thinks, to all, and valuable, he believes, because the suffering proves he is alive. On the other hand, since he oscillates between the poles of suffering and ennui, he may very well desire extinction himself. At the end of the novel, Stencil will call Profane "devil" (424), and wonder if annihilation is the schlemihl's goal. Perhaps Profane has little choice in the matter. By adopting the protective coloration of the alienated of the streets, he can defend himself from chaos only at the price of being a form of chaos himself; he is accident incarnate. If Stencil chases an abstraction, Profane already is one.

The Alligator Patrol is run by a lunatic named Zeitsuss, or "Sweet-time," and the sewers in which the operation is conducted form another time-zone, another world for Profane. In a symbolic sense, the underground is the unconscious of Jungian psychology or archetypical mythology, to which the hero is supposed to penetrate in order to understand his psyche. It is the underground of Dennis Flange and Eliot's Phoenician Sailor, and is associated with death and resurrection. Pynchon laughingly makes this association explicit. In an effort to seduce three girls they spot in front of "the Wheel of Fortune" at a street fair in Little Italy, Profane, Angel, and Geronimo embroider their exploits as alligator hunters until they resemble myths of dead and

114

reborn fertility gods like those told by Frazer in *The Golden Bough:*

> Together on the stoop they hammered together a myth. Because it wasn't born from fear of thunder, dreams, astonishment at how the crops kept dying after harvest and coming up again every spring, or anything else very permanent, only a temporary interest, a spur-of-the-moment tumescence, it was a myth rickety and transient as the bandstands and the sausage-pepper of Mulberry Street (128).

Profane himself asks "what goes on underground. Do we I wonder come out the same people at the other end?" (281). Unfortunately, he does come out the same. Reborn and transfigured by his sojourn in an underground grave, the Redeemer should be able to fertilize and regenerate the waste land. Profane, because no experience ever alters him, cannot, but reminders of his mock-function swirl about him as he sloshes through sewage beneath the streets. Another redeemer has preceded him: Father Fairing, the English priest who left Malta for America in 1919, the year Sidney Stencil died. During the crisis atmosphere of the Depression—Profane's era—in "an hour of apocalyptic well-being" (105), Fairing decided that the rats were to be the inheritors of the waste land. He climbed down into the sewers with three books: "a Baltimore Catechism, his breviary and, for reasons nobody found out, a copy of Knight's *Modern Seamanship*" (105), with the intention of converting Manhattan's rat population to Catholicism. To ensure a supply of holy water, he blessed the sewage, and then staked out the boundaries of a parish on the East Side. In his journal Fairing told how, while sustaining himself on the flesh of his rat-parishioners, he converted many, including a female, a "voluptuous Magdalen" (108) that he named Veronica. A would-be nun, Veronica was either a great saint or, since she may have become Fairing's mistress, a great sinner, the two qualities blending into the ambivalence associated with V. When Fairing died, he was somehow buried in a cairn made of a 36-inch pipe, and memorialized by his journal and his breviary. The rats absconded with the catechism and the manual of seamanship, perhaps because, as one of those who discovers the story speculates, the animals wanted to study "the best way to leave a sinking ship" (108), a phrase designed to remind the reader of Mehemet the time-traveller's metaphor for man's lot.

Various other refrains resound in this episode, not least the perversion of Catholicism and related sexual abnormalities. Considering these fruitful associations, it is not surprising to find Herbert Stencil in the sewers. Busily compiling his dossier on V., he hears of a priest's mistress named Veronica. He does not know she was a rat and, although he hears Fairing's name, does not know the priest came from Malta. At this point it would make no difference if he did, since he also does not know of the circumstances of his father's death. But he begins to lurk underground.

In the meantime, Profane has begun to think of himself as "a St. Francis for alligators," as if he were come to redeem the creatures below, "as if there had been . . . a covenant, Profane giving death, the alligators giving him employment: tit for tat" (133). The alligators had been consumer objects, children's toys. Were they captured alive, they would only be turned into other consumer goods like shoes and pocketbooks, and Profane persuades himself that they could not want that. They would prefer to return to pure Being, "and the most perfect shape of that was dead . . ." (133). He ends their limbo in purgatory by shooting them. Profane brings death, not life.

Near the end of his tenure on the Patrol, Profane comes as close as he ever does to epiphany. Alone, pursuing an alligator through Fairing's Parish, he notices that the walls of the sewer are glowing with posphorescence, presumably the radiance of randomly discharged energies associated with V. Profane anticipates Pentecostal revelation: "Surely the alligator would receive the gift of tongues, the body of Father Fairing be resurrected, the sexy V. tempt him away from murder" (110). Nothing happens. He apologizes to his prey, the alligator: "Sorry . . . it was a schlemihl's stock line"

116

(110), and lets fly with the shotgun. His flashlight goes out. Profane has achieved no understanding—he has merely shot the skulking Stencil in the ass.[8]

Fortune offers Profane other chances, however. In myth, and in T. S. Eliot's adaptation of myth in *The Waste Land,* the potential redeemer is proffered a necessary love by a female. Hardly has Profane moved in with the Mendozas before Josefina, the daughter of the family, becomes enamored of the schlemihl. Fina is a classic case of woman viewed in terms of a machismo double-standard. On the one hand, she is pure, so pure that she serves as a "Joan of Arc," a sort of saintly mascot, "punchy with grace" for a gang of delinquents called The Playboys, "a strangely exhausted group" (124) who worship her. Profane sees her avert a gang-rumble by her mere presence: the two rival gang-leaders clasp hands, "and Fina was borne up by a swarm of pneumatically fat, darling cherubs, to hover over the sudden peace she'd created, beaming, serene" (131). Fina's position relative to The Playboys is analogous to Rachel's vis-a-vis the Whole Sick Crew.

On the other hand, tiring of her virginity and reaching out for love, Fina offers herself to Profane. He refuses. Willing enough to go wenching with Angel and Geronimo, so long as the girls are "hollow-eyed" (126) and undemanding, Profane resists Fina's attempts to draw him up out of the sepulchre of the sewer, back to the street. Fina sets up an interview for him with Roony Winsome, for whom she works, hoping to get Profane a better job, but he cannot tolerate the prospect of involvement, normality, and affluence. "Where was the depression?" he asks himself, out of his element. He bolts the interview. Still, he worries about the girl, fearing that when The Playboys catch "a glimpse of the wanton behind the saint, the black slip beneath the surplice, Fina could find herself on the receiving end of a gang bang" (131). Profane is a better prophet than redeemer. In the midst of a riot Fina, like Sarah the concubine, is mass-raped by her followers, and like Victoria Wren, "ruined," is cast off by her family. She leaves the city on the plane taking Esther Harvitz to Havana.

Then it is Rachel's turn to attempt to make a silk purse out of the sow's ear. Profane yo-yos back to her, led by an instrument of pure chance, his erect penis, which creases a newspaper in his lap at an ad for Space-Time Employment Agency, where, unknown to him, Rachel works. She mothers him. With her, Profane feels like a yo-yo that has had "its own umbilical string reconnected" (200), or a clock under control. Still, Rachel insists that he get a job, and finds him one at Anthroresearch Associates, a subsidiary of Yoyodyne. Here, as nightwatchman, Profane talks with two mechanical manikins, SHOCK, an acronym for Synthetic Human Object, Casualty Kinematics, and SHROUD, or Synthetic Human, Radiation Output Determined. They are designed to measure the effects of bodily injury and radiation on human beings. To Anthroresearch Associates, these figures are evidence of man's "progress." By introducing them, Pynchon underlines the idea that man confuses "progress" with mechanical extensions of himself by which he has attempted to improve nature. For at the same time man has not improved his inner self. He simply projects human attributes on to his machines, so that they become analogues of himself; as they are inanimate, so will he become so, as he continues to identify with them. Although they are inanimate, Profane quickly recognizes them as fellow schlemihls.

SHROUD is the talkative one of the pair. "Me and SHOCK are what you and everybody will be someday" (266), it tells Profane. SHROUD compares American junkyards filled with waste cars to the stacks of Jewish corpses at Auschwitz: "It's already started." Profane protests: "Hitler did that. He was crazy," to which SHROUD replies: "Hitler, Eichmann, Mengele. Fifteen years ago. Has it occurred to you that there may be no more standards for crazy or sane, now that it's started" (275). What has "already started," of course, is man's decline toward the inanimate.

One night, betrayed by an inanimate object, his alarm clock, Profane arrives at Anthroresearch Associates to find that because of his tardiness the laboratory has erupted into chaos. He is fired on the spot. As he leaves, SHROUD gives him parting advice: "Keep cool but care. It's a watchword, Profane, for your side of the morning. There, I've told you too much as it is" (345). Bonehead that he is, the schlemihl does not understand.

Nor can he care. Rachel—her eyes "all rainy"—does her best, but cannot reach him. The basic pigment of his personality is visible to her, and she confronts him with it: "Can't you stop feeling sorry for yourself? You've taken your own flabby, clumsy soul and amplified it into a Universal Principle" (359). He insists that he is hollow, that "there's nothing inside" (347), that he can only take, not give. Moreover, he fears that women want to enclose him "with spiderwebs woven of yo-yo string" (268). They threaten him with inanimateness. In one scene, Profane lies with his head in Rachel's naked lap, listening to her vagina (a V.); he hears the voice of SHROUD. Rachel herself admits that women can clutch: "All right. We're all hookers. Our price is fixed and single for everything. . . . Can you pay it, honey? Bare brain, bare heart?" (360) But Rachel, being Rachel, will not charge. Women, she claims, " 'can all be conned because we've all got one of these,' touching her crotch, 'and when it talks we listen' " (360). She needs to care for others to complete her self. She has her own Universal Principle: "You have to con each other a little, Profane" (346). It is her version of the Great Lie. It works for her, and it seems preferable to Profane's cultivated schlemihlhood. He is bewildered by it nonetheless and momentarily wishes for a really inanimate woman: "any problems with her, you could look it up in the maintenance manual" (361).

Not all women are connable, and Fortune gives Profane one final crack at redeemerhood through the agency of a girl who is not. For reasons that are never made clear, save only that she appears to be the mysterious bearer of Fortune's blessing, so strong is Paola Maijstral's power that she almost prods Profane into animation. Having served her own apprenticeship in the underworld by becoming a "black" prostitute—"a whore isn't human" (271), she tells McClintic Sphere

—she has reached the level of awareness voiced by Sphere and SHROUD. Paola has left her musician-lover amicably and is preparing to return to Malta to see her father, or perhaps just to accomplish the final stage of her mythic development. Pig Bodine, who has followed Paola about lecherously for weeks, finally tries to rape her. Profane intervenes, cashes in a debt Pig owes him, and rescues her. In gratitude, and because she has always felt drawn to him, Paola immediately offers Profane the prize Pig had sought. He says no:

> "Anyway I say it is nasty. But I'm not looking for any dependents, is all."
> "You have them," she whispered. No, he thought, she's out of her head. Not me. Not a schlemihl.
> "Then why did you make Pig go away?" He thought about that one for a few weeks (355).

Nevertheless Rachel understands that Profane is slipping from her grasp, a yo-yo too heavy to hold. He flirts briefly and superficially with the pseudosophisti-cation of the Whole Sick Crew, while Rachel transfers her attention to the flipped-out Roony Winsome, who needs "her sanity and aloofness from the Crew, her own self-sufficiency" (264). Paola has persuaded Her-bert Stencil to accompany her to Malta, "the cradle of life" (358), as she calls her home. Because he is afraid of what he might discover there, knowing that his fa-ther died there but not how, Stencil persuades Profane to come along. Once he has made his decision to go, Stencil begins to doubt the sense of his quest and comes very close to acknowledging that Fortune has more to do with it than anything. Obsession and drunk-enness submerge his doubts, however, especially when he remembers the dossier he has compiled. He lists for Profane further appearances of V. in France, Mallorca, Spain, Crete, Corfu, Holland, and Asia Minor.

To hedge his bets, Stencil decides to take along a "peace offering" (365) to V. Both of them drunk, Stencil and Profane burglarize Eigenvalue's office for the teeth of precious metals. They make a hilarious job of the crime,[9] and it is followed by several other comic scenes designed to delay climax. Pig Bodine and Profane shack up with two girls named Flip and Flop, who are interchangeable to the two men—which suggests that they lack the hard-won wisdom of McClintic Sphere—and yo-yo into a party of "interesting" people, including a man searching for the Lost Vivaldi Kazoo Concerto. The latter is almost a signature for Pynchon, who refers to the Kazoo Concerto in each of his novels. Finally, Profane, Paola, and Stencil leave for the "immovable rock in the river Fortune" (305).

Within the framework of allusions to Eliot in which Pynchon appears at times to be working, Malta is perhaps like that "red rock" in the first section of *The Waste Land* which provides some "shadow" and safety. In mythic terms, Malta may be "the world-navel," the center of the universe, a place of constant renewal of energy. Or perhaps it is merely the metaphor of "delusion" Fausto has claimed it to be. In any case, Paola need only touch base again there to find her destiny.

The trio reaches Valletta after comic adventures against obstacles typical of a mythic hero's quest. On Malta a balloon is going up; it is the Suez Crisis of 1956, one of the last gasps of a dying British colonialism. British troops are preparing to land in Suez. Aside from Profane, the only Americans on the island are the crew of the schlemihl's old ship, the *U.S.S. Scaffold,* which is in drydock for repairs at the whim of fortune, and the chapter opens with the sailors going on liberty. The focus is on Pappy Hod, whose buddies are worried about his mental health now that they are in Malta, where he had met and married Paola. Sailors at their sentimental best, two of them follow Pappy from bar to bar to look after him. "Pappy's brother," says Johnny Contango, "brother's keeper" (413). They are on the Gut in Valletta, a "bad street" (408).

The predictable fight ensues, with unpredictable results. American sailors square off against British commandoes and threaten to riot in the streets. But this is Malta, hub of Fortune's wheel, and Paola, heir apparent to her blessing, has returned. Fortune also receives an assist from Dahoud, who has averred that "life is the most precious possession you have, because without it you'd be dead." Significantly a Negro and a musician like McClintic Sphere, Dahoud quells the riot by singing songs in the manner of Billy Eckstine. When Pappy Hod's protectors get him back safely to the *Scaffold*'s dock, Paola is waiting. She offers love to the husband who needs it, vows to be waiting for him like a Penelope in Norfolk when his tour is over, and gives him an ivory comb as a pledge. It is a relic of V., and Paola has "had it a long time," having obviously taken it from the Bad Priest when she helped the other children disassemble the machine-woman: "Five crucified Limeys—five Kilroys—stared briefly at Valletta's sky" (417) until Pappy pockets it.

Presumably the comb has been purified, and carries no evil with it. There is nothing ambiguous about the scene, although Paola is curiously stoic. She will not kiss her husband, she says, until they meet in Norfolk. In his "Confessions," her father had prayed for her: "May you be only Paola, one girl: a single given heart, a whole mind at peace" (294). She has been whore, lover, and wife, but she appears to have achieved peace. Having gone through a purgatory of sorts herself, the implication is that she can lead others out as well, a Beatrice in truth. She is a frail bearer of redemption for the waste land, however, and probably Pynchon intends to say only that she is merely human, which is more than can be said for most of the other characters. "Keep cool but care" is her watchword, and it is seemingly the best option available. If old values have lost their savor, they are the only values we have. Paola knows that. She can not be conned, and will not stoop to con her husband. She will trust to Fortune, which is to trust to life.

Profane watches this exchange; Stencil does not, and does not see the comb. Having learned nothing from Fausto Maijstral that he does not already know, Stencil nearly admits that his quest reduces "only to the recurrence of an initial and a few dead objects" (419). Fausto himself concludes that his new acquaintance is obsessed, "and that such an obsession is a hothouse . . ." (422). Stencil begins to pray to Fortune to keep him from insanity. Then he meets Father Avalanche, who tells him of Father Fairing, and Profane fills in the gaps by recounting the story of the sewer parish, Veronica the rat, and "the chamber lit by some frightening radiance" (424) just before the schlemihl shot the quester. Repeating to himself the phrase "events seem to be ordered into an ominous logic" (423) to keep his sanity, the suspicious Stencil confronts Maijstral, who first mocks him: "Yes, yes. Thirteen of us rule the world in secret" (425), then more kindly whispers, pointing at Valletta: "ask her. . . . Ask the rock" (435). After all these years, a new metaphor can not replace the one he had made his own, and when Stencil hears of a Madame Viola, an "oneiromancer," or diviner of dreams, who left a trail to Stockholm, he is off, the hothouse of his paranoia in full bloom.

That leaves Profane, in the street. On walls along it are chalked Kilroys, the sign of the "schlemihl or sad sack." According to the narrator, the image has undergone evolution. Originally Kilroy had been a schematic for "a band-pass filter. . . . inanimate" but had become disguised as a human face:

> The foolish nose hanging over the wall was vulnerable to all manner of indignities: fist, shrapnel, machete. Hinting perhaps at a precarious virility, a flirting with castration, though ideas like this are inevitable in a latrine-oriented (as well as Freudian) psychology.
>
> But it was all deception. . . . It was a masterful disguise: a metaphor. . . . But Grandmaster of Valletta tonight (410).

Profane's sign is in the ascendant, but it is not a promising omen. His virility, i.e., his potential for redeeming the wasteland, is precarious indeed, since it turns on the degree to which he himself is vulnerable. His schlemihlhood remains impervious, perhaps because Kilroys are only the inanimate barely masquerading as human. Rachel has predicted that his virility will give no life: "there'll always be a woman for Benny. . . . Always a hole to let yourself come in, without fear of losing any of that precious schlemihlhood" (360).

123

The woman this time is Brenda Wigglesworth, an undergraduate WASP on a European tour, accompanied only by thirty-six pairs of Bermuda shorts, a Puritan making the decadent scene before the inevitable degree and marriage. Brenda and Benny agree that they belong on the street and that

> this was nowhere, but some of us do go nowhere and can con ourselves into believing it to be somewhere: it is a kind of talent and objections to it are rare but even at that captious (427).

They have no such talent, although Brenda is a poet. She reads Profane a Sandburg-like piece beginning "I am the twentieth century," an admixture of the novel's motifs, which she promptly folds into a paper-plane and sails away. It is phony, she says, "things I've read for courses" (428). Profane must possess *real* experience, more than girls ever acquire. No, he replies, "offhand I'd say I haven't learned a goddamn thing" (428).

Without vulnerability, virility, or virtú, and without any delusions, let alone a Great Lie, he has learned only that he has lost something. In a moment of typical schlemihlhood prompted by a rising phosphorescence on the island, he thinks of Paola:

> It made him sadder: as if all his homes were temporary and even they, inanimate, still wandering as he: for motion is relative, and hadn't he, now, really stood there still on the sea like a schlemihl Redeemer while that enormous malingering city and its one livable inner space and one unconnable (therefore hi-value) girl had slid away from him over a great horizon's curve comprising, from this vantage, at once, at least one century's worth of wavelets? (427)

The radiance notwithstanding, he drops back into his minimal humanity, at best a holding action against the inanimate, a running in place. He and Brenda are running down the street, when, as once they had in a sewer, the lights of Malta go out.

CHAPTER FOUR

Excluded Middles and Bad Shit:
The Crying of Lot 49

Structurally, Pynchon's second novel is his finest, written as if to answer critics who charged *V.* with formlessness. *The Crying of Lot 49* is a tightly plotted, symmetrical narrative of great compactness, enhanced by the author's light tone and feeling for American popular culture. His attention to symmetry, Alfred Kazin has said, sets Pynchon above most "absurdists."[1] To call Pynchon an absurdist is to misconstrue him, particularly with reference to a book so carefully predicated on logic. *The Crying of Lot 49* is both funny and difficult, but it is not an example of absurdism.

Besides its greater compression, *The Crying of Lot 49* is a considerably more mature novel than *V.* Thematically Pynchon has traveled quite a distance—roughly that between Henry Adams and Alfred North Whitehead. In place of the collegiate antipathy to the machine age that characterized *V.* is an awareness that machines are not man's real problem, that, indeed, another historical epoch has slipped up on the Henry Adamses of this world. Superficially about a conspiracy, *The Crying of Lot 49* deals not so much with a plot as with a *process* developing from power and necessity—

which Pynchon expresses as possibility in a series of scenarios. In short, it contains an enormously more sophisticated world view than *V.*, and anticipates the still more sophisticated view of *Gravity's Rainbow*.

Almost to a greater extent even than *V.*, *The Crying of Lot 49* centers on questing, or more accurately here, on sleuthing. Part of Pynchon's appeal lies in his assimilation of the detective-spy genre of fiction and comic book alike, which makes his manipulations of clues and plots sinister and playful at the same time. In *Gravity's Rainbow*, for instance, references to Sax Rohmer's Nayland Smith and Fu Manchu abound, and in *V.*, Pynchon's use of the Mediterranean generally and Malta specifically may be bows in the direction of Eric Ambler and Dashiell Hammett (although the places are eminently suitable for other reasons). In *The Crying of Lot 49*, the source of intrigue is Pierce Inverarity, a name Pynchon probably intends as a play on that of Professor Moriarty, arch foe of Sherlock Holmes—a master of nefarious design. Inverarity, recently deceased, has left an estate of bewildering complexity, and in his will has designated his former lover, Oedipa Maas, as executrix (and presumed heir); the plot of the novel revolves around Oedipa's efforts to unravel the skein of the legacy. One of Inverarity's favorite alter-egos had been Lamont Cranston, "The Shadow" of radio fame. His last words to Oedipa, almost a year before his death, were spoken over the telephone in imitation of Cranston. Even Oedipa's attorney, alternately envious and resentful of mystery-solving television lawyers, is surreptitiously writing a brief called *The Profession v. Perry Mason, a Not-So-Hypothetical Indictment*. In such an atmosphere it is only moderately strange that Oedipa should become the Sherlock to Inverarity's Moriarty. Her name, however, suggests that the relationship is something more.

That name is a touchstone of Western Civilization, and in using it Pynchon can draw on a welter of associations. The most relevant, of course, are those stemming from Sophocles's *Oedipus Rex*, whose protagonist is tormented by the question of man's place in a universe he does not understand. The problems he faces are religious, metaphysical, political, and epistemological. He is forced to make choices, but he never achieves control over his destiny; with none of the problems resolved at play's end he must go on seeking. Oedipa Maas faces similar problems and a similar lack of resolution. The religious, metaphysical, political, and epistemological aspects of the world she encounters overlap and intertwine with one another, and to explore them is difficult. We shall begin at her own starting point, Pierce Inverarity.

Inverarity is never seen directly, but his presence in the novel is pervasive. Oedipa remembers him as an entrepreneur of classic American dimensions, a role symbolized by his keeping a bust of the financier Jay Gould over his bed. So perfectly did he embody the American Capitalist that to a Mexican revolutionary of faltering faith he was a "miracle," "another world's intrusion" (88),[2] or perhaps, to employ a ubiquitous term in the novel, an Other. Pierce, Jesus Arrabal tells Oedipa, was "too exactly and without flaw the thing we fight . . . as terrifying to me as a Virgin appearing to an Indian" (89). Inverarity restores Arrabal's belief in his cause and gives order to his world, as only a vision of the enemy can do for the paranoid. For Arrabal, Inverarity fills some sort of void and almost in a religious sense provides an opposition against which Arrabal can define himself. For a while Pierce had functioned somewhat differently for Oedipa. Having romantically "conned herself into the curious, Rapunzel-like role of a pensive girl somehow," she had imagined her lover as a knight come to free her from her tower, to give intensity to her life, which up until his arrival had seemed a "movie, just perceptibly out of focus, that the projectionist refused to fix" (10). Now she realizes that the "tower, its height and architecture, are like her ego only incidental: that what really keeps her where she is is magic, anonymous and malignant, visited on her from outside and for no reason at all" (11). She is sensitive to voids also, and on a trip to Mexico with Pierce had been devastated when she saw a painting of frail girls weaving tapestries which spilled out the windows of *their* tower, trying futilely "to fill the void," for "the tapestry was the world" (10). Pierce's energy could sustain her just so far and no further; it is ultimately no proof against the magic of the void. Now she too must search for a miracle.

Such language indicates the religious nature of Oedipa's quest. Religious imagery actually frames the novel. On the first page, having just heard of Inverarity's death, "Oedipa stood in the living room, stared at by the greenish dead eye of the TV tube, spoke the name of God, tried to feel as drunk as possible." On the last page, a part of Inverarity's estate is being auctioned off by a man who "spread his arms in a gesture that seemed to belong to the priesthood of some remote culture; perhaps to a descending angel." In between are numerous religious allusions, the most common of which are Oedipa's invocations of God. In each case she seems to be appealing not so much to the Christian Deity as to some force she hopes will manifest itself. Hers is a vague but deep longing of the type described by Mircea Eliade in *The Sacred and the Profane:* "Whatever the historical context in which he is placed, *homo religiousus* always believes that there is an absolute reality, *the sacred,* which transcends this world but manifests itself in this world, thereby sanctifying it and making it real."[3]

Pynchon also assigns religious significance to the conspiracy Oedipa believes she has uncovered, and makes it explicit by inventing an extreme seventeenth-century Puritan sect called the Scurvhamites, whose

> central hangup had to do with predestination. There were two kinds. Nothing for a Scurvhamite ever happened by accident, Creation was a vast, intricate machine. But one part of it, the Scurvhamite part, ran off the will of God, its prime mover. The rest ran off some opposite Principle, something blind, soulless; a brute automatism that led to eternal death. The idea was to woo converts into the Godly and purposeful sodality of the Scurvhamite. . . . But the brute other, that kept the non-Scurvhamite universe running like clockwork, that was something else again. Evidently they felt Trystero [the conspiracy] would symbolize the other quite well (116-117).

As with any religious sensibility, Oedipa's runs afoul of the question of evil, which is somehow connected with Inverarity. Good and Evil—whether in Manichean, Deistic, or Calvinist terms—oppose each other, but Oedipa has difficulty deciding which side is which, particularly since Inverarity may have had a foot in each camp. Was he a member of the Elect, according to some doctrine of predestination, or did he, like the Scurvhamites, end by going over to the other side, being attracted by "the glamorous prospect of annihilation" (116)? Before the book appeared, Pynchon published a lengthy excerpt in *Esquire* entitled "The World (This One), The Flesh (Mrs. Oedipa Maas), and The Testament of Pierce Inverarity," which would seem to make the mogul a Devil. But again the matter is not so simple. On the one hand, the "conspiracy" would appear to function in opposition to everything Pierce stood for. On the other, he may have subsidized, or even created, the conspiracy.

This confusion is a fairly late development in the novel, however; in the beginning Oedipa is merely ripe for epiphany, disposed to see designs around her. In San Narciso, Inverarity's legal residence, she experiences "an odd, religious instant" (13) when the tract houses remind her of a printed circuit in a transistor radio. It is the first of many such moments, each brought on by her open attitude to people and events. "You're trying to tell me something" (110) is her typical response. As she gradually learns of Pierce's holdings, specifically a real-estate development known as Fangoso Lagoons, she realizes that "some immediacy was there again, some promise of hierophany: printed circuit, gently curving streets, private access to the water, Book of the Dead . . ." (18). Gradually, in meeting people involved in various forms of communication and media, she discovers that patterns *do* surround her and impinge upon her life and those of others connected with Inverarity.

From a metaphysical and political angle, Pierce's roles are only slightly less perplexing. Before the end of the novel it becomes apparent that Inverarity's legacy —whatever else it may be—is America, an America in transition. Like America, Pierce had been confronted with a "cul-de-sac he'd tried to find a way out of," an "enigma his efforts had created" (134). Oedipa knows that her lover had been driven by a "need to possess, to alter the land, to bring new skylines, personal antagonisms, growth rates into being" (134). Inverarity had a Calvinist approach to enterprise, had been caught up in the desire to transform nature into buildings and bureaucracies; he was the Protestant Ethic incarnate. Pynchon had probably read Max Weber's *The Protestant Ethic and the Spirit of Capitalism* at this point; he makes explicit reference to Weber in *Gravity's Rainbow*. Weber perceived causal relationships between Calvinist doctrine and the establishment of economic and political structures in America. Thus, Inverarity represents the best and the worst in America—or, to put it in Faustian terms, he is possibly an evil from which good may come. The enigma he and his fellow capitalists have created is awesome, and Oedipa, his figurative daughter and literal lover, like her namesake must try to solve it.

The America Inverarity personifies is, to put it mildly, in the throes of change. In *V.* Pynchon presented a world that was running down and concluded that the outlook for regeneration was bleak. In *The Crying of Lot 49* he turns his attention to an America also wasted by loss of energy but decides that options remain. The capitalist-industrialist society is succumbing to randomly dispersed energy and is becoming a system in which inertia and homogeneity are increasingly evident, a condition aptly illustrated by the endless tract houses of Southern California and the maze of similar desks and jobs at the Yoyodyne Corporation, both phenomena created by Inverarity and his kind. As might be expected, Pynchon draws visible parallels between theories of physics and societal circumstances. In physics, Newton's orderly universe has given way to quantum theory and the recognition of randomness and indeterminacy in systems. Without an orderly system, one has reduced ability to predict future states and perceive causal connections between events; physical determinism, or causation, no longer operates smoothly. The classic textbook example of this older vision of determinism, alluded to several times in *The Crying of Lot 49,* is the collision of billiard balls. One can predict the behavior of the balls as they react to forces, just as, given the state of a closed system, one can within the framework of Newtonian mechanics predict its future states and causal relationships—provided that no external forces act on the system. Oedipa's world, however, *is* subject to external forces—or at least she believes that it is. Magic surrounds her. Oedipa speculates that "If miracles were, as Jesus Arrabal had postulated . . . , intrusions into this world from another, a kiss of cosmic pool balls" (92), then there must be forces at work beyond her ken. But, she also knows, the forces might be illusory; they are certainly difficult to discern. Too much order may not even be desirable, as she discovers when she decides that she can think only in the "madness" of a California freeway. "You think a man's mind is a pool table?" Emory Bortz asks her. "I hope not," she replies (115).

The Second Law of Thermodynamics reigns, and Oedipa quickly senses its primacy. Early in the novel she is nearly brained by a run-away aerosol can, one of Pynchon's amusing applications of classical physics to his heroine's situation. The broken valve on the can propels it about Oedipa's bathroom; as it flies, it recapitulates Joule's experiments with the expansion of gases, which led him to the kinetic theory of gas. "The kinetic theory of gas is an assertion of ultimate chaos," said Henry Adams (*The Education,* 451). In other words, it is a corroboration of the Second Law. Nevertheless Oedipa feels that the can's flight can be predicted: "The can knew where it was going, she sensed, or something fast enough, God or a digital machine, might have computed in advance the complex web of its travel; but she wasn't fast enough . . ." (23). Disorder and potential chaos affect Oedipa and the other characters in the novel, but the meaning of the book hinges on whether or not the threat is inevitable or irreversible.

Several important observations are necessary at this point. For all his emphasis on the Second Law, in *The Crying of Lot 49* Pynchon is moderating his views on entropy. America, he seems to be saying, may no longer be a closed system, so that while it is possible to speak of that system as becoming disordered, it may also be true that the system is being acted upon by other forces, which conceivably could have the effect of resisting the entropy that afflicts it. In *V.* Pynchon adopted Henry Adams's pessimistic belief that entropy within our civilization was irreversible, that our civilization was running down irrevocably to final equilibrium. Said Adams: "The physicists had a phrase for it, unintelligible to the vulgar: 'All that we win is a battle —lost in advance—with the irreversible phenomena in the background of nature'" (*The Education,* 458). In *The Human Use of Human Beings*, however, Norbert Wiener has observed that human beings are *not* closed systems in any real sense, if only because they take in food, and especially because they take in information. Information itself is related to entropy, of course, and Pynchon does make use of this aspect of entropy in *The Crying of Lot 49,* a factor we shall deal with later. Wiener puts it this way: "While the universe as a whole, if indeed there is a whole universe, tends to run down, there are local enclaves whose direction seems opposed to that of the universe at large and in which there is a limited and temporary tendency for organization to increase. Life finds its home in some of these enclaves."[4]

Since Wiener published his reflections, sophisticated theories of systems made Adams's perspective even more obsolete. Scientific opinion still holds that the physical world is an irreversible closed system, which means, according to the Second Law, that it is running down, that energy will continually dissipate itself or become unavailable, that entropy will increase. This heat-death of the universe, while a virtual certainty, is a most remote event. For those of us concerned with the here and now the question is whether human institutions and systems are susceptible to the same end. From a broad perspective they are, for they are a part of the universe. From a narrower one they are also, for all things are subject to decay. But at the same time, in another sense we are applying artificial metaphors when we refer to closed societal systems. Strictly speaking, there are none. Each such system is part of a larger system, which is part of a still larger, and so on. No man is an island, and no human institution is entirely isolated either—although, to be sure, men sometimes try to make systems and themselves so, like the Inamorati Anonymous in *The Crying of Lot 49*. That is not to say that we should ignore the larger systems of which our institutions are a part. Only recently Americans have experienced a very real example of entropy in the discovery that the energy which fuels a massive social-political-economic system is finite, running out, becoming unavailable. (Even should we harness the power of the sun, that too will eventually run out.) We learned, however, that ours was not the closed system we thought—that we are dependent on energy from other systems, which is getting close to the theme of Pynchon's book. Even more significant in this context is that our search for new sources of energy demonstrates that systems can be altered.

Humans can change systems. As a post-Wiener authority, Ervin Laszlo, says in *The Systems View of the World:* "You must keep yourself running against the odds of the physical decay of all things, and to do so you must perform the necessary repairs, including (if you are a very complex system) the ultimate one of replacing your entire system by reproducing it from one special part of it."[5] Meatball Mulligan resisted entropy by making repairs in his apartment in "Entropy." In *The Crying of Lot 49* the task is enormously more difficult: America must use special parts to alter or reproduce or create anew a much larger system. The task is complicated further by what seems to be the appearance of a new kind of energy which must be recognized for what it is, and which may already be altering the system. The process may be the result of human choice or historical evolution; the new system may come about by conscious decision or through immanence. Can human choice resist entropy or alter systems? Pynchon now apparently believes it can. Appalled by what she sees in her country, Oedipa says to herself, "This is America, you live in it, you let it happen" (112). Or,

133

to put it another way, can we learn from history? Again Pynchon seems to think that we can, if we pursue "the track of the energy." Along that route lies confusion, but there might also lie hope.

It is clear that the capitalist-industrialist system has laid waste America. Everywhere Oedipa looks the landscape is garish and uniform, sprawling and sterile. Lining the highways are prefabricated buildings, "auto lots, escrow services, drive-ins, small office buildings and factories whose address numbers were in the 70 and then 80,000's. [Oedipa] had never known numbers to run so high. It seemed unnatural" (14). The cities are worse. San Francisco is "infected" (86). San Narciso is "less an identifiable city than a grouping of concepts—census tracts, special purpose bond-issue districts, shopping nuclei . . ." (12). Dominating them all is Los Angeles. Oedipa thinks of the freeways as hypodermics plunged into the veins of this urban monstrosity, linked to its environs, nourished by them, but narcotized, narcissistic, insensitive to the people who live there: "But were Oedipa some single melted crystal of urban horse, L. A., really, would be no less turned on for her absence" (14). Pynchon emphasizes this condition by naming Pierce Inverarity's domicile San Narciso and the motel where Oedipa stays Echo Courts. Both names suggest narcissism, isolation, and indifference.

Aggravating the sickness of the land is the paradoxical nature of entropy. To remain viable, a system must be organized, but too much organization hastens entropy. Healthy organization permits multiplicity and diversity. Unfortunately, industrialized, capitalized America has enforced conformity. "How had it ever happened here," Oedipa asks herself, "with the chances once so good for diversity?" (136). The greatest waste has thus been of people, not just of those down and outs, the rejects, the counterparts of Mucho's used cars, but of all those alienated and disaffected citizens who feel themselves disinherited. Pynchon elaborated slightly on this situation in the two short pieces he published before and after *The Crying of Lot 49*. How does a system assimilate its disparate elements: It is the problem recognized by Grover Snodd in "The Secret Integration"; differentiation must be offset by integration. Or, as Pynchon asks in "A Journey into the Mind of Watts," how can Los Angeles permit a separate world to exist within itself, both part and no-part of the larger whole? Something must be done; some new system must evolve, or the old one will not survive. The system must be reproduced, or modified, from some special part, to allow for multiplicity *and* diversity.

Given this sickness and sterility, the waste land waits for deliverance: "The waiting above all; if not for another set of possibilities to replace those that had conditioned the land to accept any San Narciso among its most tender flesh without a reflex or a cry, then at least, at the very least, waiting for a symmetry of choices to break down, to go skew" (136). San Narciso is America; it loses its uniqueness for Oedipa and is subsumed into the continent. In the California of *The Crying of Lot 49* Pynchon has found the perfect waste land—he need no longer imitate Eliot's. Nevertheless there are similarities between California and some of Pynchon's earlier landscapes. For one thing, like Dennis Flange of "Low-lands," Oedipa looks to the sea "as redemption for Southern California . . ., some unvoiced idea that no matter what you did to its edges the true Pacific stayed inviolate and integrated or assumed the ugliness at any edge into some more general truth" (37). And there may be another kind of redemption available, not necessarily on the same order as that brought by Cleanth Siegel in "Mortality and Mercy in Vienna." If the waste land requires a new mythology, there may be one in the offing, with the ironic initials W.A.S.T.E., an Other with roots in history. And finally, as in "Low-lands," the advocates of the new, of the opposition, seem to be an underground conspiracy, waiting for an opportune moment.

As a sleuth tracking down a conspiracy, or as a hierophant in search of a manifestation of the sacred, Oedipa is both ill-suited and well-prepared for her function. She has "no apparatus except gut fear and female cunning to examine this formless magic, to un-

135

derstand how it works, how to measure its field strength, count its lines of force . . ." (11). A product of the fifties, she is out of her element in the sixties, where students have learned to protest against an American establishment. America has changed since her schooldays:

> Where were Secretaries James and Foster and Senator Joseph, those dear daft numina who'd mothered over Oedipa's so temperate youth? In another world. Along another pattern of track, another string of decisions taken, switches closed, the faceless pointsmen who'd thrown them all transferred, deserted, in stir, fleeing the skip-tracers, out of their skull, on horse, alcoholic, fanatic, under aliases, dead, impossible to find ever again. Among them they had managed to turn the young Oedipa into a rare creature indeed, unfit perhaps for marches and sit-ins, but just a whiz at pursuing strange words in Jacobean texts (76).

She also proves to be a whiz at history. Her very inexperience is an asset, for she has few preconceptions that might interfere with her search. One she does have is a disposition to sense lines of force, and in this respect she resembles Henry Adams ("Adams never knew why, knowing nothing of Faraday, he began to mimic Faraday's trick of seeing lines of force all about him . . ." [*The Education*, 426]). The magic that keeps Oedipa isolate in her tower is energy, power flowing in patterns and systems she does not understand and can not be sure exist. Scattering iron filings in an electromagnetic field reveals the configurations of the forces. A cloud chamber shows the track of an electron. Oedipa must deal with energy which effects us all, but its paths are invisible. To counteract the magic, to comprehend the energy, she needs a Word, a Text, a Sign; this is what Pierce may or may not have left her.

Behind Pynchon's crypticism is a holistic view of the world roughly analogous to Alfred North Whitehead's concept of process. Nowadays it is called theory of systems, and has led to a discipline which studies the energy which binds the parts of a system into a whole.

Nineteenth-century scientists thought of forces as causes, some form of motion acting on something. Twentieth-century scientists have come increasingly to think of force not as motion or cause but as a relationship between things, as energy which integrates. This view has been made possible by various connected developments: relativity in field physics, quantum theory in micro-physics, parallel modes of thought in other disciplines like biology, chemistry, economics, sociology, and political science, the rising hegemony of mathematics, the invention of the digital computer, and so on—all of which may be subsumed under the general category of technology.

In historical terms, the age of technology is displacing the age of machines, with effects more profound and disturbing than those Adams perceived in the displacement of earlier epochs by the age of machines. The new symbol is not Adams's Dynamo but the Computer, and Oedipa will eventually perceive reality as the "matrices of a great digital computer" (136). So complex are the energies that only mathematics can describe them, and so complex are the mathematics that only computers can deal with them: "God or a digital machine," says Oedipa. And, once again, so complex are the energies that not even a computer suffices as metaphor. Pynchon requires another, more embracive one, and he finds it in communications. To reiterate, technology involves not so much machines as systems, systems in which energy functions in interaction and interdependence, with incredible density. Moreover, it is energy of a particular sort:

Communications in the broadest sense of that term is replacing work as the foundation of the technological system. Energy is still utilized, but increasingly it is used to affect states of consciousness rather than to move physical objects. . . . Not levers and pulleys exerting force but sounds in the air, lights flashing on the computer, are the archetypal symbols of the new era, and electronics rather than mechanical physics is supreme.[6]

A television set, for example, is not really a machine, and the rocket of *Gravity's Rainbow* is even less so: Both are systems in which energy is in process. Electronic media are everywhere in *The Crying of Lot 49*, from the electronic guitars of the Paranoids to the omnipresent television set. "Filthy machine" (66), Mr. Thoth calls the latter, as well he might, since his name is that of the Egyptian god of speech and letters. Time has passed Mr. Thoth by; he does not understand the new age. For that matter, hardly anybody in the novel does, unless it be Pierce Inverarity.

Many readers have assumed that *The Crying of Lot 49* deals merely with the failures of communication in its conventional sense. Since such a theme was already hackneyed in 1966, if that were all Pynchon were saying the novel would have no great significance. What he is concerned with are the larger implications of the technological age and the alterations of reality it has brought as it mutates industrialism. The dislocations in the wake of change require, quite literally, new ways of looking at the world, and few people agree on what that involves. For example, Mike Fallopian of the Birch-like Peter Pinguid Society is opposed to "industrial *anything*" (33). Fallopian and his fellows know that industrialism is moribund, that its institutions and mechanics are in decline. Their reaction is to retreat into an insane ideological position which shades into crypto-fascism in order to assert order. Adopted to correct the dehumanization they associate with industrialism, their solution also dehumanizes. They begin by speaking of freedom and end by denying it; Fallopian will come to hate Oedipa because she is free. Like Hitler, who also hated industrialism and wanted to return to a primitive order but who could coopt the technology of Albert Speer, Fallopian and the Pinguids know how to grasp the essential quality of the new technology—communication. They do not know how to use it yet (they send each other letters devoid of content), but they are a threat.

While Fallopian's right-wing turn to the past illustrates the dangers attendant on the advent of the new forces, in a broader sense it suggests the dimensions of the dilemma. On the one hand, caught as she is between the older Calvinistic industrialism and the newer unknown technology, America persists in clinging to values from the past which no longer suffice to explain or govern the new circumstances. For instance, Yoyodyne, the defense plant, manufactures destructive technological weapons but markets them in classical capitalist fashion, as if they were ordinary industrial products. At business meetings the stockholders sing company songs to the tune of Cornell's Alma Mater. The values of the past are inappropriate. As another example, Stanley Koteks, like Fallopian an employee of Yoyodyne, complains bitterly that the corporation does not honor the individual inventiveness of "Tom Swifts" like himself. "Isn't it all teamwork now?" (61) Oedipa asks.

On the other hand, the technological era and the communication which informs it are historical phenomena to be understood fully only by reference to the past. Pynchon thus differs from those prophets of the new technology who hold that history is irrelevant. Since he is concerned with communication, Pynchon might have chosen a modern electronic conspiracy to provide structure for *The Crying of Lot 49*. For some years now, so-called "black-boxers" have been ripping off the telephone monopoly in America by means of Ma Bell's own technology. With a device duplicating the sonic tones that trigger telephone circuits, the user can call anywhere in the world free. So widespread and so bold is this "conspiracy" that in 1973 the membership surfaced in New York City for a convention; Pynchon, attuned to underground networks, would almost surely have known of its existence much earlier.

He chose instead to fabricate a conspiracy with roots in history, in order to unite the various levels of meaning in his novel. Oedipa takes history as seriously as does Henry Adams. By contrast, Mike Fallopian treats historical questions quite casually, intent only on using the past for his own purposes. Fallopian does not try to reconcile contradictions in the career of the legendary Peter Pinguid. Oedipa will try to make scripture out of her historical research, for she is looking for a manifestation of the sacred to revive the waste land.

It is a lovely creation, "a metaphor of God knew how many parts" (80), as Oedipa says, in language Pynchon chooses carefully. The conspiracy and the clues by which Oedipa becomes aware of it structure the novel like the clockwork mechanism the Scurvhamites believe operates the universe, and were we to disassemble all the parts we should have a chapter longer than the book itself. Without attempting to recount the ways in which Oedipa learns of the Tristero, and without trying to reconcile some apparent contradictions in the information she receives—which are properly *her* difficulties rather than the reader's anyway —we can sum up what she knows, or thinks she knows, at the conclusion of *The Crying of Lot 49*.

The Tristero takes its name from its founder, a sixteenth-century Spaniard called Hernando Joaquín de Tristero y Calavera, "perhaps a madman, perhaps an honest rebel, according to some only a con artist" (119). Calavera is Spanish for skull, an image of which adorns the cover of Oedipa's principal text, a mysterious paperback anthology of Jacobean revenge tragedies. The name Tristero itself is subject to interpretation, with some authorities associating it with "a pseudo-Italianate variant on *triste* (wretched, depraved)," and others with a complicated pun on *dies irae,* the Day of Judgment (74-75). These religious connotations ripple out from the mysterious origins of the organization, which began as an opposition to a "junta of Calvinist fanatics" (119). In 1577, at the conclusion of a successful struggle for independence from the Holy Roman Empire, the Protestants of the Low Countries dispossessed the Thurn and Taxis family of its postal monopoly by awarding it to an adherent of William of Orange, Jan Hinckart. Hinckart's cousin, Tristero, advances a claim to this postmastership, arguing that he is the legitimate heir, and continues to urge his claim even after Thurn and Taxis regains its monopoly. Styling himself The Disinherited, Tristero creates a surreptitious rival mail service, dresses his riders in black, and adopts as his symbols perversions of Thurn and Taxis's own: the *muted* post horn and the *dead* badger suggest his triumph over his enemy. To mock Thurn and Taxis further, his system uses forged and distorted stamps from the other system, and his riders justify their methods with a variation on a familiar motto: "neither tempest nor strife, nor fierce beasts, nor the loneliness of the desert, nor yet the illegitimate usurpers of our rightful estate, can deter our couriers" (118). In addition, the Tristero agents wage a campaign of harassment, murder, and destruction against Thurn and Taxis all over the Continent.

This information Oedipa receives from the "tabernacle" of history texts. To fill in the gaps of the organization's history in the centuries that follow she must speculate, and here she is assisted by Emory Bortz, a professor who holds "a mirror-image theory, by which any period of instability for Thurn and Taxis must have its reflection in Tristero's shadow-state" (122). Since disorder racked Thurn and Taxis in the seventeenth century, Bortz postulates dissension in the ranks of Tristero also. One faction, he says, must have pushed for continued sub rosa attacks on the rival system, another for an immediate takeover, and still another, made up of "men above the immediacy of their time who could think historically" (123), for a merger. Surely, Bortz thinks, at least one man could see the approaching break-up of the Holy Roman Empire and the chaos that would entail. Like Herbert Stencil, Bortz allows his imagination to play in a Hollywood-style scenario in which a visionary named Konrad tries to shout down the militants of other Tristero factions:

"The salvation of Europe . . . depends on communication, right? We face this anarchy of jealous German princes, hundreds of them scheming, counter-scheming, infighting, dissipating all of the Empire's strength in their useless bickering. But whoever could control the lines of communication, among all these princes, would control them. That network someday could unify the Continent. So I propose that we merge with our old enemy Thurn and Taxis. . . . Together . . . our two systems could be invincible. . . . We, who have so long been disinherited, could be the heirs of Europe!" (123)

But the factionalism is too great. The Holy Roman Empire crumbles, leaving Thurn and Taxis even more unstable, and the traditionalists inside Tristero persuade the others to continue the depredations against the weakened monopoly. Since Tristero has never publicly revealed itself, Thurn and Taxis still have "no clear idea who their adversary is." That being the case, Bortz thinks, "then many of them must come to believe in something very like the Scurvhamite's blind, automatic anti-God" (124). All the monopolists know is that the enemy has ghostly powers for disrupting their system.

Over the next century or so, however, as evidence of Tristero's existence surfaces, the Thurn and Taxis "paranoia recedes, as they come to discover the secular Tristero" (124). It has moved out of the realm of the quasi-sacred to a visible political plane: "Power, omniscience, implacable malice, attributes of what they'd thought to be a historical principle, a Zeitgeist, are carried over to the now human enemy" (124). This growing historical awareness of Tristero's secular role parallels Oedipa's discovery of the conspiracy. First apprehended as religious revelation, it has gradually appeared to her in profane manifestations.

According to Bortz it is even possible that Tristero, grown powerful, "staged" the French Revolution for the express purpose of revoking the Thurn and Taxis monopoly in France and in the Lowlands, but this view is at least partially contradicted by another text given Oedipa by Genghis Cohen, the philatelist who is appraising Inverarity's curious stamp collection for the estate. This manuscript speaks of another internecine conflict which shook Tristero at the time of the French Revolution, when once again one faction wishes to ally Tristero with Thurn and Taxis to subsidize the enemy. The attempt fails. Because of its mirror-image relationship, the decline of Thurn and Taxis is matched by "historical eclipse" for Tristero. The latter is reduced to transmitting the correspondence of anarchists as they sow chaos across Europe in the early 1800's. The author of the manuscript believes that the greater number of the survivors of Tristero left Europe for America in 1849 and 1850.

After that, Oedipa knows a good deal of the organization's history. In America also Tristero set up a secret rival mail service, forged or altered official U.S. stamps, and generally employed the tactics it had used with success in Europe, this time under the banner of free enterprise. From Mr. Thoth, for instance, Oedipa has learned that Tristero riders either dressed in black or disguised as Indians had attacked his grandfather when he rode for the Pony Express in 1860. Moreover, to Oedipa's consternation, the evidence suggests that in contrast to other private mail services suppressed by the Federal Government, the 800-year-old Tristero still functions, at least in California and probably all across America, and may be on the point of another secular appearance. The modern Tristero's symbols are two: the muted post horn and the acronym W.A.S.T.E. (We Await Silent Tristero's Empire). And as one might guess, the mail drops for the system are the familiar green WASTE containers found on the streets of major cities.

Assuming that the underground communications system really exists, what underground people use it? By the end of the novel, Oedipa finds it easier to ask what underground groups do *not,* since she has found the Tristero symbols everywhere among the alienated and disaffected of California:

> For here were God knew how many citizens, deliberately choosing not to communicate by U.S. Mail. It was not an act of treason, nor possibly even of defiance. But it was a calculated withdrawal, from the life of the Republic, from its machinery. Whatever else was being denied them out of hate, indifference to the power of their vote, loopholes, simple ignorance, this withdrawal was their own, unpublicized, private. Since they could not have withdrawn into a vacuum (could they?), there had to exist the separate, silent, unsuspected world (92).

The last word in that passage is the important one,

since it adds weight to what Pynchon has been hinting at. The metaphorical conspiracy is an anti-world, a mirror-image from which forces seem to emanate, although for the most part the forces are invisible. Oedipa senses them. While on her quest she puts up at a Berkeley hotel which is host to a convention of deaf-mutes, and there participates in a dance party. A young deaf-mute sweeps Oedipa on to the ballroom floor where they dance for half an hour among other deaf-mutes:

> Each couple on the floor danced whatever was in the fellow's head: tango, two-step, bossa nova, slop. But how long, Oedipa thought, could it go on before collisions became a serious hindrance. There would have to be collisions. The only alternative was some unthinkable order of music, many rhythms, all keys at once, a choreography in which each couple meshed easy, predestined (97).

Since no collisions do occur, predestination would seem to be the reason for this music of the spheres. Two conceptions come to mind; Pynchon will use them both in *Gravity's Rainbow*. The first is metaphysical: Leibnitz's view of the universe as a collection of "monads," each of which apprehends the others in some mysterious way according to a preestablished harmony. The second is religious: the Calvinist doctrine of predestination, which holds that a preordained Elect shall be saved by God's mysterious Grace. The Elect, which includes all those so predestined, and the Preterite, those passed over, form two separate worlds, made up in each case of the living and the dead.

If an anti-world exists, it may be sinister—or not. Perhaps it is just the Other that keeps the universe running, like the counterweight on the pendulum of a clock. The conspiracy's religious overtones, however, are commensurate with America's Calvinist origins. The other world, whatever it is on a religious or metaphysical level, apparently contains the "disinherited," the alienated and the disaffected of America, and thus may function on a political level as well. Were that other world to intersect with "this world" on any of the three levels, perhaps regeneration might result. Contact between spiritual worlds might provide supernatural harmony. Friction between metaphysical worlds might furnish the energy to renew systems. Finally, an intersection between political worlds might rejuvenate American democracy. At least once during a period of crisis, and probably twice, if Emory Bortz's surmise is correct, Tristero has come close to an alliance with an established order. The potential remains. But how do worlds intersect? For that matter, how do we apprehend the Other? Pynchon borrows a second metaphor from physics, and joins it to the conspiratorial communications system to provide the medium.

Since it crowds in upon her, the information Oedipa receives must be sorted, and value must be assigned to each bit she has. The process of sorting is related to the concept of entropy within systems. In the very beginning of his novel Pynchon has described his heroine as "shuffling back through a deckful of days which seemed more or less identical" (2), unable to remember all that she knows of Pierce Inverarity. The allusion to a card deck is another from classical physics, one of the favorites of Sir William Dampier. In his *A History of Science* he writes that an increase of entropy in a system "is analogous to shuffling a pack of cards, originally in order of number and suits, by a mechanical shuffler. The shuffling can never be undone, save by conscious sorting, or by the indescribably remote chance of the cards happening to fall into their original order again."'

Where information is concerned, however, the process grows more complicated. Augmenting this example from physics in *The Crying of Lot 49* is another: Maxwell's Demon. In 1871, James Clerk Maxwell, a Scotch physicist, proposed a metaphor which theoretically contravened the Second Law of Thermodynamics. Oedipa learns of it from Stanley Koteks, the disgruntled Yoyodyne engineer. He tells her about John Nefastis, who has invented a machine based on Maxwell's Demon, and gives her a quick outline of the theory, which we can expand on slightly. The Demon is an intelligence capable of sorting molecules. In Maxwell's hypothetical situation, this little being controls a door (frictionless) separating two chambers in a larger chamber filled with gas. The Demon can distinguish between slow-moving and faster molecules and, by opening and closing the door, can concentrate the faster molecules of higher energy—or heat—in one chamber and the slower in the other. According to the laws of thermodynamics, heat provides force and work, so the difference in temperature between the hotter chamber of high-speed molecules and the cooler chamber of low-speed molecules can furnish the force to power a heat engine. Because the Demon can continue the process indefinitely, energy can be reconcentrated continually in a perfectly balanced system organized for efficiency; it thus becomes in effect a perpetual motion machine in which entropy does not prevail. And since the Demon is inside the system, the system is closed off from other forms of energy from outside the system—at least as Maxwell theorized. Koteks sums up: "Since the Demon only sat and sorted, you wouldn't have put any real work into the system. So you would be violating the Second Law of Thermodynamics, getting something for nothing, causing perpetual motion" (62).

Physicists have debated Maxwell's hypothesis endlessly by raising objections which usually involve the question of perception: The Demon would hardly be able to sort without light, for instance, and the introduction of light energy into the chamber would "open" the system. Oedipa's immediate objection is more trenchant: "Sorting isn't work? . . . Tell them down at the post office, you'll find yourself in a mailbag headed for Fairbanks, Alaska . . ." (62). Sorting *is* work, which means that the Second Law is operative and that you don't get something for nothing. Although she thinks Kotecks is crazy, Oedipa decides to visit John Nefastis, chiefly because she suspects he and Koteks are communicating by the W.A.S.T.E. system. Nefastis's fervid lecture on the concepts behind his machine is sufficiently forceful to make Oedipa feel like a "heretic" for doubting him. The word "entropy" "bothered him as

146

much as 'Trystero' bothered Oedipa" (77). Both the religious allusion and the association between the two words are significant. Much of his exegesis escapes her, but

> She did gather that there were two distinct kinds of this entropy. One having to do with heat-engines, the other to do with communication. The equation for one, back in the '30's, had looked very like the equation for the other. It was a coincidence. The two fields were entirely unconnected, except at one point: Maxwell's Demon. As the Demon sat and sorted his molecules into hot and cold, the system was said to lose entropy. But somehow the loss was offset by the information the Demon gained about what molecules were where (77).

So far, so good, except that the discovery that the equations were the same was not entirely coincidental. Basically, Nefastis is correct. He has incorporated the argument against Maxwell's hypothesis into his account: The loss of entropy in the system is more than balanced by the energy required for perception, which must come from outside the system. Nefastis's machine gets around this problem in wacky fashion; it is predicated on a new system involving a "sensitive," a person who can communicate with the Demon. "Communication is the key" (77), he asserts:

> "The Demon passes his data on to the sensitive, and the sensitive must reply in kind. There were untold billions of molecules in that box. The Demon collects data on each and every one. At some deep psychic level he must get through. The sensitive must receive that staggering set of energies, and feed back something like the same quantity of information. To keep it all cycling."

If the sensitive does communicate, he will see "on the secular level" the pistons on top of the machine moving. "On the secular level" implies that there is a sacred level also. Nefastis does not elaborate. Entropy is a metaphor, he says, which has something to do with

147

one world's intrusion on another: "It connects the world of thermodynamics to the world of information flow. The Machine uses both" (77). Clearly Pynchon is returning to the theme of his story "Entropy." Information theory is one aspect of the broader subject of communications and raises questions which affect Oedipa. The equations in the fields of thermodynamics and communications are similar, yet beyond that superficial resemblance are crucial differences, and the differences make the relationship complex.

The flow of information is measured by what Norbert Wiener calls "negative entropy." In thermodynamics, entropy "is a measure of disorganization" but "the information carried by a set of messages is a measure of organization."[8] Another pioneer of information theory, Warren Weaver, clarifies the connection:

> That information should be measured by entropy is, after all, natural when we remember that information is associated with the amount of freedom of choice we have in constructing messages. Thus one can say of a communication source, just as he would also say of a thermodynamic ensemble: "This situation is highly organized; it is not characterized by a large degree of randomness or of choice—that is to say, the information, or the entropy, is low" . . . The word information relates not so much to what you *do* say, as to what you *could* say. That is, information is a measure of your freedom of choice, when you select a message. . . . The greater this freedom of choice, the greater is the uncertainty that the message actually selected is some particular one. Thus greater freedom of choice, greater uncertainty and greater information all go hand in hand.[9]

Put another way, the two worlds—the world of thermodynamics and the world of information theory—are in fundamental opposition to one another, and may possibly be mirror-images of each other, a kind of dualism Pynchon also speaks of in *V*. When entropy increases in a thermodynamic system, disorganization, confusion, and uncertainty increase. But the greater the uncertainty in the system, the more information available, because entropy in informational terms is a measure of uncertainty. What happens in Nefastis's machine, then, is the production of energy—to drive a piston—as a result of the almost combustible reaction of positive and negative entropies: "One little movement, against all that massive complex of information, destroyed over and over with each power stroke" (77).

When we discount the loony features of this Rube Goldberg apparatus, we are left with several important considerations. The first is that an increase in entropy in a thermodynamic system can be offset by greater information about the system. The more information available, the greater the possibility of the Meatball Mulligans and Oedipa Maases of this world doing something about it. A second is that the possibility of two worlds intersecting is here made manifest. If a "sensitive" like Oedipa can establish communication with some intelligence (being, force), then an ordered vision of the universe might result. Driblette taxes Oedipa with an exaggerated respect for words, but that attention to the accuracy of communications may enable her to counter the "evil" of disorganization. Wiener discourses at some length on the tendency man has to see entropy—the loss of order—as a Manichean evil. On a more prosaic level, Oedipa is left with another metaphor, the Demon, that she can apply to her own situation. Before long she will think of Pierce Inverarity as a Demon. But there is still a third consideration, and it has to do with the way Oedipa sees the world.

Reassuring as Weaver's emphasis on the relationship of freedom of choice to information is, the relationship applies primarily to the *source* of information. While that might attribute purpose to those who put information in her way, Oedipa herself is not formulating messages; she is receiving them. Moreover, information theory has to do with the transmission of messages and their possible distortion (at one point Oedipa's husband pronounces her name as "Mrs. Edna Mosh" to allow for the distortion on the tape recorder into which he is speaking); it has nothing to do with the meaning or value of messages. To sort the messages out, she

149

must perceive them, and she must assign values to her perceptions. Once again she runs up against the Second Law. Gregory Bateson, who has explored the psychiatric dimensions of communication, has amplified the dilemma:

> The relation between information and value becomes still more evident when we consider the asking of questions and other forms of seeking information. We may compare the seeking of information with the seeking of values. In the seeking of values it is clear that what happens is that a man sets out to "trick" the Second Law of Thermodynamics [like Maxwell's Demon]. He endeavors to interfere with the "natural" or random course of events, so that some otherwise improbable outcome will be achieved. . . . Briefly, in value seeking he is achieving a coincidence or congruence between something in his head . . . and something external. . . . He achieves this coincidence by altering the external objects and events. In contrast, when he is seeking information, he is again trying to achieve a congruence between "something in his head" and the external world; but now he attempts to do this by altering what is in his head.
>
> Negative entropy, value, and information are in fact alike in so far as the system to which these notions refer is the man plus environment, and in so far as, both in seeking information and in seeking values, the man is trying to establish an otherwise improbable congruence between ideas and events.[10]

This sums up Oedipa's epistemological problem. When worlds intersect, how do we distinguish between them? The world of thermodynamics is the "natural" world. The world of information theory is *our* world, the way we apprehend input. As philosophers have traditionally reminded us, the two worlds may not coincide, although they may "intrude" on one another at one or both of two junctures: the mind of God (Maxwell's Demon, Pierce Inverarity?) and the mind of man (Oedipa or Everyman). Always with us is the possibility that there is only *our* world, our way of seeing it, that the universe exists only in our selves, because wish can be father to perception. This is the philosophical position known as solipsism: a man can know with (relative) certainly only that the self exists. Soon Oedipa will come to think herself paranoid, which is another way of saying the same thing. And paranoia recoils upon the other half of the dual nature of "communication" as we have been using the term. In *Gravity's Rainbow* Pynchon will define paranoia as "the onset, the leading edge, of the discovery that *everything is connected,* everything in the Creation." It is possible, in other words, that all the clues to the existence of Tristero are "something in her head," with no objective reality outside her self.

Although reduced to essentials Maxwell's Demon is only a metaphor, to Pynchon scientific metaphors go much further toward representing the human condition than do conventional literary types. This one is central to the book, with ramifications that spread all through it. Were we to say it is pregnant with associations, we would only be emulating Pynchon, who will have Oedipa tell a doctor that she thinks she is pregnant, this after Oedipa adopts the masculine name Arnold Snarb for a time. A symbolic virgin birth is aborted when she uses the name of Grace Bortz, but she will not emulate Mike Fallopian, whose ideas are stillborn. To the end, Oedipa is free to choose, free to interpret, and free to be wrong.

Although she does not at first recognize it as such, Oedipa's first clue to the existence of the conspiracy comes from her husband, Mucho Maas. In addition, Oedipa may owe him part of her heightened receptivity to clues. Mucho is a disk jockey for Station KCUF (when read backwards, one of Pynchon's bad jokes) and is tormented by the ethics of his present and past occupations. Formerly a used-car salesman, he still feels guilty for his responsibility in contributing to the waste of a civilization, particularly since he is aware that the used cars he traded were sad extensions of his customers. If any evidence is needed that Pynchon has moved beyond the hostility to machines and objects evident in *V.*, it is here, in the compassion with which he views human love for man-made things in *The Cry-*

ing of Lot 49—his most compassionate book. The trading stamps, the old rags, the combs, the lost or forgotten flotsam left behind in traded automobiles had sickened Mucho because they symbolized the futility of the owner's attempt to trade an old life for a new, "to exchange a dented, malfunctioning version of himself for another, just as futureless, automotive projection of somebody else's life" (5). Mucho too feels himself at the mercy of forces beyond his control—each day is "another defeat" (3)—but he can see only confusion. Perhaps he should have been in a war, Oedipa speculates, where the battle lines would have been recognizable. Now Mucho has come close to despair over his role as a peddler of the "fraudulent dreams of teenage appetites" (6). Ostensibly a communications expert, as a disk jockey he conveys only naked lust to his adolescent listeners.

Until she learns of Inverarity's testament, Oedipa has been a housewife circumscribed by routine: Tupperware parties, Muzak in the supermarkets, her herb garden, occasional glances at book reviews. More from fashionable impulse than from any serious attempt to allay the magic around her, she has a psychiatrist, Dr. Hilarius, who, like Geronimo Diaz of "Low-lands," teeters on the edge of insanity. Oedipa's encounters with Hilarius are suffused with Pynchon's laughing contempt for analysts. In Pynchon's world, the self, the ego, *is* "incidental"; it is a function of the "reality" outside the self and the manner in which the outside world impinges upon consciousness—a conception which puts Pynchon closer to R. D. Laing than Freud. Implicit in the construction of his characters is the idea that the self is really an endless fluctuation of sensibility, rather like a film sprocketing through a projector. At any given moment the focus or the frame changes. The self is thus not so much thought as lived; its existence is predicated on shifting multiple states of consciousness.

The problem is that one doesn't—or doesn't always —control the projector; Oedipa sometimes wakes to find "the camera's already moving" (29). The significance of any event as a consequence lies at least in part outside the self, unless the character, like Randolph Driblette, resolves to "project a world." This is one reason why Pynchon's figures seem so two-dimensional, as if they had stepped from cartoons. Cartoons are frequent in *The Crying of Lot 49,* perhaps because Pynchon wants to underline his vision of modern reality; every time Oedipa sees a television set in operation Magilla Gorilla or Yogi Bear sooner or later scampers across the screen. Pynchon may be following Conrad, who has Marlow say of Kurtz: "To him the meaning of an episode was not inside, like a kernel, but outside, enveloping the tale which brought it out only as a glow brings out a haze. . . ."[11] One can try to see what he thinks is there, and failing that, impose his own design or pattern on reality, which in turn becomes his reality. Not surprisingly, paranoia—an attempt to impose design on the outside world—is a common response of Pynchon's characters. To perceive accurately the nature of the outside world requires courage, patience, and intelligence—qualities which Oedipa has where others do not. She is willing to sort her impressions in the face of mounting confusion.

Dr. Hilarius is fascinated by Oedipa and calls her at three in the morning, in humorous reversal of the usual analyst-patient relationship, to ask her to join his experimental LSD program. Aware that the line between perception and paranoia is thin, she refuses. Nor will she take any of the pills he has prescribed for her, believing that she would be "literally damned" (8) if she did. A partially reconstructed Nazi who had artificially induced insanity in Jewish inmates of Buchenwald, Hilarius has since done penance by subscribing to the theories of the Jewish Sigmund Freud, although they do violence to his own views. Instead of seeing printed circuits in inanimate objects, Hilarius assigns symmetry to human faces and claims to effect cures by twisting features into "Fu Manchu" shapes. Hilarius's face reminds Oedipa of Uncle Sam's, in the portrait "that appears in front of all our post offices, his eyes gleaming unhealthily, his sunken yellow cheeks most violently rouged, his finger pointing between her eyes. I want you. She had never asked Dr. Hilarius why, being afraid of all he might answer" (7).

At first Oedipa declines to ask many things, her desire to fill the void being subordinate to her fear of the magical forces around her. When she meets Metzger, Pierce Inverarity's lawyer and the co-executor of the estate, he remarks that Inverarity had spoken of her only once: "Don't you want to know what he said?" (17). Oedipa does not. Her reluctance also indicates her courage, however; she wishes to keep her options open.

By way of emphasizing the paranoia which threads the lives of his characters, Pynchon throws in a teenage rock group called The Paranoids, one of whom is the manager of Echo Courts, where Oedipa stays while she works with Metzger. The Paranoids play electric instruments, alternately imitate and placate their elders, and sing about loneliness. While he is obviously an authority on the counter-culture, Pynchon puts no great trust in it. If anything, the youngsters here are more entitled to paranoia than adults, for adults do exploit them and appropriate their youth. Three of the male characters in the book dote on young girls in misguided hope of reversing the entropy that affects them as they grow older. Metzger eventually elopes with the girlfriend of one of the Paranoids.

If Oedipa has difficulty focusing on her void, if she wishes to reserve judgment on the lines of force, Metzger's problem is more acute. He is a former child movie star known as Baby Igor whose stint as an actor has left him anxious to recapture his youth, unsure of the parameters of his personality, and enchanted at the "extended capacity for convolution" (20) in his life. Having perceived the narcissistic and dramatic facets of an actor turned lawyer, he has sold the story of his career as a TV pilot film, with himself played by Manny di Presso, a lawyer turned actor. Metzger is proud of his film and keeps it in a Hollywood vault, where "light can't fatigue it, it can be repeated endlessly" (20). To film one's life is to preserve it. So long as the movie stays in the vault, it is eternal; no one can see it, but it does not run the risk of Baby Igor movies shown on television. When that happens, the reels get mixed up.

Interestingly enough, a movie is one of the few devices that can actually reverse entropy, since it can be run backwards, or shown over and over again—always assuming that someone doesn't mix up the reels.

Metzger pretends that the end of a film is not predetermined, and makes a wager with Oedipa: that she sleep with him if she cannot guess what happens in a Baby Igor movie running on TV the night they meet. "The movie's made," she protests. "But you still don't know," he returns (20). She accepts the bet, and of course loses it in a hilarious seduction scene made sinister by the sudden surge of forces. The Paranoids, jamming outside, blow all the fuses in the motel with their electric guitars just as Metzger and Oedipa reach a climax. Power is restored in time for Oedipa to see Baby Igor electrocuted at the conclusion of the film. The sexual act itself seems fraught with danger; one is reminded of the medieval definition of orgasm as "le petit mort," the little death. Considering the limited effectiveness Pynchon permitted so basic an act of communication as love in *V.*, the outlook for it in *The Crying of Lot 49* does not appear promising. But the affair has "sensitized" (21) Oedipa and prepared her for ending "her encapsulation in the tower" (29).

Oedipa's willingness to be seduced grows out of her disintegrating relationship with Mucho, whose guilt and obsessions have taken him along paths she cannot follow. Although she and her husband exchange dutiful notes while she is at San Narciso, she does not confess the liaison with Metzger, believing that somehow Mucho will know without her telling. Of *his* affairs she has long been aware; they have familiar patterns and always involve high-school nymphets. She had mentioned Mucho's proclivities to him once, but softened by the tenderness with which she accepts his obsessions and which is her dominant characteristic, she decided not to reproach him again. When Pynchon says, "like all their inabilities to communicate, this too had a virtuous motive" (29), he is reminding us that love does not overcome all barriers, and that the failure to communicate is sometimes a matter of choice. Considering the theme of the novel, it is an important observation.

For a brief period Metzger serves as Watson to Oedipa's Sherlock. She has already seen a strange postmark on a letter from Mucho, "Postmaster" having been misspelled as "Potsmaster." When Metzger can throw no light on it, she temporarily forgets it, although Pynchon has already signalled the reader to watch for clues involving stamps: "Much of the revelation was to come through the stamp collection Pierce had left, his substitute often for her—thousands of little colored windows into deep vistas of space and time ... he could spend hours peering into each one, ignoring her. She had never seen the fascination" (28). As she quests deeper into those vistas, Oedipa will understand the fascination. And the stamps offer one more fragment of Pierce's Calvinism, his habit of substituting cosmic vision for love.

Metzger takes Oedipa to the Scope, a bar frequented by employees of Yoyodyne. Another of Pynchon's decadent scenes, the Scope offers exclusively electronic music by and for the weird habitues of the place. There Oedipa meets Mike Fallopian and sees on the ladies room wall the first of what will be many emblematic graffiti, a muted post horn juxtaposed with the word WASTE and an ad for a swinger's club. She also sees Fallopian receive a letter by a private mail delivery system but does not connect the two "revelations." Fallopian, obviously embarrassed by her as yet mild interest in the idea of a private mail service, passes it off as an amateurish enterprise, justifies it by his Peter Pinguid Society's ideological opposition to government mail monopoly, and explains that he is writing a history of federal suppression of independent mail delivery services in America: "He saw it all as a parable of power, its feeding, growth and systematic abuse, though he didn't go into it that far with her, that particular night" (36). Even oblique references to power and forces elicit responses from Oedipa; she copies down the ad from the restroom wall.

At this point Oedipa is hardly obsessed; Fallopian is easily dismissed as a curious paranoid of the type Southern California spawns so prolifically. But another paranoid, Manny di Presso (one of Pynchon's lowest puns), the actor who plays Metzger in the lawyer's TV pilot, provides thickening for the plot. Oedipa meets him in company with Metzger and the Paranoids, who have tagged along on an inspection tour of Fangoso Lagoons, one of Inverarity's real-estate ventures. Di Presso vents his paranoia—"All the time, somebody listens in, snoops; they bug your apartment, they tap your phone" (43)—with more reason than most. He is involved with the Mafia, a real underground criminal organization, which held the contract for delivering human bones to Inverarity's industries, in one case for making charcoal filters for cigarettes, in another for providing ornamental underwater skeletons for the pleasure of skin-divers at Fangoso Lagoons. Metzger assumes that they come from an American cemetery ripped up by the builders of a superhighway. Not so, says Di Presso. They come from the bottom of Lago di Pàie (Lake of Piety) in Italy, recovered by an Italian Mafioso who remembered how they got there, having been attached to a German army which annihilated a squad of American soldiers and threw the bodies in. Familiar with "the American cult of the dead" (42), he salvaged them with an eye to profit. Now he wants to be paid from Inverarity's estate. The frequent references to death in the novel are reminders that the quests of Pynchon's characters are either open-ended, never to be realized, or that they end in death. They also suggest the decadence of American culture and the serious and sinister implications of the conspiracy Oedipa seems to be stumbling upon.

In itself the story seems to mean little, but it reminds one of the Paranoids of a Jacobean play they've seen which has a plot strangely similar to Di Presso's tale. The Paranoids give unintelligible accounts of Richard Wharfinger's seventeenth-century drama, one of the first indications that information, as it becomes more available, also becomes less understandable. Oedipa drags Metzger to a theater in San Narciso to see for herself "the landcape of evil Richard Wharfinger had fashioned for his 17th century audiences, so preapocalyptic, death-wishful, sensually fatigued, unprepared, a little poignantly, for that abyss of civil war that had been waiting, cold and deep, only a few years ahead of them" (44). Pynchon refers to the decadent twentieth century as "Neo-Jacobean" in *V.*; he concludes *Gravity's Rainbow* with the threat of apocalypse hanging over a theater audience. Here, in *The Crying of Lot 49*, the description of Wharfinger's play is prophetic. America too is only a short distance from an abyss.

Pynchon provides a deadpan synopsis which reads like a Marx Brothers script directed by Bela Lugosi, or, as Metzger says, like "a Road Runner cartoon in blank verse" (53). The hilarity of the summary almost obscures the brilliance of Pynchon's parody of Jacobean drama; it is laughter of the blackest hue. In terms of a fiction within a fiction, the play furnishes parallels with the larger plot of the novel and provides Oedipa with leads, some of them secondary but important, like the bones in the lake. Rather than summarize it ourselves —which would take forever—we need only point out that the most significant motif in the bloody story involves the Thurn and Taxis postal system and an Adversary which goes unnamed until the very end. The Adversary is a dreaded force obviously known to the play's characters and to Wharfinger's original audience but not to Oedipa and her companions in the Tank Theater.

Mounting fascination and apprehension rivet Oedipa as the acts unfold. The reader finds himself in approximately her position when Oedipa goes to the ladies room during intermission. The walls are blank: "She could not say why, exactly, but felt threatened by this absence of even the marginal try at communication latrines are known for" (48). Oedipa is particularly disturbed by the mystery of the dreaded assailants: "It is at about this point in the play, in fact, that things really get peculiar, and a gentle chill, an ambiguity, begins to creep in among the words. Heretofore the naming of names has gone on either literally or as metaphor. But now, . . . certain things, it is made clear, will not be spoken aloud . . ." (49-50). The naming, when it finally does come, is linked to the Thurn and Taxis postal monopoly; the silent adversary is symbolized by a "once-knotted horn" and is called "Trystero." The name "hung in the dark to puzzle Oedipa Maas, but not yet to exert the power over her it was to" (52).

She is puzzled enough to seek out the play's director, Randolph Driblette, amid the backstage's "soft, elegant chaos" (54), as if the play's cast and crew form a perfectly integrated, harmonized—and non-entropic—system. Driblette's appearance and manner reinforce this impression. His eyes in particular attract her, for she seems to see circuits again: "They were bright black, surrounded by an incredible network of lines, like a laboratory maze for studying intelligence in tears. They seemed to know what she wanted, even if she didn't" (54). He tells her the script derives from an anthology of Jacobean drama he picked up at Zapf's Used Book Store, lets drop a remark that others have asked about the text, and advises her not to get caught up in textual analysis: "You're like Puritans are about the Bible. So hung up with words, words. You know where that play exists, . . . not in any paperback you're looking for, but. . . . the reality is in *this* head. Mine. I'm the projector at the planetarium, all the closed little universe visible in the circle of that stage is coming out of my mouth, eyes, sometimes other orifices also" (56). If he were to disappear, he says, she would be left with facts without meaning, although so far as he knows, the facts—the existence of the Thurn and Taxis monopoly, for example—are accurate. He admits that she could try to track down the elements of his personality which gave life to the play, perhaps fall in love with him, in order to learn what she wants—and he does seem to know what she wants.

In Driblette several motifs merge. Wary of words, he illustrates the dangers of solipsism. He "projects" the world as a "closed little universe" at sacrifice of knowing what the broader universe is like. In one way he is the counterpart of Mike Fallopian in his reconstructions of history; in another he differs sharply, for his motives are better. Driblette wants to give life to the seventeenth-century world—after his own moral fashion. According to one of his admirers, Driblette was "a peculiarly moral man. He felt hardly any responsibility toward the work, really; but to the invisible field surrounding the play, its spirit, he was always intensely faithful" (113). Measured against the religious feelings that grip Oedipa, Driblette is a nonbeliever—and he places Oedipa firmly in the Calvinist/Puritan framework with his charge that she is hung up on words. He can integrate elements into a system, hold it together with his own spiritual energy, and keep it functioning for night after night, but he will not survive the play's closing. Just after the set for *The Courier's Tragedy* is struck, he commits suicide by walking into the "integrated Pacific."

For the remainder of her quest, three pairs of things elicit responses from Oedipa: cemeteries and references to vengeful death, the Thurn and Taxis monopoly and Trystero (or Tristero), the word WASTE and the emblematic muted post horn. Unlike the "clues" in *V.*, which depend on sometimes awkward juxtaposition in the narrative, the clues in *The Crying of Lot 49* proliferate and intertwine in a plot worthy of Agatha Christie. Moreover, in contrast to Stencil in *V.*, Oedipa is intent on "bringing something of herself" to her search (65), despite her essential passivity. In part her efforts stem from loyalty to Inverarity. As the clues swirl and cohere around what she comes to know as the Tristero, they appear connected to her former lover's estate. His will guides her: "If it was really Pierce's attempt to leave an organized something behind after his own annihilation, then it was part of her duty, wasn't it, to bestow life on what had persisted, to try to be what Driblette was, the dark machine in the center of the planetarium, to bring the estate into pulsing stelliferous meaning . . ." (58). She writes in her notebook: *"Shall I project a world?"* (59).

She vows to order the multitudinous business interests of Inverarity's estate. But it is not easy; each time she tries, some allusion to Tristero crops up. At Vesperhaven House, an old folks home Inverarity controlled, she hears tales of Tristero's battles with the Pony Express from the aged Mr. Thoth, who also tells her that he can feel God close to him on days "of a certain temperature . . . and barometric pressure" (66), as if God too were a matter of energy somehow

160

manifest in a chamber of gas. From Genghis Cohen, she acquires information about Pierce's collection of Tristero forgeries of Thurn and Taxis and U. S. stamps, about odd postmarks—such as the one on Mucho's letter—and about Thurn and Taxis itself, which began, he tells her, in the thirteenth century.

Cohen is affable if sinister in appearance, but when he offers Oedipa some homemade wine distilled from dandelions he picked in a cemetery since macadamized into a freeway, she senses another world's intrusion:

> She could, at this stage of things, recognize signals like that, as the epileptic is said to—an odor, color, pure piercing grace note announcing his seizure. Afterward it is only this signal, really dross, this secular announcement, and never what is revealed during the attack, that he remembers. Oedipa wondered whether, at the end of this (if it were supposed to end), she too might not be left with only compiled memories of clues, announcements, intimations, but never the central truth itself, which must somehow each time be too bright for her memory to hold; which must always blaze out, destroying its own message irreversibly, leaving an overexposed blank when the ordinary world came back (69).

The passage is heavy with motifs. First, the destruction of information recalls the operation of Nefastis's machine, in which formation and entropy cancel each other to move the piston. Second, the reference to overexposure revitalizes another motif, that of film moving through a projector. And finally, the religious language reasserts the prominence of that aspect of the novel. Edward Mendelson has pointed out that the epileptic seizure has often been associated with religious ecstasy[12] which would seem to be appropriate, for Oedipa is being "pierced" by some kind of "grace."

Cohen cannot—or will not—tell her very much. Primed by the Wharfinger play and her other clues, Oedipa completes connections herself, and leaves Cohen's office feeling that the spirits of the dead are persistent. Mike Fallopian in the meantime serves as Devil's Advocate to challenge her interpretation of evidence. (It is worth remarking that Fallopian belongs to a private mail service apparently separate from the conspiratorial Tristero.) His expressed doubts are contagious. Mindful of the possibility that she may be fantasizing, one evening Oedipa decides "to drift . . . , at random, and watch nothing happen, to be convinced it was purely nervous, a little something for her shrink to fix" (80). Within an hour of her plunge into the street crowds of North Beach she is washed into a homosexual bar called The Greek Way by a wave of "guided tourists" out to cover sinful San Francisco. One of the tourists, having had enough, pins his ID badge on her as he leaves, and Oedipa, resolved to float, becomes "Arnold Snarb." Among the milling tourists and homosexuals she spies a lapel pin shaped like the muted horn. The man who wears it does not respond to Oedipa's veiled hints about Tristero, but does listen as she pours out her frustration: "You have nobody else to tell this to. Only somebody in a bar whose name you don't know?" (82). The pin, he tells her, is the symbol of an organization called Inamorati Anonymous, whose purpose is to prevent its members from falling in love. Having been hurt by love before, each member will sit with and strengthen any other member on the verge of succumbing again; it is the same technique Pynchon attributes to the Alcoholics Anonymous of "The Secret Integration." In contrast to the methods of the AA, however, IA treats each case individually and anonymously: "Nobody knows anybody else's name; just the number in case it gets so bad you can't handle it alone. We're isolates, Arnold. Meetings would destroy the whole point of it" (83).

The anonymous founder of IA, a Yoyodyne executive replaced by an IBM 7094, had lost his faithless wife along with his job, and decided to commit suicide, but wavered long enough to have his mind changed by a quasi-religious experience. He placed an ad in the L.A. paper to ask for reasons why he should not kill himself. The answers arrived in a batch, delivered by an odd messenger. None of the letters offered compelling reasons for staying alive. After soaking himself in gasoline preparatory to striking a match, he heard his wife and her lover enter his house, where they proceeded to make love. He found the scene so absurd, particularly when the lover sneers at the suicide decision—" 'Nearly three weeks it takes him,' marvelled the efficiency expert, 'to decide. You know how long it would've taken the IBM 7094? Twelve microseconds' " (85)—that he broke into hysterical laughter. Moreover, he discovered that the gasoline had loosened the stamps on the batch of letters to reveal the muted horn postmark. "If he had been a religious man he would have fallen to his knees," says Oedipa's confessor-confidant.

As it was, he only declared, with great solemnity: "My big mistake was love. From this day I swear to stay off of love: hetero, homo, bi, dog or cat, car, every kind there is. I will found a society of isolates, dedicated to this purpose, and this sign, revealed by the same gasoline that almost destroyed me, will be its emblem." And he did (85).

The founder's reaction is curious. Actually he is a victim not of love but of the same magic that has oppressed Oedipa, represented here by the computer. He thinks of suicide when he loses his job but before he loses his wife: "trained to do absolutely nothing but sign his name to specialized memoranda he could not begin to understand and to take blame for the running amok of specialized programs that failed for specialized reasons he had to have explained to him, the executive's first thoughts were naturally of suicide" (83). In short, it is not love that makes the world go 'round, but a different kind of communication, the kind that flows through a computer in twelve microseconds. By blaming his trouble on love, the man humanizes forces he does not understand. Although equally a perversion, the IA founder's conception of love is the reverse of John Nefastis's. For example, just after Oedipa had unsuccessfully tried to make contact with Nefastis's Demon, the inventor proposed that they have intercourse in front of his TV set, hopefully during a newsreel on the "teeming" masses of China. Nefastis's madness is consistent: Both sex and spirituality for him require the mediation of a communications device. When the IA founder receives his "sign," he draws his own conclusions, creates a self-repairing, "steady-state" system, and uses communication to suppress and disrupt love. The IA thus becomes a closed system of isolates who achieve community, however unorthodox and however pathetic.

The tourists have left. The tale of the IA's founding seems to mock Oedipa as she sits, the only female in a bar crowded with homosexuals, none of whom have any "sexual relevance" to her, none of whom "could do her any good" (86), although she feels sorely the need for communication. She wanders out into the streets again, to find that she can not escape what has become her nemesis. The muted post horn emblem is everywhere: displayed in a shop window, chalked on the sidewalks, sewn on the jackets of a gang of juvenile delinquents. In one neighborhood she sees children out much too late but secure in "their own unpenetrated sense of community" singing—

"Tristoe, tristoe, one, two three
Turning taxi from across the sea"

—and playing hopscotch on the chalked image of a muted horn: She runs across Jesus Arrabal, Mike Fallopian's counterpart at the other end of the political spectrum, who has just received a radical newspaper dated 1904 bearing the postmark of the mysterious system. The paper's name may be significant; it is *Regeneración*. The papers just arrive, Arrabal tells Oedipa: "Have they been in the mails that long? Has my name been substituted for that of a member who's died. Has it really taken sixty years? Is it a reprint? Idle questions, I am a footsoldier. The higher levels have their reasons" (89). Oedipa goes on.

On the back of a bus seat is the post horn and the word DEATH, another acronym someone has obligingly spelled out as Don't Ever Antagonize the Horn. The symbol replicates, always connected with the freakish and the disaffected; and always testifying to Pynchon's knowledge of American subcultures. As just one example, Oedipa sees a Tristero horn in an ad for AC-DC, Alameda County Death Cult, whose weird sexual rites resemble those of groups in *The Family,* Ed Sanders's study of Charles Manson and the bizarre California scene. She sees the muted horn so many times that she comes to expect it, and thus fears that she might not be seeing it that often. And yet she feels safe, as if something—Grace, perhaps—protects her from the night:

> She touched the edge of its voluptuous field, knowing it would be lovely beyond dreams simply to submit to it; that not gravity's pull, laws of ballistics, feral ravening, promised more delight. She tested it, shivering: I am meant to remember. Each clue that comes is *supposed* to have its own clarity, its fine chances for permanence. But then she wondered if the gemlike "clues" were only some kind of compensation. To make up for her having lost the direct, epileptic Word, the cry that might abolish the night (87).

The revelations border on the mystic; as yet they are merely hints of unity, of energy in "voluptuous field," not quite direct, not quite the ecstatic ("epileptic") visions of the saint. The Tristero shimmers in ever-changing colors. Heretofore the mystery that encompasses it has been "sacred." That aspect will persist, slowly giving way to a "secular" hue of social and political pigmentation. And in each case, with each clue, Pierce Inverarity, "the dead man, like Maxwell's Demon, was the linking feature in a coincidence" of two worlds (89).

As night becomes morning, a disheveled Oedipa has her most poignant encounter, with an old sailor turned wino. On his hand is tattooed the Tristero emblem. He gives Oedipa a letter for the wife he has not seen in years, and asks her to drop it in a WASTE box under the freeway. Clearly he is on his last legs. Motivated by her usual compassion, Oedipa cradles him against her breast, holds him as she sinks exhausted to rest, needing to touch him lest she not believe in his reality, and almost overcome by what she imagines is the experience to be lost when the man dies. The "circuits" in his eyes are bursted veins, his mind "the memory bank to a computer of the lost" (93).

Oedipa helps him to his flophouse bed, a mattress some match or cigarette will someday fire. As she looks at him lying on the bed, motifs vector together:

> She remembered John Nefastis, talking about his machine, and massive destructions of information. So when this mattress flared up around the sailor, in his Viking's funeral: the stored, coded years of uselessness, early death, self-harrowing, the sure decay of hope, the set of all men who had slept on it, whatever their lives had been, would truly cease to be, forever, when the mattress burned. She stared at it in wonder. It was as if she had just discovered the irreversible process. It astonished her to think that so much could be lost . . . (95).

Wryly she thinks of his hallucinations, his DT's, which leads her to metaphor:

> Behind the initials was a metaphor, a delirium tremens, a trembling unfurrowing of the mind's plowshare. The saint whose water can light lamps, the clairvoyant whose lapse in recall is the breath of God, the true paranoid from whom all is organized in spheres joyful or threatening about the central pulse of himself, the dreamer whose puns probe ancient fetid shafts and tunnels of truth all act in the same special relevance to the word, or whatever it is the word is there, buffering, to protect us from. The act of metaphor then was a thrust at truth and a lie, depending where you were: inside, safe, or outside, lost. Oedipa did not know where she was (95).

Pynchon is speaking once again in the language of *V.* "A device, an artifice," Fausto Maistral defined a metaphor. Only metaphor—even in so low a form as puns—can penetrate the vistas of time and space, and Oedipa has recourse to a pun on the mathematical symbols for time and space, the correlatives for those vistas: "She knew that a sailor had seen worlds no other man had seen if only because there was that high magic to low puns, because DT's must give access to dt's of spectra beyond the known sun, music made purely of Antarctic loneliness and fright. But nothing she knew of would preserve them, or him. She gave him goodbye . . ." (96). Oedipa's vision is shading into metaphysics. The old man—everyman—comes in contact with other worlds, but at great cost. Some Demon's machine cycles, and to know, to see other worlds is to be destroyed in ceaseless motion. Finally, death itself will become the medium by which one reaches the other world.

She does find the mailbox, an ordinary green waste box, with nearly invisible dots separating the letters W.A.S.T.E. Oedipa waits until a carrier appears to empty the drop. Stealthily she follows as he makes his deliveries. The last stop is John Nefastis's home. Although her suspicions would now seem to have empirical verification, a succession of events revives her paranoia. When she arrives at Dr. Hilarius's office for a much-needed session, her psychiatrist is peppering the neighborhood with rifle fire, flipped out—convinced that Israeli agents are pursuing him. Freudianism has not mitigated the guilty memory of his atrocities. In fact, he tells Oedipa, that is Freudianism's great failure, that it has no satisfactory explanation for the evil of the concentration camps. He had wanted to believe that once light and rationality were let into the unconscious evil would disappear, that "at Auschwitz the ovens would be converted over to petit fours and wedding cakes, and the V-2 missiles to public housing for the elves" (102). He himself had created an absolutely evil face, his most successful experiment at Buchenwald; it haunts him yet. Oedipa, taken hostage by the madman, keeps him talking as the police arrive. Once again in the reversal of role that has been their relationship, she counsels pragratism and prudence: "Face up to your social responsibilities. . . . Accept the reality principle. You're outnumbered and they have superior firepower"

(101). And he has advice for her, when she tells him that she came to be talked out of a fantasy:

> "Cherish it! . . . What else do any of you have? Hold it tightly by its little tentacle, don't let the Freudians coax it away or the pharmacists poison it out of you. Whatever it is, hold it dear, for when you lose it you go over by that much to the others. You begin to cease to be" (103).

He never took any LSD himself, he confesses, preferring "to remain in relative paranoia." Drugs erase the boundaries of the self, break down distinctions between one's self and others.

That is what has happened to Mucho, whom Oedipa finds outside in a KCUF mobile unit after the cops rescue her. At the radio station, Mucho's boss confides that his colleagues have been calling Mucho "The Brothers N [Brothers to the nth power]. . . . He's a walking assembly of man" (104). The DT's—and dt's —have Mucho too. Like the old sailor, he hears "music made purely of Antarctic loneliness and fright." In the past a nightmare associated with the used car lot terrified him: "We were a member of the National Automobile Dealer's Association. N.A.D.A. Just this creaking metal sign that said nada, nada, against the blue sky" (107). The word, Spanish for nothing, should remind Pynchon's readers of the lady V., who takes pleasure in contemplating "Nothing."

Desperate to believe in himself and his job, wanting to broadcast "with movements stylized as the handling of chrism, censer, chalice might be for a holy man" (13), Mucho, thanks to the LSD he got from Hilarius, has lost himself in hallucination. Not only have the boundaries of his self broken down, but also his ability to distinguish time and energy spectra. For Mucho, communication flickers along a closed circuit; the elements of his world are approaching final equilibrium. "You're an antenna, sending your pattern out across a million lives a night, and they're our lives too," he tells Oedipa (107). He cannot even project a world, like Driblette. In Mucho's world, all energy spectra coincide, and his vision of God, deliberately invoked, is an advertising slogan: "Then you'd have this big, God, maybe a couple hundred million chorus saying 'rich, chocolaty goodness' together, and it would all be the same voice" (106). Which is another way, it would seem, of saying "Nothing." Mucho has become Echo.

This double insanity is followed by a third defection from her world, when Metzger elopes with the teenage girlfriend of one of the Paranoids, and by still a fourth, the worst. Driblette walks into the Pacific wearing the costume in which he spoke the name of Tristero. Oedipa learns of his death from Emory Bortz, an authority on the plays of Wharfinger, from whom she also learns that Driblette may have spoken that word only on the single evening she saw the play. That possibility, in addition to the falling away of the men in her life, pushes her toward a paranoiac edge.

Oedipa sits on Driblette's grave in a futile endeavor to communicate with the dead director. Her "signal" goes "echoing down twisted miles of brain circuitry" (122). She can not reach him: "But as with Maxwell's Demon, so now. Either she could not communicate, or he did not exist" (122). She can not communicate with anyone. "Her men" are slipping away from her as she rushes toward an abyss.

Fallopian, dressed in his para-military outfit and full of hate, asks if she has considered the possibility that Inverarity has pulled a joke, that the Tristero is a gigantic hoax he set up before he died. Oedipa has, but it is "like the thought that someday she would have to die" (126). She can not face that; to do so would be to succumb to Mucho's vision of nada. Nevertheless she knows that every clue can be traced back to Inverarity's estate. Inverarity owned everything: Yoyodyne, Vesperhaven House, Fangoso Lagoons, the Tank Theatre, Zapf's Used Books. He had even heavily endowed the college at which Bortz teaches. All of her informants, in fact, may be Inverarity's agents.

Oedipa tries to apply logic to her situation. The alternatives open to her are four. First, Inverarity has mounted a plot of elaborate proportions, perhaps

169

to survive death, as a paranoia; as a pure conspiracy
against someone he loved. Would that breed of per-
versity prove at last too keen to be stunned even by
death, had a plot finally been devised too elaborate for
the dark Angel to hold at once, in his humorless vice-
president's head, all the possibilities of? Had something slipped through and Inverarity by that much
beaten death? (134)

Second, she is plain crazy. Third, she is hallucinating,
the most attractive possibility. Finally, she has blun-
dered

onto a secret richness and concealed density of dream;
onto a network by which x number of Americans are
truly communicating whilst reserving their lies, recita-
tions of routine, arid betrayals of spiritual poverty, for
the official government delivery system; maybe even
onto a real alternative to the absence of surprise to
life, that harrows the head of everybody American . . .
(128).

Nobody can help her decide. Oedipa has left her
tower; she confronts the void. Cohen aggravates her
anxiety by telling her that a mysterious, unknown bid-
der will be on the scene when Inverarity's collection of
Tristero stamps is auctioned as Lot 49. Almost suicidal, Oedipa drives on the freeway at night with her
lights out, "but angels were watching" (132). She tele-
phones the Inamorato Anonymous at the Greek Way,
tells him everything, and asks if he is party to some
practical joke:

"It's too late," he said.
"For me?"
"For me."

An organization dedicated to isolation can help no one.
When her anonymous connection hangs up, she is left,
"her isolation complete" (133), trying to face the sea,
the integrated Pacific which laps the waste land. She
cannot see it, cannot see the mountains either, but she
hears the music of the spheres, "the sound of a stainless

chime held among the stars and struck lightly" that obliterates all barriers to a vision of a unified America. She knows that Inverarity's legacy is America. And she knows then "that it [is] all true. That Inverarity had only died" (134).

In one of Pynchon's most beautiful scenes, Oedipa walks along railroad tracks, one great symbol of the Calvinist spirit in America, the communications system founded by the prototypical Inveraritys of the last century: Track spurs lead off to the factories Inverarity probably owned, and beyond them lace into the webs and networks that embrace the country. There follows a lovely vision of Americans dwelling in communication grids: squatters who have set up shacks along the highways, camped in abandoned Pullman cars near cinderbeds, or slung themselves hammock-fashion aloft on telephone poles, "living in the very copper rigging and secular miracle of communication" (136), disinherited all, linked but not linked to their fellows, still waiting for "the Word" to emerge from "the roar of relays." Should she try to give them their inheritance from Pierce's estate by redistributing his wealth? She knows she cannot, if only because the establishment would be "on her ass in a microsecond" (136).

She deplores the alternatives that confront America, just as she balks at "the symmetry of choices" facing herself: "How had it ever happened here, with the chances once so good for diversity?" Everything seems to break down into dualities, into either-or propositions, and Oedipa wants answers that will transcend dialectics. She rebels against the law of logic which says that statements must be either true or false: "She had heard all about excluded middles; they were bad shit, to be avoided . . ." (136). Her knowledge of Tristero may be the means of transcending alternatives, but she does not know enough, and in the meantime she walks "among matrices of a great digital computer" with the alternatives hanging before her, balanced, as ones and zeros in the binary math that is the language of computers. One or zero, either-or, one world or another, these are the choices with which she must deal until the final revelation, for only revelation, Pynchon implies, can bring transcendence.

Oedipa's quest has led her to the final impasse of her namesake, the meaning of the human condition, and confusion and mystery seem to restrict her options:

> Behind the hieroglyphic streets there would either be a transcendent meaning, or only the earth. . . . Another mode of meaning behind the obvious, or none. Either Tristero in the orbiting ecstasy of a true paranoia, or a real Tristero. For there either was some Tristero beyond the appearance of the legacy America, or there was just America and if there was just America then it seemed the only way she could continue, and manage to be at all relevant to it, was as an alien, unfurrowed, assumed full circle into some paranoia (137).

Depending on that final revelation, however, may be many options, whose import Oedipa imperfectly senses, but which Pynchon intends the reader to grasp. If there is meaning it resides in the two metaphors Pynchon has developed in the novel as "a thrust at truth and a lie," for metaphors are our only access to meaning. The Tristero and Maxwell's Demon are arresting conceptions which both urge and defy interpretation. As Robert Sklar has remarked, this enigmatic quality of Pynchon's second novel distinguishes it from his first:

> V. is like a riddle that once correctly answered never taxes the mind again; The Crying of Lot 49 is founded in an emotion of mystery, an emotion which remains, inviolate and mysterious, even when the outward mystery is solved. V. is a complex novel that gets simpler with each rereading, The Crying of Lot 49 a simple novel that reread grows more complex.[13]

It is not that Pynchon's ideas in The Crying of Lot 49 are so radically different from those in V., but simply that they are given new weight and pattern. In the earlier book the cynical colonialist Van Wijk says to Kurt Mondaugen: "We are, perhaps, the lead weights of a fantastic clock, necessary to keep it in motion, to keep an ordered sense of history and time prevailing against chaos." In *The Crying of Lot 49* the Tristero is the counterweight, the mechanism necessary for motion. Anti-worlds, once the property of religious thinkers, are now a serious possibility to scientists, and both aspects of the concept appeal to Pynchon.

On a secular plane, the Tristero can interact with established systems without an intermediary. Throughout history it has done so, always in opposition to the vested interests. Even so, the organization contained men with historical perspective, the Konrads—"gutsy" name, according to Emory Bortz—who could conceive of alliances to make larger systems function. In terms of what Oedipa discovers, the gutsy-named Pierce may be such a man, Pierce the American visionary determined to rejuvenate a flagging system. The momentum of the America of the sixties is slowing. Having disinherited countless numbers of her citizens, she too may be in process of disintegration, like the Holy Roman Empire, or she may be on the verge of revolution, like the France of the eighteenth century. Inverarity may have been trying to achieve an alliance, because whoever controls communications, particularly communications in the sense of energy, controls America. Such an alliance could seize and maintain the lines of communication, lay the magic, and understand the patterns of force, possibly even integrate America like the Pacific at her shores.

Or Inverarity may have been deliberately subsizing the Tristero simply because it does provide the opposition necessary to keep the American system in motion, "to keep an ordered sense of history and time prevailing against chaos." In this respect he would function as a Maxwell's Demon. John Nefastis tells Oedipa that the Demon bridges the two worlds of thermodynamics and information flow "to keep it all cycling" (77). Oedipa remembers Inverarity's explanation for the success of his empire: " 'Keep it bouncing,' he'd told her once, 'that's all the secret, keep it bouncing' " (134). To sort molecules, to make distinctions, to concentrate energy, as the Demon does, is to behave like the human who must keep his system running by repairs and realignment, by conscious choice, by resistance to entropy, death, meaninglessness, nothingness. Whatever the lines of force, they have to do with communication, with energy in process, whether it flow between individuals, between individuals and the state, or between individuals and the universe. Like the wino-sailor, we all travel in a space-time continuum, but among different coordinates, and our common fate is "the massive destruction of information." Yet that information is our only hope of community, and when we fail to communicate, we remain isolates, our separate worlds closed to one another. By communicating, by establishing connections between worlds, we share our dt's, and open up new "vistas of time and space."

On the other hand, the connections may not be possible. If so, paranoia is the only sense of community open to us. Perhaps the patterns of our existence are predestined. Like Leibnitz's monads we recognize others, but can not alter our relations. Perhaps some Calvinist scheme obtains, in which the Elect and the Preterite have long since been predetermined. Or perhaps some limited grace is available to us, like that which seems to be Oedipa's, which permits some knowledge of Other Worlds, some note of music given off by the motion of spheres—which may be sufficient to reestablish faith in possibilities.

Should W.A.S.T.E. be a promise of spiritual salvation for the waste land, it would derive from American tradition, and function as a quasi-sacred "ordered sense of history and time prevailing against chaos," to use Van Wijk's phrase once again. In such an instance, Inverarity might represent a Protestant devil or deity rather than Maxwell's Demon. Besides being "gutsy," Pierce Inverarity's name might be significant for another reason. Inverarity is a village in Scotland, near Dundee, a seat of the Protestant Reformation under John Knox. Max Weber theorized that the spirit of American capitalism arose in opposition to a postulated evil chaos, that it stemmed from a desire to order nature. The Other, however, according to the Scurvhamites and Calvinists generally, is necessary; it is the pendulum of the clock of the universe. Without it there would be no motion: no evil, no good. None of this terminology necessarily commits Pynchon to a Calvinist theology (although he returns to it in *Gravity's Rainbow*); he may simply be working within a specifically American framework. Nevertheless, the problem of evil is difficult to explain, and Hilarius goes mad trying to cope with the demonic through fealty to Freud, who assumed that evil was merely a human aberration.

Pynchon appears to be saying that good and evil are dialectic partners, mirror images of each other which can be transcended. Inverarity may symbolize that transcendence, and for that reason be devil *and* deity. Mike Fallopian accuses Metzger of thinking like the John Birchers: "Good guys and bad guys. You never get to any of the underlying truth" (33). Because energies are always changing their configurations, even Jesus Arrabal finds it hard to recognize the "enemy." The Tristero may be evil, or it may not. As an anti-world, its energies predestined, it may intersect with our world only to remind us that the clock is ticking smoothly, perpetually.

Inverarity's legacy, then, may be a political alternative to a flagging American system, a metaphysical potency for integrating energies, a spiritual salvation bringing health and power to a waste land, or at the very least, a corrective to "the absence of surprise to life." But it may also be a joke, a hoax. Oedipa fears what the revelation may bring, and she should, for Mucho's vision of homogeneity and nothingness may be the accurate one. Balancing her fear, however, is her courage. She goes to the auction, knowing that agents of Tristero will be there.

The final scene of *The Crying of Lot 49*, which places Oedipa in a locked auction room, surrounded by black-suited men, recalls the conclusion of Herman Melville's *The Confidence Man*. That earlier novel closes on an imminent revelation involving multifaceted alternatives also. Pynchon adds one redeeming note of humor—when Oedipa tells Genghis Cohen that his fly is open—to soften his heroine's terror and to suggest that the alternatives are endless and exciting. Until the final revelation, excluded middles do not apply: They are bad shit indeed.

CHAPTER FIVE

Living on the Interface:
Preterition in Gravity's Rainbow

As if Pynchon had been planning his third novel from the beginning of his career, in *V.* Lieutenant Weissmann, the fascist, tells Mondaugen, the sferics engineer, "Someday we'll need you . . . for something or other, I'm sure. Specialized and limited as you are, you fellows will be valuable" (*V.,* 224). Mondaugen builds rockets for Weissmann in *Gravity's Rainbow.* They are two of several characters carried over from Pynchon's early work and but two of a cast of over three hundred. This Tolstoyan number is matched by the book's enormous length and sweep. A detailed summary of the book would run as long as (if not longer than) *Gravity's Rainbow* itself. Our limited approach will of necessity omit many interesting areas, some of them problematic. Our discussion is further complicated because *Gravity's Rainbow* is about *connectedness:* Pynchon has created a universe in which everything is related to everything else, and he demonstrates relationships with a vengeance. Within the space of a very few pages the reader can be charmed, amused, or annoyed at the novel's symmetries, but, whatever his reaction, the symmetries are so thorough that to consider aspects in isolation is to tear the book's fabric.

Pynchon is again working with systems of which humans are barely conscious. According to the novel's narrator,

> we have to look for power sources . . . and distribution networks we were never taught, routes of power our teachers never imagined, or were encouraged to avoid . . . we have to find meters whose scales were unknown in the world, draw our own schematics, getting feedback, making connections, reducing the error, trying to learn the real function . . . zeroing in on what incalculable plot? (521)[1]

Those characters who do perceive the connections dream them, confess to paranoia, blunder on revelation, or hallucinate after taking drugs. The principal narcotic in the novel, Oneirine (as in *oneiromancer*, one who divines through dreams), induces "the dullest hallucinations known to psychopharmacology," paranoiac visions which, like all forms of paranoia, are "nothing less than the onset, the leading edge, of the discovery that *everything is connected*, everything in the Creation, a secondary illumination not yet blindingly One, but at least connected . . ." (703).

For the characters the hallucinations and the dreams can sometimes be "mindless pleasures," which was the original title of *Gravity's Rainbow*.[2] For the narrator they are both comic and sinister. Implicit in his narrator's posture is the similarity between paranoia and art and understanding. To understand existence and to create art is to extract order from chaotic experience or to impose order upon it, and the thinking man or the conscious artist is always aware of the process. The very seriousness of the endeavor is comic, perhaps because laughter is the only reward for what costs so much effort. "You will want cause and effect. All right" (663), the narrator addresses the reader, knowing that no causal explanation will be convincing; or the narrator remarks, "perhaps you know that dream too" (287). He might invite the reader to take his pick of several songs for "bridge music" (222) between scenes, or insist on an aria from *Madame Butterfly*. Pynchon frequently has his characters break into songs, most of them set to popular tunes, partly because the musical comedy keeps serious themes from becoming too solemn, partly because music is itself a theme, and partly because the novel is structured like a play or a film, and "bridge music" does help establish continuity.

The tunes and the humor also relieve the frightening nature of the novel, which opens with the terrifying image of a V-2 rocket—in a very real sense the true protagonist of the story—descending on London in 1944, during World War II. As Pynchon sees it, an older order is passing in apocalypse. The rocket arcs in parabola, an annunciation of a new technology, while beneath it a man dreams of a railroad train—the same symbol Pynchon uses for the old industrial order in *The Crying of Lot 49*—disgorging swarms of refugees from all over Europe into a huge glass and trusswork Bahnhof. The latticework of this giant "theater," another stage away from the actual Theater of the War, is the first of innumerable chains, linkages, networks, and systems to follow. The rocket, a system itself, will dominate them all.

Gravity's Rainbow rests on the plot device that has become Pynchon's trademark: a conspiracy. This one —identified as "Them" or "The Firm"—is cosmic, its reach virtually unlimited, its most discernible components the huge corporations and cartels like General Electric, Siemens, Shell and Standard Oil, I. G. Farben and so on. These organizations, multi-national and therefore supra-national, ignore geographical and political boundaries; accountable to no one government, they circumvent the laws of all nations, and operate as states themselves, even though the men who direct the companies may be politicians and leaders in their own countries. Without constitutional or national allegiances, the business state ignores ideologies to conclude deals with friend or foe. In *Gravity's Rainbow*, Germans, Americans, Russians, and Englishmen form commercial chains, sell products and buy patents, and generally determine the orderliness of markets before,

during, and after World War II. As has often been remarked, war is good for business, or, as Pynchon's
narrator maintains:

> The real business of the War is buying and selling.
> The murdering and the violence are self-policing, and
> can be entrusted to non-professionals. . . . mass
> death's a stimulus to just ordinary folks, little fellows,
> to try 'n' grab a piece of that Pie while they're still
> here to gobble it up. The true war is a celebration of
> markets. Organic markets, carefully styled "black" by
> the professionals, spring up everywhere (105).

Since "They" include generals and admirals as well
as politicians on boards of directors in the interlocking
companies, the cartels can control the actual destruction during the war, either by direct command or simply by exchanging the matériel of war between themselves. By a coincidence which illustrates Pynchon's
topicality, a few weeks after the appearance of *Gravity's Rainbow* Anthony Sampson published *The Sovereign State of ITT*, which revealed the operations of that
global company in detail. Among those who have sat
on the board of directors or served ITT in an important
capacity are Paul Henri Spaak of Belgium, Harold
Macmillan and two members of the British House of
Lords, one member of the French Assembly, Lester
Pearson of Canada, and John McCone of the CIA.
ITT, founded by Sosthenes Behn, a name Pynchon
might have dreamed up, had by World War II become
so powerful and so international that it could literally
serve both Axis and Allies. Sampson uses this example:
"While ITT Focke-Wulf planes were bombing Allied
ships, and ITT lines were passing information to German submarines, ITT direction finders were saving
other ships from torpedoes."[3]

On a less dramatic but more important level, the supranational business states facilitate technology, invention, production, and the creation of jobs all over the
world, and in the process homogenize, dehumanize,
and control their employees; they also interfere in the
lives of people they do not touch directly. Or perhaps,

as Pynchon suggests, "They" do "control" just about everybody. In the terminology of Max Weber, human community *(Gemeinschaft)* has given way to business alliances *(Gesellschaft)* oppressive in their power to determine the course of events. In *Gravity's Rainbow* Pynchon uses the word *Gesellschaft* several times, mentions other Weberian terms, and refers to Weber himself. For this reason we had better pause to review the pertinent aspects of Weber's thought.

That Pynchon should discover an affinity with the German sociologist is not surprising. Writing in the first two decades of this century, Weber began to move along lines superficially similar to Fausto Maijstral's in *V.* According to Weber, man counters alienation through a combination of "objectivity" and "rationalization." With objectivity he strips away illusions about the meaning of life; with rationalization he creates values and new meaning. Having no illusions, he is free to design his world. In fact, human freedom lies precisely in the ability to see life for what it is, to create meaning, and to act with purpose. But the discipline and asceticism which make possible rationalization can also lead to oppressive systems that control men. Weber identified the discipline and asceticism in our era as essentially Calvinistic, and found its most exemplary stage in America, although he observed its progress in Germany and the Low Countries as well. Put perhaps too simply and in somewhat more Pynchonian language than Weber's, the Calvinist, faced with the blankness and chaos of nature, transforms nature after his own design by bureaucratizing it and turning it to profit. The capitalist system he thus creates becomes oppressive; the bureaucracies reify and control their individual members. For Weber there was something tragic about this process of rationalization, of imposing design and pattern on nature, if only because he believed the process irreversible and inevitable in its homogenizing effect on humans. While he spoke in sociological constructs, Weber was postulating a theory of systems analogous to theories of thermodynamics: Closed systems decline into entropy.

If nothing can halt the process, however, it can be

slowed by what Weber referred to as charisma. Systems can be altered, perhaps even repaired or rejuvenated by the appearance of "irrational," charismatic figures and the movements they engender. The narrator of *Gravity's Rainbow* observes with apparent regret that John F. Kennedy and Malcolm X, had they not been assassinated, might have been such charismatic leaders. Sooner or later, Weber said, rationalization will assimilate the charismatic movements, "routinize" them, but while they retain their novelty and irrationality they offer potentiality for change.

Charisma can be dangerous, since it can induce disorder, and some people oppose such irrationality for sound reasons. The "Fuhrer-principle" grips Germany during the war; men of good will can deplore it:

> if personalities could he replaced by abstractions of power, if techniques developed by the corporations could be brought to bear, might not nations live rationally? One of the dearest Postwar hopes: that there should be no room for a terrible disease like charisma . . . that its rationalization should proceed while we had the time and resources . . . (81).

Pynchon's novel is predicated not on Hitler but on another charismatic candidate: the V-2 rocket. The significantly named Miklos Thanatz (to suggest "Thanatos") thinks of the missile

> "as a baby Jesus, with endless committees of Herods out to destroy it in infancy. . . . It really did possess a Max Weber charisma, . . . some joyful—and deeply irrational—force the State bureaucracy could never routinize, against which it could not prevail . . . they did resist it, but they also allowed it to happen. . . . You [Slothrop] and I perhaps have become over the generations so Christianized, so enfeebled by Gesellschaft and our obligation to its celebrated 'Contract,' which never did exist, that we, even we, are appalled by reversions like that" (464-465).

For Weissmann, the tormented genius who gives it birth, "the Rocket was an entire system *won,* away from the feminine darkness, held against the entropies

181

of lovable but scatterbrained Mother Naure" (324). The Rocket has two aspects. Conceived for death, ostensibly evil, it offers life. It is a "star," an "angel," a "Text." It is the means by which man can escape Gravity and Earth itself. It is the pinnacle of man's technology, symbol of a new state, or at the very least, a new city, the "Raketen-Stadt," a hope for those dispossessed by the entropic systems which have caused the War. The Rocket also bridges dual worlds.

The dualities in Pynchon's first two novels have been multiplied. Chief among them are the Elect and the Preterite, the Calvinist polarity of *The Crying of Lot 49,* by which Pynchon extends the ramifications of his Weberian structure. The "Them" of the conspiracy in *Gravity's Rainbow* are, or seem to be, the Elect. To Them are opposed the Preterite, the disinherited, the "passed over," those not touched by grace, those controlled by the Elect. As does Weber, Pynchon regards America as the course where Calvinist rationalization has run most true, and the majority of his direct allusions to Preterition have to do with New England Puritanism and the Calvinist assault on the western frontier. The landscape of *Gravity's Rainbow* is global, however, with characters from Africa, South America, Japan, Central Asia, Russia, and Europe. Calvinist impulses govern the majority of them, and to make the connection more convincing the narrator forces parallels. A village in the Kirghiz steppes resembles a town in "a Wild West movie" (339); a Russian rides a horse from Midland, Texas; Albert Speer looks "remarkably like American cowboy actor Henry Fonda" (448); Mickey Rooney ("Judge Hardy's son") puts in an appearance at the Potsdam Conference. . . .

The Preterite have their champions, from William Slothrop, of the Massachusetts Bay Colony—who wrote *On Preterition,* in which he "argued holiness for these 'second sheep,' without whom there'd be no elect" (555)—to Bryon the Bulb, an immortal light bulb who defies the cartel-controlled electric grid of Europe, who holds back the darkness, one of "the great secret ikons of the Humility, the multitudes who are passed over by God and History" (299). Before the novel ends, some of the characters organize themselves into a Preterite Counterforce, a "We-system" to combat the "They-system" (638). The legions of the Preterite also include allies among the dead, for the living and the dead are still another duality only hinted at in *The Crying of Lot 49* but made much of in *Gravity's Rainbow*. . . .

This is a startling conception, to be sure, although it is inherent in Calvinism itself; the Elect are a community of saints, living and dead, and the Preterite include souls on both sides of this "interface" as well. Pynchon legitimizes the idea by beginning the book with a quotation from Wernher von Braun to the effect that life persists after death. Like the living, the dead are organized into rationalized bureaucracies, having been killed by "death-by-government, a process by which living souls unwillingly become the demons known to the main sequence of Western magic as the Qlippoth, Shells of the Dead" (176), and still capable of "collaboration" with the living. Among the spirits of the nether world, the most prominent are the Angels. From the many invocations of the *Duino Elegies,* it is apparent that Pynchon thinks of angels in much the same way as Rainer Marie Rilke. J. B. Leishman and Stephen Spender have described the Angel of the *Elegies* as

the hypostatisation of the idea of a perfect consciousness—of a being in whom the limitations and contradictions of present human nature have been transcended, a being in whom thought and action, insight and achievement, will and capability, the actual and the ideal, are one. He is both an inspiration and a rebuke, a source of consolation and also a source of terror; for, while he guarantees the validity of Man's highest apsirations and gives what Rilke would call a "direction" to his heart, he is at the same time a perpetual reminder of man's immeasurable remoteness from his goal.[4]

Weissmann, having renamed himself Blicero, can still not accept Wittgenstein's "The world is all that is the case." Now a captain in the Nazi SS, that most perversely rationalized of systems, a "master" of the rocket, Blicero conceives the perfect Rocket, number 00000, with which to penetrate reality. "Self-enchanted by what he imagined elegance, his bookish symmetries" (101), Blicero dotes on the *Elegies,* particularly the first, which begins

> Who, if I cried, would hear me among the angelic orders? And even if one of them suddenly pressed me against his heart, I should fade in the strength of his stronger existence. For Beauty's nothing but beginning of Terror we're still just able to bear, and why we adore it so is because it serenely disdains to destroy us.[5]

In the second *Elegy* Rilke suggests that our lovers might be able to make the Angels hear: "Lovers, if Angels could understand them, might utter/strange things in the midnight air."[6] "I want to break out," Blicero tells his lover Gottfried, "to leave this cycle of infection and death. I want to be taken in love: so taken that you and I, and death, and life, will be gathered, inseparable, into the radiance of what we would become . . ." (724). Then he places Gottfried in the Rocket, and fires it into heaven. The message of his *Elegies,* Rilke told a friend, is that "affirmation of life and affirmation of death reveal themselves as one."[7] The charismatic Rocket offers death and life, and what man can become.

Pynchon makes use of the *Elegies* and to a lesser extent Rilke's *Sonnets to Orpheus* for *Gravity's Rainbow* in much the same way he draws on Eliot's *Waste Land* for his story "Low-lands." While the limitations of space will not permit us to consider the parallels in detail, we shall note a few in appropriate places. For the present, suffice it to say that the main characters of the novel suffer from a romantic alienation that owes its expression to the German poet. For that matter, the seedbed of many of Pynchon's ideas and conceptions in his third novel is the post-war period in Germany which culminated in the Weimar Republic. Weber wrote during the early phases of this period, of course, and so did Rilke, but other developments are important also: the economics of Walter Rathenau, who appears as a spirit in a seance; the music-hall innovations of Bertold Brecht and the films of UFA, the major German film company; the agitations of the communists and the rise of the fascists; and the achievements of German science, especially those in physics and chemistry. When *Gravity's Rainbow* appeared, most critics dwelled on Pynchon's similarity to Joyce. However, we should note that a more logical affinity would be with Thomas Mann, also a product of this period. In the irony of his narration, his mastery of the leitmotif, and his similarity of theme, Pynchon has much in common with Mann, who has many times been called a literary equivalent of Max Weber. It is perhaps no accident that the first appearance of the Angel in *Gravity's Rainbow* takes place in the sky over Lübeck, Mann's home.

Like Mann, Pynchon is interested in the polarities between Northern and Southern cultures. In the fiction of both writers, North stands for rationality, discipline, civilization, alienation from nature; with South are associated irrationality, freedom, nature, fertility. The movement of characters in *Gravity's Rainbow* is toward the rationalized North, which for the Hereros, the South West African tribe Pynchon first introduces in *V.,* is the land of the dead. In *V.,* by contrast, Hugh Godolphin had his vision of annihilation in the South, in Antarctica; his was a death of the unconscious rather than the ego. When Blicero fires Rocket 00000, he aims it true north, at the "zero at the top of the world" (340).

The zero at the top of the world is a "final zero," an "interface" between life and death, but there are other interfaces and other zeroes throughout the novel. Oedipa Maas conceives choices as zero or one, in the binary language of computers; so do characters in *Gravity's Rainbow.* Excluded middles are still bad shit, and there are more of them. Dualities and antimonies rival North and South: love and death, paranoia and anti-paranoia, sky and underground, the living and the dead, freedom and control, black and white, the Outside and the Inside of the self, gravity and flight, grace and

185

damnation, zero and one, even Rossini and Beethoven: "a person feels *good* listening to Rossini. All you feel like listening to Beethoven is going out and invading Poland" (440). The majority have to do with the Elect and the Preterite. Usually they are referred to as "worlds," just as in *The Crying of Lot 49,* and the worlds connect at interfaces—edges or intersections in systems or switching paths in energy grids. In *Gravity's Rainbow,* no Maxwell's Demon governs the flow of energy between worlds. Nevertheless, in speaking of the great chemist T. H. Liebig, whose achievements were so essential in the development of technology, the narrator observes that

> Liebig himself seems to have occupied the role of a gate, or sorting-demon such as his younger contemporary Clerk Maxwell once proposed, helping to concentrate energy into one favored room of the Creation at the expense of everything else . . . (411).

Because they believe in Manichean extremes, many characters endorse the principle of excluded middles. The most sinister of these, the Pavlovian zealot Edward Pointsman, whose name suggests his function as a pointsman or switchman of decisions and energies, owns a complete set of "the books in Sax Rohmer's great Manichean saga" of Fu Manchu (631), and ignores a voice which whispers "Yang and Yin" (278) to suggest that excluded middles do not always apply. Other characters are not so blind; they clutch at "the leading edge of a revelation" (631), which often comes as light, whenever they encounter it. Even the most humorous episodes furnish perceptions of interfaces. For example, the hilarious Keystone Kops sequence in which Tyrone Slothrop, aloft in a balloon, throws pies at a pursuing biplane culminates in a vision of the edge of the earth's shadow sweeping by at 650 miles an hour.

To sharpen these dualities, Pynchon—again like Mann—invests his work with mythological associations on a vast scale, in a manner both deliberate and mocking, utilizing both central myths of Western civilization and popular culture myths. Orphic myths, manifested in various descents into the underworld, jostle against Faustian legend, which calls for trips up the Brocken, the Walpurgisnacht mountain, and these in turn are juxtoposed with fairy tales like Hansel and Gretel, children's stories like *Alice in Wonderland* or *The Wizard of Oz,* and archetypical figures from movies, such as Dracula, King Kong, and Jack Slade. In addition, there are allusions to classical, kabbalistic, and Christian contexts. By far the most significant are references to Norse and Teutonic myth. Swirling in the background of the novel are the trappings of Northern epic: runes, the Northern Lights (the flickering light given off by the Valkyries), dwarves, the Titans Etzel and Utgarthaloki, and rainbows (the bridge to the abode of the gods), the distillation of mead in the novel's first scene. Two of the principal figures are Blicero, or "white," and his former love, the Herero Enzian, or "blue," a name Blicero borrowed from Rilke; the body of the Norse goddess of death, Hela, is half white, half blue.[8]

Often the allusions are treated comically, lest they become too ponderous. At one point, Pynchon even introduces a Committee on Idiopathic Archetypes to check their validity. At another, when Pynchon makes an imaginative connection between the benzine ring, the vision of which came to the chemist August Kekulé as a dream of a serpent with its tail in its mouth, and the cosmic serpent of Norse mythology, which encircles the earth in the same fashion, he has the narrator remark that "one of these archetypes gets to look pretty much like any other" and laugh at those who discover them for the first time: "You hear some of these new hires, the seersucker crowd come in the first day, 'Wow! Hey—that's th—th' *Tree of Creation!* Huh? Ain't it? Je—eepers!' but they calm down fast enough . . ." (411). Because this serpentine ring recurs throughout the novel, it echoes Pynchon's chief source of mythological allusion, the operatic works of Richard Wagner, who made his own adaptation of Norse and Teutonic motifs.

Of these the most important is *The Ring of the Ni-*

belungen cycle. The final opera of that cycle, *Die Göt-terdämmerung,* recounts the death of the gods when their enemies storm the rainbow bridge to Valhalla. During a surrealistic sequence in *Gravity's Rainbow,* the disaffected servants of the Elect ("Them," the gods), before deciding to form a Preterite Counter-force, speculate on their chances for rebellion:

It is possible that They will not die. That it is now within the state of Their art to go on forever—though we, of course, will keep dying as we always have. Death has been the source of Their power. It was easy enough for us to see that. If we are here once, only once, then clearly we are here to take what we can while we may. If They have taken much more, and taken not only from Earth but from us—well, why be-grudge Them, when they're just as doomed to die as we are? . . . But is that really true? Or is it the best, and the most carefully propagated, of all Their lies, known and unknown? (539)

The Elect do not die in *Gravity's Rainbow,* but the possibility of apocalypse remains, enhanced by the Wagnerian framework.

Pynchon's use of it results in a mythic *tour de force,* splendidly complex. In Wagner's operatic cycle, the gods doom themselves by their own avarice; they steal the ring of the Nibelungs, the black pygmies who labor beneath the earth, hating the gods. Pynchon transforms that ring into a literal great chain of being; it is the car-bon ring, the foundation of organic chemistry, the ring of life itself—which is related to virtually every other ring, chain, latticework, grid, and system in the novel. It is the Ring of Creation, of the "Preterite" earth, as the spirit of Walter Rathenau, made wise by being translated to the "other side," tries to tell a seance of I. G. Farben executives:

"Imagine coal, down in the earth, dead black, no light, the very substance of death. Death ancient, prehis-toric, species *we will never see again.* Growing older, blacker, deeper, in layers of perpetual night. . . . A thousand different molecules waited in the preterite dung. This is the sign of revealing. . . . There is the other meaning . . . the succession . . . I can't see that far yet. . . .

But [industry] is all the impersonation of life. The real movement is not from death to any rebirth. It is from death to death-transfigured. The best you can do is to polymerize a few dead molecules. But polymerizing is not resurrection" (166).

The passage synthesizes various motifs. The chain of life spirals from death (Rilke: "The affirmation of life and the affirmation of death [are] . . . one"); excluded middles do not apply, for life is cyclical. The earth belongs to the Preterite; it is the fruit of their labors and their lives. If "They" cannot really die, it is also true that "They" have never lived, for cartellization, industrialization, the design the Calvinist ethic imposes on nature, are not life. "They" have stolen the ring of the Preterite, which is a metaphor for colonialism and exploitation. Another passage makes this clear; it refers to August Kekulé's dream of the benzine ring:

Kekulé dreams the Great Serpent holding its own tail in its mouth, the dreaming Serpent which surrounds the World. But the meanness, the cynicism with which this dream is to be used. The Serpent that announces, "The World is a closed thing, cyclical, resonant, eternally-returning," is to be delivered into a system whose only aim is to *violate* the Cycle. Taking and not giving back, demanding that "productivity" and "earnings" keep on increasing with time, the System removing from the rest of the World these vast quantities of energy to keep its own tiny desperate fraction showing a profit: and not only most of humanity— most of the World, animal, vegetable and mineral, is laid waste in the process. The System may or may not understand that it's only buying time. And that time is an artificial resource to begin with, of no value to anyone or anything but the System, which sooner or later must crash to its death, when its addiction to energy has become more than the rest of the World can supply, dragging with it innocent souls all along the chain of life (412).

Sooner or later, apocalypse, the Götterdämmerung, will arrive, when the saturation point of exploitation is reached, or when the Preterite rebel. The "succession" Rathenau cannot yet "see" concerns that revolt. Although the Preterite includes the passed over of all nations, considered in Wagnerian terms the Herero Preterite are the Nibelungs. The Hereros of the novel are the survivors of von Trotha's 1904 South West Africa atrocities; they have a mantra which means " 'I am passed over.' To those of us who survived von Trotha, it also means we have learned to stand outside our history and watch it, without feeling too much" (362). The Hereros are not pygmies, but they are associated with them, and they are also associated with undergrounds. Their tribal totem is the Erdschwein ("earthpig") or aardvark, which digs holes in the earth. One of their rituals back in Africa was to bury a woman up to her neck in the earth to increase her fertility:

> In preterite line they have pointed her here, to be in touch with Earth's gift for genesis. The woman feels power flood in through every gate: a river beneath her thighs, light leaping at the ends of fingers and toes. It is sure and nourishing as sleep. It is a warmth. The more the daylight fades, the further she submits—to the dark, to the descent of water from the air. She is a seed in the earth. The holy aardvark has dug her bed (316).

The Hereros of *Gravity's Rainbow* are Schwarzkommandos, the black Rocket Corps, former colonial subjects drafted into the service of the Third Reich apparently at the behest of Blicero, the driven and shadowy Weissmann. Blicero shimmers; at the time of the novel's action he may already be dead, for he is referred to as "Dominus Blicero," the "Lord of the Night." In Africa during the twenties, Weissmann had taken as his protege and lover Enzian, now leader of the Schwarzkommandos. Enzian remembers Blicero then as "a very young man, in love with empire, poetry, his own arrogance"; he loves the German still:

"my slender white adventurer, grown twenty years sick and old—the last heart in which I might have been granted some being—was changing, toad to prince, prince to fabulous monster. . . . 'If he is alive,' he may have changed by now past our recognition. We could have driven under him in the sky today and never seen. Whatever happened at the end, he has transcended. Even if he's only dead. He's gone beyond *his* pain, *his* sin—driven deep into Their province, into control, synthesis and control . . . I haven't transcended. I've only been elevated" (660-661).

For Enzian, Blicero was a "Jesus Christ," a "Deliverer," the "white faggot's-dream body" (324). The Herero is the colonial black victimized by the Christian white; now he can find his identity only in the death-wish of his oppressor. Before he fires Rocket 00000, Blicero remembers Enzian wanting "to fuck, but . . . using the Herero name of God. . . . creator and destroyer, sun and darkness, all sets of opposites brought together, including black and white, male and female . . ." (100). "What did I make of him?" Blicero wonders (100). What he had made is the first priest of the Rocket. Having brought the boy with him when he returned to Germany, Blicero has taught Enzian well that love among the Europeans "had to do with masculine technologies, with contracts, with winning and losing. Demanded, in his own case, that he enter the service of the Rocket" (324). Understanding the Rocket, Enzian believes, will permit him to understand himself.

Now Rocket technician and leader of his people, having drifted away from his lover, Enzian tries to comprehend his destiny, tries to find the "Real Text" (520), which the Hereros have assumed must be the Rocket. Infected by "Their" Christianity, Enzian hopes somehow to effect a rebirth, but he does not know how and suspects that the mission he has set himself may even be in the control of others. Complicating his problem is a schism in the ranks of the Schwarzkommandos, one faction of which endorses the "doctrine of

191

the Final Zero" (525). These are the "Empty Ones," who opt for tribal suicide, and Enzian himself finds the desire attractive:

> It was a simple choice for the Hereros, between two kinds of death: tribal death, or Christian death. Tribal death made sense. Christian death made none at all. . . . But to the Europeans, conned by their own Baby Jesus Con Game, what they were witnessing among these Hereros was a mystery potent as that of the elephant graveyard, or the lemmings rushing into the sea (318).

In his heart Enzian knows that all gods—Herero or Christian—are far away, that there is "no difference between the behavior of a god and the operations of pure chance" (323). For that reason he can sympathize with the Empty Ones, who dream of Nature as Void, pristine, without design, of the proto-continent "Gondwanaland, before the continents drifted apart, when Argentina lay snuggled up to Südwest . . ." (321). They wish to reverse the Calvinist ethic, to re-create *"their* time, *their* space" (326), even if that time and space be death. Only by so doing can they rediscover the world-navel, "the Center without time, the journey without hysteresis, where every departure is a return to the same place, the only place . . ." (319). The Eternal Center is the Final Zero, to be achieved by the ultimate erotic act which embraces "all the Deviations" (319) men employ to break through the prison of their selves. Although the "Schwarzgerät," Gottfried, the boy Blicero shrouds in Rocket 00000, remains a mystery until the end of the novel, the Hereros know what Blicero has done before they learn what the secret component of the Rocket is. The Act is the ultimate Act of Christianity itself: the Sacrifice-Suicide, glamorous in its annihilation. The Hereros are the people of the Rocket.

Ritualizing their new religion, they adopt a mandala patterned after the shape of a Herero village, "the gathered purity of opposites" (321), in which male and female principles are symbolized. The mandala contains the letters KEZVH, the initials of the German words for the five positions of the launching switch for the V-2. Knowing that Blicero fired Rocket 00000, the Schwarzkommandos are determined to emulate him; they travel always North (across the Netherlands and Germany, the area of the original *Nibelungenlied*) toward the Herero "land of the dead," unearthing from their "graves" V-2's that misfired, to salvage parts for their Rocket 00001—as if collecting pieces of the True Cross. Appropriately, the V-2 itself is described both metaphorically and literally as rising from beneath the earth; it is the final form of the ring, and it is also physically put together in tunnels. The Schwarzkommandos may or may not actually fire the 00001 in the novel. By book's end they have constructed it, and Enzian presumably intends to be in it, an imitation Christ in place of the original, an abortive and sterile savior, doomed to eternal Preterition—or perhaps not. Until the last Enzian argues against suicide. If he succumbs to the death-wish of his tribe, the Elect will have bought more time. In any case, the oppressed of the earth are a threat to those who have sinned against them. One rocket may bring down no Valhalla in flames (although it may be descending on us all in the final scene of the novel), but the possibility of successors to it frightens "Them" so badly that they send a member of the elect to destroy the Schwarzkommandos.

He is Tyrone Slothrop, and his passage is also set to the music of Richard Wagner. If Blicero yearns for a love-death, Slothrop plays a comic Tristan whose Isolde is the Rocket itself. This sexual love of death thematically integrates the novel, just as Slothrop's search for the Rocket unites the multiple subplots. When the novel opens, Slothrop, brother to the Hogan Slothrop of "The Secret Integration," native of Minge-borough, Massachusetts, and graduate of Harvard, is an American Army Lieutenant working for ACH-TUNG (Allied Clearing House, Technical Units, Northern Germany, one of innumerable acronym-named agencies in the book) in London in 1944. Although Slothrop and the reader learn of it only gradually, he has been under surveillance by The Firm for years because of a famous—to everyone but Slothrop, who knows nothing of it—experiment in which he was the subject as a baby. Laszlo Jamf, a Pavlovian before he phased into chemistry, conducted a study of stimulus and response for I.G. Farben at Harvard in 1920 by conditioning the infant Tyrone to respond sexually to a "mystery stimulus." While Jamf attempted to extinguish the response after the experiment, it is apparent that he did not succeed, for Slothrop's penis erects even now in peculiar places, just before a V-2 rocket falls on those same locations in London. Because the V-2 travels faster than sound, Slothrop can not possibly hear its approach, so he must be responding to the rocket itself or to one of its components. Just what the "mystery stimulus" is we never learn, although it is almost certainly one of the aromatic rings—smelling like bananas—which Jamf later sythesizes into the polymer called Imipolex G.

Whatever its cause, Slothrop's seeming ability to predict the fall of a V-2 comes to the attention of PISCES ("Psychological Intelligence Schemes for Expediting Surrender. Whose surrender is not made clear" [34]), an Allied agency which is part of a larger Firm-controlled agency known as "The White Visitation," with headquarters in a mental asylum. Composed of "a few token lunatics, an enormous pack of stolen dogs, cliques of spiritualists, vaudeville entertainers, wireless technicians, Couéists, Ouspenskians, Skinnerities, lobotomy enthusiasts, Dale Carnegie zealots" (77), The White Visitation pursues a bewildering variety of methods designed to increase The Firm's control over individuals, including astral projection and communication with the dead on both sides of the War. One of the reasons that Pynchon chooses the War as his setting is that it was a conflict in which the battle lines between good and evil seemed clearly drawn. The White Visitation and other organizations demonstrate that those divisions are tenuous.

On a map of London Slothrop has placed stars to designate the inordinate number of his sexual conquests (over a thousand V-2's fall on London from 1944 to

1945); they correspond exactly with the impact points of the V-2's. That perplexes The Firm, especially the Grey Eminence of The White Visitation, Dr. Edward Pointsman, a behaviorist who has chosen Pavlov's *Letters to Pierre Janet* as his Holy Text. Pointsman believes in "the stone determinacy of everything, of every soul" (86), and concludes that Slothrop illustrates a theory laid down by Pavlov himself:

> Not only must we speak of partial or of complete extinction of a conditioned reflex, but we must also realize that extinction can proceed *beyond* the point of reducing a reflex to zero. We cannot therefore judge the degree of extinction *only* by the magnitude of the reflex or its absence, since there can still be *a silent extinction beyond the zero* (85).

According to Pointsman, Laszlo Jamf must have extinguished the young Tyrone's erection-response to the "mystery stimulus" only to zero and not beyond, so that the man still reacts to something in the rocket. Since Pointsman is an adherent of cause and effect, and since not to know the cause is not to be able to determine and control, he fears Slothrop:

> "he is, physiologically, historically, a monster. *We must never lose control.* The thought of him lost in the world of men, after the war, fills me with a deep dread I cannot extinguish..." (144).

He would like to operate on the American, to investigate his cortex, the interface between Outside and Inside; eventually he will attempt to castrate Slothrop.

Without realizing his affinity for the rocket, Slothrop has begun to fear being blown to "just zero, just nothing" (25) by the V-2's landing all over London; he nearly succumbs to what his friend Tantivy Mucker-Maffick—who is being used, also unawares, by The Firm to keep tabs on Slothrop—calls "operational paranoia" (25). Slothrop has always shown "a peculiar sensitivity to what is revealed in the sky" (26), and for that matter so have his ancestors, who lie buried in

Massachusetts beneath tombstones on which is chiselled the hand of God emerging from a cloud. Puritans, i.e., Calvinists, the Slothrops have over the years done their bit toward turning New England countryside into "necropolis." Over generations the family business became paper—"toilet paper, banknote stock, newsprint—a medium or ground for shit, money, and the Word" (28). To get it they have levelled forests and hillsides—without prospering. For all their Protestant ethic labors, and ostensible membership in the elect, the Slothrops lean toward the Preterite, that class toward which the book's sympathies are directed. Moreover, they produce paper, the medium of the Word, and the narrator has a soft spot for those who deal in Texts; later he will praise the German printers' union for resisting Hitler when other unions did not, an act of courage which "touches Slothrop's own Puritan hopes for the Word, the Word made printer's ink, dwelling along with antibodies and iron-bound breath in a good man's blood . . ." (571). Slothrop's respect for the Word recalls Oedipa Maas, and so does his openness to revelation, which as a child he thinks might emanate from the Aurora Borealis, "the ghosts of the North." If and when it comes, the narrator suggests, revelation will come as a rocket to the New England landscape:

> slender church steeples poised up and down all these autumn hillsides, white rockets about to fire, only seconds of countdown away, rose windows taking in Sunday light, elevating and washing the faces above the pulpits defining grace, swearing *this is how it does happen—yes the great bright hand reaching out of the cloud* . . . (29).

Although a member of the Elect, Slothrop is thus Preterite on two counts. (1) His ancestors are visibly unsuccessful in business, and according to the peculiar Calvinist schizophrenia which holds that God's grace is mysterious and never visibly manifested in the living and, on the other hand, that business triumphs are signs that the Calvinist is a member of the Elect, their failure damns them. As if to cinch the matter, "no other Slothrop ever felt such fear in the presence of Commerce" (569); his ineptitude renders him helpless to cope with the "real business" of the world—which *is* business. (2) Slothrop has been victimized by "Them" and will continue to be; he was "sold" to Harvard and Laszlo Jamf, although he was "paid" for his unwitting participation in the original experiment with a four-year scholarship to Harvard.

Jamf is an ambivalent figure, a genius who stands in direct line of succession to Liebig and is thus a sort of Maxwell's Demon himself. His symbolic relationship to Slothrop is difficult to ascertain; at times he seems to be Slothrop's "father." Having spent a night atop Jamf's grave in the German mountains, feeling that he has "passed a test" (269), Slothrop dreams that he *is* Jamf. Later, members of the Counterforce will deny that Jamf ever existed, and claim that he was Slothrop's excuse for being "in sexual love, with his, and his race's death," (738). The narrator compares his switch from psychology to chemistry to Kekulé's change from architecture to chemistry. One of his students remembers Jamf as impatient with "corporate procedures" and an advocate of a fascist chemistry. Jamf longed to move beyond the organic to the inorganic, the immortal, and the inanimate. That wish gave birth to Imipolex G, which, in its plasticity was an assertion "that chemists were no longer to be at the mercy of Nature" (249); a new surface both inanimate and almost living, Imipolex G is capable of being stimulated electronically, and highly erotic, an interface between life and death. It is identified with the Northern Lights and Rilke, with revelation and death. It is a "material of the future" (488), as Slothrop would seem to be a man of the future. Since Slothrop is good at reading Texts, The Firm can use him to "routinize" the charisma of the V-2, or at the least, to neutralize the blacks.

Among the zany projects hatched at The White Visitation is the scheme to plant in Germany evidence of the existence of a black Rocket Corps in Hitler's Aryan army, in the hope that the news will demoralize the *Herrenvolk*. Numerous agencies combine to fabricate documents—including a spurious film of the blacks in action with the elite weapon. When the war is almost over in Europe and The Firm learns that the Schwarzkommandos *do* exist, it views them as an immense postwar threat. "They" know that Enzian's troops are searching for rockets amid the chaos of the war zone, and knowing also of Slothrop's peculiar precognition of V-2's, plan to use him as a homing device to lead "Them" to the blacks. Pointsman injects Slothrop with sodium amytal to learn that he shares the American male's association of blackness with excrement and buggery, a motif that is carried forward in several directions in the novel; most notably in the narrator's reflections on King Kong, the gigantic black ape on the phallic Empire State Building—which in turn of course is linked to the image of Negroes with phallic rockets— and in the fear and hatred several major characters exhibit in the presence of Negroes. "They" assume that Slothrop's fear can be converted to hate and that he will willingly betray the Schwarzkommandos.

Slothrop and Tantivy are transferred to the Riviera, where they stay at the Casino Hermann Goering, a nightclub-resort once occupied by the Germans, who decorated it Nazi-style, complete with a Heinrich Himmler gaming-room which allows the narrator to play with Pynchon's perennial motif, the Wheel of Fortune. Fortune hardly has a chance (if we may be permitted one pun against Pynchon's dozens), for "They" are determined to control Slothrop. "They" engineer a scenario in which the unwitting Slothrop rescues a beautiful girl from a Pointsman-trained octopus (a perfect symbol of The Firm). The girl is Katje Borgesius, a double agent—or a triple, considering The Firm's manipulation of her—who has been one of Blicero's lovers, and whose name (apparently compounded from Borgia and Jesus) suggests her sacrificial role and the sexual perversions she specializes in. Slothrop's rescue scene derives from the movies; at times *Gravity's Rainbow* seems to be about modern man as conditioned by the Late Show. Katje naturally seduces Slothrop. Her job is to keep him under surveillance and to reinforce his conditioning by furnishing him with captured Nazi documents on the V-2. The documents cause erections for Slothrop, and Katje is there to fix those too.

Despite the madcap overtones of the affair, it backfires. Suspecting a plot, Slothrop confides to Tantivy that there is a "peculiar *structure*" to his life traceable somehow back to Harvard. None of his experiences can be laid to chance; everything has been controlled, like "a fixed roulette wheel" (209). At first the suspected conspiracy shows no "edge." Then Tantivy disappears, presumably removed by "Them"; Slothrop reads of his death in a newspaper. Next he inveigles a confession out of a drunken Sir Stephen Dodson-Truck, who shares with Slothrop "a love for the Word" (207), a confession regarding Slothrop's penis, "The Penis He Thought Was His Own" (216). And to cap his growing paranoia, Slothrop stumbles across a secret document on Imipolex G and bones up on it by surreptitiously using a private Royal Dutch Shell Teletype, in the process learning something about the supranational aspect of that corporation and himself. Shell and I. G. Farben have an interest in Slothrop, and Jamf has been at the center of it. Perhaps, the narrator observes, Slothrop is "genetically predisposed" to paranoia, to a sudden apprehension of other worlds, a phrase that recurs frequently here, like

> all those earlier Slothrops packing Bibles around the blue hilltops as part of their gear, memorizing chapter and verse the structure of Arks, Temples, Visionary Thrones—all the materials and dimensions. Data behind which always, nearer or farther, was the luminous certainty of God (141-142).

A sense of helplessness overtakes him; "Fuck you" is the "only spell he knows" (203), and while it is appropriate for his rocket-lover role, it seems inadequate. "Grace" is what he really needs, and grace he begins vaguely to associate with the rocket, or with one Rocket, the 00000, whose designation appears on the secret manifest for Imipolex G. The 00000 will become his "Grail." It is toward Slothrop's sexual affinity for the V-2 that Katje responds. As Blicero's lover, she had watched the phallic rocket ascend as the SS Captain fired each one, thought of it rising in its multi-colored flame like a courting peacock, "programmed in a ritual of love." She apprehends the erotic nature of a rocket and its fascination:

> Katje has understood the great airless arc as a clearer allusion to certain secret lusts that drive the planet and herself, and Those who use her—over its peak and down, plunging, burning, toward a terminal orgasm . . . which is certainly nothing she can tell Slothrop (223).

The "bridge music" in these scenes is Rossini (love), as opposed to Beethoven (power), and at first it suggests hope for Slothrop. Ironically, however, neither *La gazza ladra* or *Tristan and Isolde* are as relevant to Slothrop as the music of the harmonica and the kazoo, which are instruments of the Preterite. One of the final images of Slothrop in the novel associates him with harmonica and kazoo. Yet Slothrop is a mock-Tristan, just as he is a mock-Redeemer, the latest in the line of Pynchon's saviors, and just as flawed as his predecessors. He is also significantly American. Slothrop has come East, back across the Atlantic, to reverse the western passage of his ancestors to America, where they "penetrated and fouled" the "virgin sunsets" and the "purity" of that land (214). For one of his identities, Slothrop will become Ian Scuffling, British War Correspondent, in order to "escape" "Them," although he will not ultimately circumvent his fate: "Presto change-o! Tyrone Slothrop's English again! But it doesn't seem to be redemption exactly that . . . They have in mind . . ." (204).

Some of Slothrop's shortcomings he shares with Benny Profane. In spite of his more elegant title of Holy Fool, Slothrop is a schlemihl. A victim like Profane, he is equally unable to learn from experience. Nor can he understand his mission in the world; he will never find the paradigmatic Rocket, nor discover what the "Schwarzgerät," the payload of that missile, is. Since Laszlo Jamf's code-name for the infant Tyrone was "Schwarzknabe" (black boy), and since he possesses a "Schwarzphänomen" (black spirit or aura) which "choreographs" his movements, it seems likely that his destiny lies with Rocket 00000. "They" may wish him to routinize the charisma of the rocket, but as a Redeemer he has the potential to bring love to the new technology the Rocket has called into being, a real love, not a love of death, for in spite of his conditioning Slothrop does not love death. In two sequences Slothrop is pursued by men singing bawdy limericks about a man having intercourse with a rocket, but "Slothrop does not know that they are singing to him, and neither do they" (306). A veteran of countless couplings, he is unable to love, let alone transcend love and death, which is what we must do. Enzian wants to transcend, as he believes Blicero has, but at a terrible price—extinction. Slothrop's fate will be better—and worse. In searching for a Text, the Word, he will in a sense become a Text, but it—and he—will be forgotten as he loses his self without having found his Grail, and without having succored the Preterities.

The ability to love is given only to a few in *Gravity's Rainbow*. Slothrop is offered love by Geli Tripping, an "apprentice witch" in touch with chtonic powers and with Metatron, the Angel of the *Kabbala* who inhabits the world of spirit and governs the visible world. When he refuses because he can not accept the involvement, she bestows her love on Tchitcherine, to redeem the Russian from *his* destructive Schwarzphänomen. Roger Mexico, the statistician who tries futilely to save Slothrop from his fate, can love because the War is his "mother"; the stress of crisis and the temporary absence of "control" sensitizes him to understanding where it only bewilders Slothrop. Mexico's girl can love only so long as the war lasts; after the hostilities Jessica Swanlake (a name which is probably a play on Wagner's *Lohengrin*, an opera in which the heroine betrays her love), separated from Mexico by "Them," will opt for the security of a life within a rationalized system. Pynchon seems to be suggesting that love as we understand it—i.e., "normal" love rather than perversion—is possible only outside a system, in a state like war, which loosens the system's grip. On the one hand systems unite all men, and on the other isolate them, as Weber theorized. At issue also is the imperviousness of the "interfaces" of the human self, about which we shall have more to say later. Mexico works at love; Slothrop does not.

As one final example of successful love, there is Ludwig, a German boy searching for Ursula, his lemming. *"One lemming,* kid?" Slothrop asks him (553). Knowing of the suicidal impulse of lemmings, Slothrop is skeptical of Ludwig's faith "that love can stop it from happening" (556). For all the absurdity of this episode, it is crucial to understanding Slothrop's role in *Gravity's Rainbow.* It is linked to the story of Tyrone's ancestor, William Slothrop, author of *On Preterition,* who also raised pigs, around which he constructed parables. While knowing that the pigs he loves must die, killing them himself,

> William must've been waiting for the one pig that wouldn't die, that would validate all the ones who'd had to, all his Gadarene swine who'd rushed into extinction like lemmings, possessed not by demons but by trust for men, which the men kept betraying . . . possessed by innocence they couldn't lose . . . by faith in William as another variety of pig, at home with the Earth, sharing the same gift of life . . . (555).

In the zone of the war, where systems and control are briefly in abeyance, Ludwig does find Ursula; "so not all lemmings go over the cliff. . . . To expect any more, or less, of the Zone is to disagree with the terms of the Creation" (729). Small mercies are possible—but not for Slothrop. Gradually he will forget his "Grail," the Rocket, and wander on, looking for innocence and for grace. Innocence he will find; grace he will not. Nor will he die. He literally fragments, cut to pieces by energy grids, the victim of his innocence, which is no defense against the complexities of the systems that reform after the war. In the religious and metaphysical realms which form two levels of the novel, the Preterite are conditioned, like lemmings, to love death. Because they are caught in a cycle of eternal recurrence, they are not free; they can only die. The only hope, says a member of the Counterforce, is to affirm the cycle, to affirm death as well as life. Slothrop's destiny is to escape the cycle, and he can because he also escapes control. The paradox is that in so becoming free, he loses his self. He returns not to the earth, but to the void; it is a fate worse than death.

But at first Slothrop searches for the Rocket, the Text, the Key to redemption for the Preterite, by which they can reclaim what is theirs—the technology which derives from Earth itself. He escapes from the Casino Hermann Goering after Katje quits the game, hoping that Slothrop will carry memories of her with him, "to help bring him back" from his quest (225). Recalling that she was at Blicero's side when rockets were fired at London while Slothrop was there, she thinks they have been joined by the parabola, "that purified shape latent in the sky, that shape of no surprise, no second chances, no return" which "they move forever under . . . as if it were the Rainbow, and they its children . . ." (209). As Katje tells him, "between you and me is not only a rocket trajectory, but also a life. You will come to understand that between the two points, in the five minutes, *it* lives an entire life" (209). Slothrop will carry memories of Katje only so long as he remembers the object of his quest; he will eventually forget both—as his life becomes the parabola between points, a curve in the Zone, a rainbow.

Ostensibly divided into military occupation areas, the Zone's interfaces are not yet formed. "There are no zones," says one character: "no zones but the Zone" (333). It is an Oz where "categories have been blurred badly" (303) and where the ghosts of the victims of the war rub shoulders with the living. After all, it is still a *theater* of war, and the narrator, quick to seize on puns, regards it as somewhat unreal; Slothrop must feel his way among the images and players. Other characters metaphorize the Zone as a cloud chamber in which human particles are erratically visible. More important, it is an "interregnum" (294), a moment in time when no government has control, a power-vacuum. Considered within the Weberian framework of the story, the Zone is a void not yet rationalized, without design, and thus pregnant with possibility. Out of the destruction some new society might arise. Neutral Switzerland is a part of the Zone, and ironically, in view of Calvin's association with that country, Slothrop carries a message from Zurich to Geneva for a decidedly anti-Calvinist Argentine named Francisco Squalidozzi.

In company with some comrades, "a community of grace" (265), Squalidozzi has the distinction of having sailed an interned U-boat, from Argentina *back* to Germany. The sense in his madness lies in his appraisal of the Zone's possibilities for the future. For the uncomprehending Slothrop, he analyzes the failures of rationalization:

> We are obsessed with building labyrinths, where before there was open plain and sky. To draw ever more complex patterns on the blank sheet. We cannot abide that *openness*: it is terror to us. Look at Borges. Look at the suburbs of Buenos Aires (264).

Squalidozzi believes that men want once more the "anarchic oneness of pampas and sky," and that the War has cleared away the labyrinths and bureaucracies, probably only for a few months, which makes imperative the attempt to keep the Zone in the state of anarchy he equates with freedom and serenity: "In the openness of the German Zone, our hope is limitless" (265).

According to the Hereros, Argentina once nestled close to South West Africa, before the continents split apart, and Squalidozzi's desire, although it has a different goal, is similar to that of the Hereros. Unfortunately, he will fare no better than they. If they have been corrupted by the white Europeans, Squalidozzi and his Argentine U-boat crew follow the pattern of Martin Fierro, hero of the Argentine epic *The Gaucho*, to ultimate cooption into Gesellschaft. Ironically, Squalidozzi is suckered into making a movie on the life of the rebel hero by Gerhardt von Göll, a German film-maker of considerable celebrity in the thirties, now turned entrepreneur and black-marketeer. "Even the freest of Gauchos end up selling out, you know," von Göll tells Squalidozzi. It was von Göll who made the film on the Schwarzkommandos for The White Visitation, and now, having convinced himself that he has somehow created them, he promises to bring dream into being for the Argentine: "I can take down your fences and your labyrinth walls, I can lead you back to the Garden . . ." (388).

Despite such megalomania, von Göll understands the Zone. He can see patterns and grids of power forming; he has adopted the chess knight as his symbol and "Der Springer" as his nom de guerre; he can leap over the chessboard, over the interfaces. Moreover, von Göll subscribes to the clockwork theory of William Slothrop, as he tells Tyrone:

". . . we define each other. Elect and preterite, we move through a cosmic design of darkness and light, and in all humility, I am one of the very few who can comprehend in toto. Consider honestly therefore, young man, which side you would rather be on" (495).

Von Göll generally reduces Elect and Preterite to the economic categories of Haves and Have-nots, but like Weber he knows also that the Elect are as much prisoners of the systems they construct as are the abused Preterites. By contrast, William Slothrop's position was broader and embraced all aspects of the Elect-Preterite question:

William felt that what Jesus was for the Elect, Judas Iscariot was for the Preterite. Everything in the Creation has its equal and opposite counterpart. How can Jesus be an exception? Could we feel for him anything but horror in the face of the unnatural, the extracreational? Well, if he is the son of man, and if what we feel is not horror but love, then we have to love Judas too (555).

Could William Slothrop "have been the fork in the

road America never took, the singular point she jumped the wrong way from?" Tyrone wonders. Too late for himself and too late for the Zone, Slothrop will remember Squalidozzi's dream of the Virgin Zone, when

> for a little while all the fences are down, one road as good as another, the whole space of the Zone cleared, depolarized, and somewhere inside the waste of it a single set of coordinates from which to proceed, without even nationality to fuck it up . . . (556).

The Slothrops ("Sloth"-rops) of the world are too slow, however: grids of many coordinates form quickly. Only for a short period can he move in the still unrationalized state: "Slothrop, though he doesn't know it yet, is as properly constituted a state as any other in the Zone these days. Not paranoia. Just how it is. Temporary alliances, knit and undone" (291).

One of these alliances is with von Göll, who has a critical double role in the novel. The first is as a filmmaker, master of the means for producing fantasies and purveyors of "Mindless pleasures" for audiences; we shall consider this role more fully later. The second is as a black-marketeer and proto-capitalist during a period in the Zone like "the very earliest days of the mercantile system" (336) except that information is "the only real medium of exchange" (258); this fact suggests the rise of technology, just as information and communication in *The Crying of Lot 49* come to be the "energy" of systems. Von Göll and his sidekick, Blodgett Waxwing, take Slothrop under their wings. Knowing that he is somehow important to "Them," and being in a surreptitious business themselves, they treat Slothrop kindly in hopes of showing a profit. Eventually von Göll will lead the American to the "Holy Center," the rocket base at Peenemünde, although by then Slothrop will have forgotten why he should be going there.

Before and after that experience, however, Slothrop, like any hero approaching a holy center, must undergo rites of passage, and as he does Pynchon wraps him in the mantle of various figures from myth and legend. Waxwing gives Slothrop a white Zoot suit, and since white is the color of death in *Gravity's Rainbow,* the gift is not an auspicious omen; it emphasizes the American's role as sacrifice. Another costume is that of a gigantic pig, however, as if Slothrop were fulfilling his ancestor William's expectations of a pig "that wouldn't die." In between these two appearances Slothrop spends time with Geli Tripping, the witch, who takes Slothrop to the top of the Brocken, and the Faustian motif is advanced by his affair with Margherita Erdmann ("earth being")—an Eternal Feminine by virtue of her elevation to goddess stature in the early films of von Göll. Like Goethe's Margaret, Margherita apparently murders her child, a girl named Bianca ("white"), with whom Slothrop also consorts on a "ship of all nations" (462) called the *Anubis,* after the Egyptian god who conveyed souls to the underworld. Toward the end of the novel, Slothrop becomes a symbol: a crossroads at which men are gibbetted, a mandala like Enzian's, and a Fool in the Tarot deck, the only card without a number and place. Finally he is just nothing, a soul "among the Humility, among the gray and preterite souls, . . . adrift in the hostile light of the sky, the darkness of the sea . . ." (742). All of these images overlap and overlay each other to enhance themes and to reinforce Pynchon's view of history as a layering of cultured archetypes—a mulch or carbon-bed of ideas for rings of the future.

The most important of the mythic guises Slothrop acquires is Orpheus, with whom he is associated on numerous occasions. His Eurydice is Katje, who, feeling herself "corruption and ashes" (94) because of her participation in the perversions of Blicero, the "Lord of the Night," surrenders herself to Pointsman at The White Visitation, where she becomes a "Queen of the Night" for Brigadier Pudding's obscene rituals. (Slothrop must leave her in the underworld.) This Orpheus role merges with another closely related: Tannhäuser, Wagner's operatic hero, the "Singing Nincompoop"

(364). In the opera, Tannhäuser the minnesinger spends a year under the Venusberg (the Venus mountain) with Venus, comes back to the upper world, and seeks absolution for the sin of his sensual love from the Pope. The Pope refuses with the words, "You can no more expect mercy than my staff can be expected to flower again." Tannhäuser's earthly love, Elizabeth—whom Pynchon refers to as Lisaura—is true to him, but he does not return from his pilgrimage to the Pope. Too late, of course, messengers arrive from Rome with the holy staff in full bloom.

Slothrop's sojourn under the mountain takes place at Nordhausen, in the tunnels where the V-2 was assembled. The Mittelwerke at Nordhausen, being looted by the Allied armies, contain the charismatic relics of the rocket. Here the Schwarzkommandos worked, says the narrator in a surrealistic sequence, "where Tradition sez Enzian had his Illumination, in the course of a wet dream where he coupled with a slender white rocket" (297). Here we are offered a vision of the "Rocket-City" of the future, the promise of space travel, the eschatological rocket state, in which technology has been altered by the charismatic rocket to good purpose. But there are also reminders of the uses to which the rocket has been put. Such underworlds taint and corrupt. For the pilgrim afterwards, "the Pope's staff is always going to remain barren, like Slothrop's own unflowering cock" (470). Slothrop receives no grace.

Still a third significant role begins for Slothrop when he dons a "Wagnerian" costume, complete with a helmet that looks like a rocket's nose cone, to become Raketemensch, "Rocketman," a charismatic role. A German narcotics dealer, by the simple and powerful *act of naming* (366) confers on him a charisma which is immediately recognized by Seaman Bodine (the "Pig" Bodine of *V.* and "Low-lands"), busily dealing dope while on liberty from the destroyer *John E. Badass.* In his absurd costume Slothrop meanders around the Zone, always heading North. He meets Enzian, who tells him he is "free," that he has only to stand outside history, to affirm his Preterition, and to affirm death in order to affirm life. He also encounters

Tchitcherine, Enzian's Russian half-brother, who wants to kill Enzian because he believes their kinship has made him one of the "passed over" of history.

The Russian will learn, as Rocketman will not, that history is passing them all by. Tchitcherine will see the formation of "*A Rocket-cartel. A* structure cutting across every agency human and paper that ever touched it. Even to Russia . . . Russia bought from Krupp, didn't she, from Siemens, the IG . . ." (566). The rocket's charisma is being routinized, not by Slothrop, but by "Them":

> . . . a State begins to take form in the stateless German night, a State that spans oceans and surface politics, sovereign as the International or the Church of Rome, and the Rocket is its soul (566).

The Rocket-City is turning into Rilke's City of Pain.

Slothrop can no longer perceive connections. From paranoia he has slipped into anti-paranoia, "where nothing is connected to anything, a condition not many of us can bear for long" (434). He does not know what "They" want of him: "Either They have put him here for a reason, or he's just here. He isn't sure that he wouldn't, actually, rather have that *reason* . . ." (434). He is beyond control, perhaps beyond zero; he is free, and yet he is not, not as Weber defined freedom, which consists in exercising the choice of design which paradoxically makes us prisoners. Slothrop has freed himself from karmic cycles, but he has no choices and therefore can not be said to be free. He can not affirm death and for that reason can not affirm life. Bodine gives Slothrop a T-shirt dipped in the blood of John Dillinger (a relic he thinks confers grace); Katje joins forces with Enzian in hope of finding her Orpheus; Roger Mexico tries to plot his course in order to rescue him. Slothrop can no longer be found.

The Rocket, which might have struck grace from the heavens, only falls again anyway, helpless in the grip of gravity, and like Slothrop, falls to pieces. Worse, although Slothrop does not know it, not only has the Rocket been "routinized" and coopted by "Them," but it has also been wedded to a force which explodes over Hiroshima; Slothrop sees the headline and can not understand it. That blast was America's contribution to the Rocket-City, as Blicero himself senses before he fires the 00000. "America *was* the edge of the world," Blicero thinks, now corrupted along with all Europe, and perhaps, as if Blicero foresees the moon-landings, the moon will be the new edge to which the colonists of the old order will go, carrying death, as they carried it all over earth. He will break the cycle also.

Blicero will make the Angel hear, at least, and there is something tragic in that cry. But Slothrop has his cry too, and it comes from Rilke as well. Just before Slothrop begins to fade, the narrator quotes the final stanza of the twenty-ninth *Sonnet to Orpheus* as the American stands beside a stream:

> And though Earthliness forget you,
> To the stilled Earth say: I flow.
> To the rushing water speak: I am (622).

Slothrop may say "I am," but he does not know *who* he is. Having never found the Rocket, he has never found his self. He is out of control, out of the karmic cycle, and out of touch with the world of men. He belongs to no system and therefore does not belong to history. No revelations mean anything to him, even when he sees a rainbow: "a stout rainbow cock driven down out of pubic clouds into Earth, green wet valleyed Earth, and his chest fills and he stands crying, not a thing in his head, just feeling natural . . ." (626). Slothrop has become a charismatic figure without a following, never to be rationalized, never to redirect a death-loving system.

CHAPTER SIX

The Physics of Heaven:
History, Science, and Technology
in Gravity's Rainbow

In 1912, Rainer Maria Rilke wrote to his patroness, Princess Marie von Thurn und Taxis, at whose estate, Duino, he was writing the *Elegies*, about El Greco's "Ascension":

> a great angel thrusts himself diagonally into the picture, two angels simply stretch upwards, and out of this superabundance of movement arises the sheer upward flight—it cannot help itself. This is the physics of Heaven.[1]

In *Gravity's Rainbow*, the rocket—the Angel, the star—cannot help itself either, and its inevitability represents the charisma of technology. Pynchon would agree with Andrew Hacker's observation that "the movements of technology are not matters of social policy or human choice."[2] Technology is itself a historical force, almost a Zeitgeist, viewed somewhat nostalgically in *Gravity's Rainbow* at a period in time when it lost forever whatever innocence it possessed. By the novel's end, the Rocket's charisma has been "routinized":

> But the Rocket has to be many things, it must answer to a number of different shapes in the dreams of those who touch it—in combat, in tunnel, on paper—it must survive heresies . . . and heretics there will be: Gnostics who have been taken in a rush of wind and fire to chambers of the Rocket-throne . . . Kabbalists who study the Rocket as Torah . . . Manicheans who see two Rockets, good and evil, who speak together in the sacred idiolalia of the Primal Twins (some say their names are Enzian and Blicero) of a good Rocket to take us to the stars, an evil Rocket for the World's suicide, the two perpetually in struggle (727).

The immanence of *"technologique,"* "something that had its own vitality" (401), manifests itself in accord with Pynchon's view of history as an unfolding of continuity and connection rather than as a train of cause and effect. At the seance in Berlin, the ghost of Walter Rathenau, in addition to speaking of the composting of carbon-beds in layers to form the earth, denigrates cause and effect as "secular history" which "is a diversionary tactic" (167), a kind of history that is "at best a conspiracy, not always among gentlemen, to defraud" (164). "They" would have humans believe in control and in death, in determinism. This "rational structure" is the source of "Their" power, and "They" seem to have achieved a "collaboration . . . between . . . matter and spirit" to know something "that the powerless do not" (165).

Those few characters who escape tragedy in the novel do so because they manage to escape from historical determinism. One is Tchitcherine, the Russian, a Red Army officer who nevertheless "has a way of getting together with undesirables, sub rosa enemies of order, counterrevolutionary odds and ends of humanity" as if he were a "giant supermolecule with so many open bonds available at any given time" (346). While in exile in the vast Central Asian plains, he learns of the Russian extermination of various ethnic nationalities, a barbarism Pynchon equates with the Calvinist annihilation of Indians in America and, more humorously, with the wiping out of the Dodo Bird in seventeenth-century Mauritius by Franz Van der Groov, Katje Borgesius's ancestor. The crazy Dutch Puritan killed the flightless, stupid birds because he believed they did not fit in God's scheme of things; the Russians killed Kirghiz (and others) because the communists believed they retarded the inevitability of historical development, and in that sense the Russians are Calvinists also, trying to impose order on the windswept void of Asia.

Since Tchitcherine is Enzian's half-brother, he fears that his connection with the blacks, a people who have not been assimilated into the communist scheme, will cause him to be "passed over" by history. He comes close to revelation when he sees the Kirghiz Light (presumably some phenomenon like the Aurora Borealis), but he is destined to remain always out on the "edge" of things, which is his salvation. If history be a fabric, Tchitcherine is one of the frayed threads at the edge, and thus he eventually escapes control. So long as he accepts official dialectical materialism he is not free, because "They" can require him to die for the cause, as Wimpe, the German drug salesman who latches on to one of Tchitcherine's open bonds, tells him:

"Religion was always about death. It was used not as an opiate so much as a technique—it got people to die for one particular set of beliefs about death. . . . But ever since it became impossible to die for death, we have had a secular version—yours. Die to help History grow to its predestined shape. Die knowing your act will bring a good end a bit closer" (701).

Having been a communist, Tchitcherine will be "haunted" by the fear that he is wrong, that the Marxist "theory of history," which he conceives in terms of classical physics rather than in the usual Hegelian jargon, will get him in the end. Wimpe's drug Oneirine (a creation of Jamf) enables him to perceive paranoically that things are relativistically connected instead of being causally linked, and that it is in "Their" interest to have him believe in the dialectic. Not until Geli Tripping saves him from his doubts will he forget his hatred of Enzian and achieve his freedom.

One other major character in *Gravity's Rainbow* survives the turmoil relatively unscathed. Opposed to Dr. Pointsman, the behaviorist and determinist who asserts the hegemony of cause and effect, is Roger Mexico, the statistician for The White Visitation and later a member of The Counterforce. Mexico is an "Antipointsman" (55) who rejects Calvinism. When someone suggests that death by rocket is punishment for sins, Mexico responds, "it's the damned Calvinist insanity again. Payment. Why must they always put it in terms of exchange?" (57) For the statistician-democrat, everyone is "equal in the eyes of the rocket" (57). Someday, according to Mexico, scientists may "have the courage to junk cause-and-effect entirely, and strike off at some other angle" (89), an idea which horrifies Pointsman. With men like Mexico advocating randomness, Pointsman fears, "What if Mexico's whole *generation* have turned out like this? Will Postwar be nothing but 'events,' newly created one moment to the next? No links? Is it the end of history?" (56).

Mexico is free by virtue of his ability to perceive continuity in spite of randomness. He occupies the same ground Oedipa Maas achieved: "the domain *between* zero and one—the middle Pointsman has excluded from his persuasions—the probabilities" (55). Mexico predicts rocket strikes in London during the war by plugging figures into a Poisson equation, which is based purely on probabilities. He is the twentieth-century scientist aware of indeterminacy and therefore aware of the possibilities of freedom. Mexico can be excited by a beautiful Christmas night scene in a Kentish church, a rare night of possibility which seems to "banish the Adversary, destroy the boundaries between our lands, our bodies, our stories, all false, about who we are . . ." (135). So expansive a sense of brotherhood does not hamper his relationship with Jessica Swanlake; with her he forms "a joint creature unaware of itself" (38), their bodies "a long skin interface" (121). Like many other characters he is subject to paranoia, but Mexico's is creative, allowing him to understand how things are related and to perceive the areas of freedom between the grids of control. Almost alone in "a culture of death" (176), Mexico holds to life, while Pointsman at the end is left only with his fruitless faith in cause and effect.

Once again Pynchon is using the change wrought in physics by the twentieth century to sharpen the oppositions within his thematic framework. In particular these involve relativity in field physics and quantum theory in micro-physics; together they have altered the scientist's view of reality. Less and less the scientist speaks of cause and effect and more and more, like Roger Mexico, of probabilities and of statistical or mathematical descriptions of connections between things as they move relative to one another in a space-time continuum. Concepts of determinism have been eroded by principles of indeterminacy.

In *Gravity's Rainbow*, "Their" authority stems from classical physics, which *does* rest on cause and effect relationships between forces and objects; the twentieth-century physics that has given birth to the technology embodied in the Rocket threatens to undermine "Their" tyranny because it introduces concepts of indeterminacy and reinforces the potential for free will. Thus "They" must try to coopt the newer physics for their own purposes, and in doing so "They" benefit from our confusion. For example, from time to time the narrator mentions the Aether which James Clerk Maxwell (who else?) thought flowed past the earth to provide the medium in which light waves travelled. In order to prevent this discussion from becoming too recondite, we will simply say that the theory of the

Aether—variously called Luminiferous or Soniferous, depending on whether one is dealing with light or sound waves—did not account for, among other things, the effects of gravity, a factor which is germane to Pynchon's title. Modern science says that there is no Aether, only Void, and "They" may say it too. The problem is that like Tchitcherine we do not know for sure, claims the narrator, and besides, it would be nice if there were a medium:

What if there is no Vacuum? Or if there is—what if They're *using* it on you? What if They find it convenient to preach an island of life surrounded by a void? Not just the Earth in space, but your own individual life in time? What if it's in *Their* interest to have you believing that? (697)

Our "own individual lives" are surrounded by time, and that fact makes control easier by "Them," because it reduces the possibilities of our perceiving our essential oneness with others. Pynchon multiplies metaphors from field and micro-physics. Characters move in "quantum jumps" (564), each section of the Zone "speeds away from all the others, in fated acceleration, red-shifting, fleeing the Center" (519), refugees are "particle and wave" (398). All of these metaphors and a good many more concern motion in time, and the third of those listed is particularly relevant, since it refers to the major paradox of modern micro-physics: Under certain conditions light manifests itself as if it were composed of particles and under others as if it were a wave. In *Gravity's Rainbow* Pynchon envisions human lives and human history as wavelengths, a continuous flow that we sometimes perceive as particles because we are bound by time. Waves are not objects but forms, patterns that move, and their motion is measured in wavelength and frequency—functions of time.

The idea permits Pynchon considerable latitude and much humor. One episode presents an American army private named Eddie Pensiero, a near-catatonic drug addict; he is the Company barber. As he cuts hair, while Slothrop plays his harmonica nearby, the narrator remarks:

Hair is yet another kind of modulated frequency. Assume a state of grace in which all hairs were once distributed perfectly even, a time of innocence when they fell perfectly straight, all over the colonel's head. . . . Passing through it tonight, restructuring it, Eddie Pensiero is an agent of History (643).

Wavelengths can be cut when they are separated into discrete parts, and that is "Their" secret. Long before Slothrop disappears, when he first feels the onset of paranoia, he has the sensation that "Their odds were never probabilities, but frequencies *already observed*" (208).

Tyrone Slothrop is the principal victim of a faulty perception of time. After "They" had coopted the Rocket, Slothrop's "time" had passed, or at least that is what the apologists for the failed Counterforce claim as part of his legend:

There is also the story about Tyrone Slothrop, who was sent into the Zone to be present at his own assembly—perhaps, heavily paranoid voices have whispered, *his time's assembly*. . . . He is being broken down instead and scattered (738).[3]

When Slothrop begins to disintegrate, he can communicate only on low frequencies, and he is said to lose "temporal bandwidth":

"Temporal bandwidth" is the width of your present, your *now*. It is the familiar "$\triangle t$" considered as a dependent variable. The more you dwell in the past and in the future, the thicker your bandwidth, the more solid your persona. But the narrower your sense of Now, the more tenuous you are. It may get to where you're having trouble remembering what you were doing five minutes ago, or even—as Slothrop now—what you're doing *here* . . . (509).

The $\triangle t$ or delta t, a change in time, becomes very familiar in *Gravity's Rainbow* and is the key to explanations of human isolation. In *The Crying of Lot 49*, the DT's of the alcoholic Sailor furnish Pynchon with a pun on calculus signs (dt) for those "vistas of time and space" the Sailor's mind has hurtled through. In *Gravity's Rainbow* distance and time are functions of motion also, and the calculus is that of the rocket's parabola. Scarcely a section of the novel lacks a parabola, which, like the flight of Rilke's Angel, represents the transcendence of human limitations and contradictions; it is an "inspiration and a rebuke," a synthesis of opposites, a trajectory that is a true dialectic. If one bisects a parabola, each half is a mirror image of the other. Moreover, in a sense the novel takes the form of a rocket's flight as it arcs free of the earth, ascends, then, its motion "betrayed" to gravity, plunges back toward the planet that gave it rise. The flight can be mathematically computed by using the double integral, a calculating concept on which Pynchon rests the foundation of the book's structure.

Rather morbidly the narrator equates the double integral sign $(\iint)$ with the Nazis SS emblem; with "the shape of lovers curled asleep" (302), with the old Norse "rune that stands for the yew tree, or Death" (302), and with the shape of the tunnels underneath the earth at the Mittelwerke where the V-2's were constructed. More to the point, the double integral is a method by which the rocket's parabola can be divided into time-frames, and without trying to discuss the mathematics, we can present the technique visually in the following figure:

Here the parabola is sliced up by integrals extending vertically from a base line stretched between the rocket's point of firing and its point of impact. Those lines are artificial and arbitrary. Along the parabola itself an infinite number of lines can be drawn, and each two of them—as double integrals—bound a moment in time, relative of course to distance. As the rocket moves along its path, and as it passes these artificial divisions, it has passed through a change in time—designated as $\triangle$t. Theoretically, precisely because the number of divisions can be extended infinitely, the rocket can be said to be poised in the sky ("the Perfect Rocket is still up there, still descending" [426]), approaching final zero in an asymptotic (approaching but not reaching infinity) curve, like Zeno's famous arrow. So long as it hangs there, the missile is a threat of man's destruction and a reminder of his achievement. *Gravity's Rainbow* opens with a rocket in flight over London and ends with a missile so poised at "the last delta-t" above the Orpheus movie theater in Los Angeles.

The beauty of the concept is that from it Pynchon can draw analogies of enormous variety and fertility. The most obvious is with the motion picture film, in which "time frames" sprocket through a projector and flash on a screen—as in the theater at the novel's end. Moreover, the parabola is a wave; it is also a "life," Katje tells Slothrop. And just as humans divide up a parabola into fragments for convenience and precision in measurement, so they divide up their lives into artificial frames to comprehend them. In each case they sacrifice the whole for its parts, but the continuity remains, whether they see it or not. When *Gravity's Rainbow* appeared, many readers noticed the "framed" sequences in the book, an effect heightened by sprocket-shaped designs separating them in the original edition.[4] Film has one great quality as far as Pynchon is concerned here: Scenes are obviously contingent but not necessarily linked by cause and effect. Each scene is thus a moment in time, an artificial measurement in a space-time continuum. "Do you find it a little schizoid," asks one rocket technician of another, "breaking a flight profile up into segments of responsibility?" (453).

Of the half-dozen related stories in this film-novel, Franz Pökler's most aptly illustrates the interlocking relationship of rocket mathematics, cinema techniques, and human lives, and for that reason is central to the construction of *Gravity's Rainbow*. To make the relationship clear, the narrator recounts early experiments in rocket research during which airplanes dropped models of the missile from 20,000 feet:

> The fall was photographed by Askania Cinetheodolite rigs on the ground. In the daily rushes you would watch the frames at around 3000 feet, where the model broke through the speed of sound. There has been this strange connection between the German mind and the rapid flashing of successive stills to counterfeit movement, for at least two centuries— since Leibnitz, in the process of inventing calculus,

used the same approach to break up the trajectories of cannonballs through the air. And now Pökler was about to be given proof that these techniques had been extended past images or film, to human lives (407).

Pökler, a former chemist, is one of several scientists in the novel to shift into another field of research. Through the offices of his old classmate Mondaugen, Pökler in the thirties joins an amateur league of Berlin rocket enthusiasts interested in space exploration. For Pökler and his colleagues, the rocket is a paradigm of man's most noble ambition, as Franz tells his wife Leni: "We'll all use *it*, someday, to leave the earth, to transcend. . . . Borders won't mean anything. We'll have all outer space . . ." (400). Aware of the rocket's potential for quite another purpose, the Wehrmacht drafts the technicians for weapons development. Even so, for a while Pökler can persuade himself that he is engaged in pure science, especially since at first the military agency funds projects extravagantly and permits him to work unfettered. Pökler feels that he has entered "a monastic order" of democratic scientists among whom no Weberian rationalization has as yet taken place: "it was a corporate intelligence at work, specialization hardly mattered, class lines even less" (402). Many of Pökler's fellow scientists are mystics. One draws parallels between rocketry and Zen archery. Mondaugen borrows metaphors from Stefan George and Herman Hesse; he visualizes the rocket as a resolver of paired opposites: male and female, life and death, creation and destruction. It is an outgrowth of Mondaugen's "electro-mysticism":

Think of the ego, the self that suffers a personal history bound to time, as the grid. The deeper and true Self is the flow between cathode and plate. The constant, pure flow. Signals—sense-data, feelings, memories relocating—are put onto the grid, and modulate the flow. We live lives that are waveforms constantly changing with time, now positive, now negative. Only

221

at moments of great serenity is it possible to find the pure, the informationless state of signal zero (404).

Pökler responds skeptically: "In the name of the cathode, the anode, and the holy grid?"

Mondaugen's theory of paired opposites allows him to justify Hitler as a necessary evil. By contrast, Leni Pökler opposes the Nazis on similar Manichean grounds. Unfortunately for their compatibility, Leni is a communist, while Franz is a "good" but apolitical German of the type who did not oppose the Nazis until it was too late. Because they usually degenerate into brawls between screaming agitators and club-wielding police, Pökler can not understand Leni's participation in the street demonstrations of pre-war Berlin. She tries to tell him how the fear evaporates as the mob approaches the moment of annihilation, frozen in time by its very immanence, like a rocket itself:

She even tried, from that little calculus she'd picked up, to explain it to Franz as $\triangle t$ approaching zero, eternally approaching, the slices of time growing thinner and thinner, a succession of rooms each with walls more silver, transparent, as the pure light of the zero comes nearer . . . (159).

Pökler, "the cause-and-effect man," does not comprehend; the $\triangle t$ for him is an artificial function, not real. But Leni is searching for truth, for a way to link everything together, which is why she has recourse to mysticism, to belief in other worlds and other patterns of energies. When Franz tells her that no changes in other systems can effect changes in hers, she says: ". . . not cause. It all goes along together. Parallel, not series. Metaphor. Signs and symptoms. Mapping on to different coordinate systems, I don't know . . ." (159). If Pökler does not share the obvious death-wishes of his wife and friend, neither does he see what they do: that cause and effect do not always apply to the real world. For a scientist, he is surprisingly unacquainted with the theory of relativity that his wife apprehends intuitively. She can visualize the world as a space-time continuum in which things can be described only by means of their relationship to one another. Franz is a pedestrian with a pedestrian mind on the street Leni visualizes as alive. He deals only with the graph of the intersections, and for all his talk of transcendence, contents himself with clinging to "the network of grooves between the paving stones" of the street where Leni marches:

> Pökler knew how to find safety among the . . . abscissas and ordinates of graphs: finding the points he needed not by running the curve itself, not up on high stone and vulnerability, but instead tracing patiently the xs and ys, . . . moving always by safe right angles along the faint lines . . . (399).

His rationality limits Pökler. He can not conceive the designs of the Nazis, which are also mystical, which blend love and death, which have little to do with cause and effect; he says nothing, does not protest, and his tragedy is that of his countrymen: Had he not chosen silence, "back when there was time, they all might have saved themselves" (409). Essentially passive, even masochistic, especially in his attachment to his wife, he yet believes in Destiny, as Leni knows:

> she knows about the German male at puberty. On their backs, in the meadows and mountains, watching the sky, masturbating, yearning. Destiny waits, a darkness latent in the texture of the summer wind. Destiny will betray you, crush your ideals, deliver you into the same detestable Bürgerlichkeit as your father . . . and without a whimper you will serve out your time, fly from pain to duty, from joy to work, from commitment to neutrality (162).

Franz's destiny is the Rocket, for "it was impossible not to think of the Rocket without thinking of *Shicksal* [fate]" (416).

Before he goes to Peenemünde in 1937, where he and his colleagues will be "invading Gravity itself," Leni leaves Franz for her lover Peter Sachsa, the medium who calls up the spirit of Walter Rathenau.

Sachsa will eventually be killed by a policeman in a street riot. This circumstance allows the narrator to draw parallels between Sachsa and Leni and Nora Dodson-Truck, the medium of The White Visitation, a near-goddess whose symbol is the triskelion and who will speak in the voice of Gravity itself. Leni is arrested by the Nazis and with her Ilse, her daughter by Franz.

Ilse had been conceived on the night Pökler saw *Alpdrücken* ("Nightmare"), a film by Gerhardt von Göll, in which the voluptuous Margherita Erdmann is gang-raped. So erotic was that sequence that the rape became real, and Erdmann was impregnated; the child was Bianca. In a more symbolic sense, the German males who see the film are so aroused that they "father" the children conceived after seeing the film on Margherita, since she is the stimulus to their desire when they have intercourse with their wives, and all the children so conceived are the "same" child. Pökler is one of those aroused—and there is an implied comparison between Margherita's black garter belt (all she wears in the film) and the parabola of the V-2. Ilse is thus a "movie child" from her beginning.

By the time the war starts and Pökler realizes that his talents have been suborned by the sinister forces whose existence he has refused to admit, Blicero, the chief of his rocket research unit, has a hold over Franz. Blicero arranges to have Ilse brought from her concentration camp to spend two weeks with her father each year; in return Pökler must work on the rocket. He will finally install the Imipolex G shroud in Rocket 00000 for Blicero. Pökler has convinced himself that daughter and wife are being "re-educated"; he does not know what goes on in the camps, and like many other Germans, has not tried to find out. The first year Ilse delights Pökler by prattling of rocket-trips to the moon, his own dream, which reinforces his vision of "a map without any national borders, insecure and exhilarating, in which flight was as natural as breathing" (410). On her second visit, Pökler is permitted to take Ilse to *Zwölfkinder,* a sort of German Disneyland, a place "made for innocence in a corporate State" (419).

224

Here, and again here, in the years to follow, he begins to doubt that the girl "They" call Ilse is really his daughter. Since he sees her only once a year, she may be a different child each time; "even in peacetime, with unlimited resources, he couldn't have proven her identity, not beyond the knife-edge of zero-tolerance his precision eye needed" (421). Unable to rescue her or to escape "Their" control, Pökler does what he can; he accepts the girl, whether his daughter or not: "it was the real moment of conception, in which, years too late, he became her father" (421).

It is too late. By the third year Pökler has been transferred to Nordhausen, where he works in the Mittelwerke tunnels on V-2 assembly. Nearby is the Dora concentration camp, which Pökler chooses to ignore. Ironically, Ilse and her mother are kept there. Leni will survive the war and become the prostitute Solange, one "among the accidents of this drifting Humility, never quite to be extinguished, a few small chances for mercy . . ." (610). Ilse's fate we never learn. Pökler's cause and effect mind, even after he realizes Blicero's game, will not permit him to seize the ironic pattern or recognize the "signs and symptoms" of control. His Teutonic rationality erects barriers between his knowledge and his understanding, or, as the narrator puts it: "Weissmann's cruelty was no less resourceful than Pökler's own engineering skill, the gift of Daedalus that allowed him to put as much labyrinth as required between himself and the inconveniences of caring" (428). Pökler connects circumstances only after Blicero puts him at a rocket's impact point to observe the missile's re-entry. Franz sits square in the "Ellipse of Uncertainty," a safe place only because the V-2 virtually never hits its target predictably. One must trust in probabilities, and eventually Pökler can— too late, although his love redeems his tragedy to an extent:

The only continuity has been her name, and *Zwölf-kinder*, and Pökler's love—love something like the persistence of vision, for They have used it to create for him the moving image of a daughter, flashing him

only these summertime frames of her, leaving it to
him to build the illusion of a single child . . . (422).

Pökler's story points up several important aspects of
Gravity's Rainbow. The first has to do with the continuity of the novel itself, and the way Pynchon pre-
serves it. About five-sixths of the way through, after
Tyrone Slothrop has begun to fragment, and after the
atomic bomb has been dropped on Japan, the Slothrop
plot-line becomes tenuous, and the focus of the narrator's vision must expand to cover the larger theater of
the war, including the Pacific as well as Europe. As a
result, the final hundred pages are difficult, for they
contain time-frames—sometimes specifically referred
to as movies—of wide diversity, interspersed with the
tag ends of other subplots (Enzian, Tchitcherine, etc.),
to keep the "film" going. Most of them surrealistic,
these frames include scenes from Slothrop's childhood
in Mingeborough, one of which presumably became the
short story "The Secret Integration." One frame links
Tyrone to John F. Kennedy; another reviews Oedipal
conflicts and hints at Slothrop's charismatic function
when he searches for "The Radiant Hour" hidden by
his parents; a third and fourth, "Shit 'N' Shinola" and
"An Incident in the Transvestites' Toilet," seem designed to reinforce the reader's conditioning with reminders of the American association of blackness with
death, excrement, and sexual perversion. Among the
scenes presented in slapstick fashion are a couple of
film-clips of a zany pair of Kamikaze pilots, probably
to attribute to the Japanese a love of death similar to
the Germans'. Such frames shore up themes attenuated
by the novel's length, and one of the last, "Back in der
Platz," mentions Gerhardt von Göll's "tasteless" film,
"New Dope," in which film-images run backwards so
that reality is reversed.

Although Pökler's confusion is the most obvious,
other characters in *Gravity's Rainbow* perceive reality
as frames of film, an illusion, the narrator frequently
reminds us, that is common to humans. On the last
page, in the final apocalyptic frame, he maintains that
we have all been sitting in a theater, watching the

screen, and something has just happened to the movie: "The screen is a dim page spread before us, white and silent. The film has broken, or a projector bulb has burned out. It was difficult even for us, old fans who've always been at the movies (haven't we?) to tell which before the darkness swept in" (760). Because we are limited creatures, bound by time, our lives artificially framed by double integrals as we arc between birth and death, we only believe that we see existence as continuity when we usually see the frames, the temporal flickers on the screen. Our limitations are the source of "Their" control, so that we "are trapped inside Their frame . . . ass hanging out all over Their Movieola viewer, waiting for Their editorial blade" (694).

The illusion is understandable, for if lives are wavelengths, themselves over and over again rapidly, and if each of us observes them from the fixed points of his perception past which the waves oscillate, then the frames seem to encompass all that is real. Since cause and effect have been discredited, we must settle for regularity of sequence as evidence of continuity. Our "mania for subdividing" (448), for slicing up "the Creation finer and finer, analyzing, setting namer more hopelessly apart from named" (391) is responsible. In the language of *The Crying of Lot 49,* we have disinherited ourselves from the fullness which should be ours by our fetish for analysis; we split reality into mathematics, molecules, and words, endlessly to recombine and eventually to misunderstand them. During his exile Tchitcherine is assigned to a political task force with the job of imposing a New Turkic Alphabet on the Kirghiz of Central Asia, but battles break out between the Arabists and Cyrillicists as they dispute vowels and consonants. Words and letters, says the narrator, are molecules which "can be modulated, broken, recoupled, redefined, co-polymerized one to the other in worldwide chains" (355); they are as ambivalent as chemical compounds, depending on how they are used. On the one hand, words illuminate and liberate; on the other, they obscure and restrict. So long as we continue to rationalize, to specialize, and to subdivide, we will find it difficult to see continuity.

227

Humans can hardly do otherwise, of course, and the conpulsiveness to analyze and divide contributes to man's tragic condition. The more we learn, the more we invent, the narrower the focus of the reels of our consciousness. At one point, Tyrone Slothrop protests Gerhardt von Göll's cavalier behavior by observing that they aren't in the movies, to which the director-entrepreneur replies:

> "Not yet. Maybe not quite yet. You'd better enjoy it while you can. Someday, when the film is fast enough, the equipment pocket-size and burdenless and selling at people's prices, the lights and booms no longer necessary, *then* . . . then . . ." (527).

Irreversibly developing technology will continue to alter our ways of perceiving.

For all of Pynchon's talk of edges and interfaces, the world he predicates is seamless and holistic. It is the four-dimensional universe of Albert Einstein, in which the configurations of matter cause the space-time continuum to curve back upon itself. In a sequence concerning the Rocket-City, Pynchon even invokes the elevator in the immeasurably high building that serves Einstein as metaphor in the formulation of the General Theory of Relativity, which deals with accelerated systems and revises Newton's notions of gravitation. Gravity itself is one of Pynchon's principal metaphors in *Gravity's Rainbow,* as the title indicates. The medium Nora Dodson-Truck eventually claims that her identity is the Force of Gravity and associates it with historical process, the layering of matter and time:

> "I am Gravity, I am That against which the Rocket must struggle, to which the prehistoric wastes submit and are transmuted to the very substance of History . . ." (639).

Perhaps more importantly, Pynchon's is also the universe of Alfred North Whitehead, who asserts in *Process and Reality* that everything in the world is related to everything else—to the extent that even inanimate things are "aware" of other things. From White-head Pynchon also borrows a metaphor: "sentient" rocks. Frau Gnahb, a salty, maniacal Tugboat Annie-type whose ship carries Slothrop and von Göll north to Peenemünde, possesses a unique ability, her son Otto tells Tyrone: 'She knows by instinct—*exactly how* to insult *anybody*. Doesn't matter, animal, vegetable—I even saw her insult a *rock* once" (496). *Gravity's Rainbow* concludes with an affirmation of a "Soul in ev'ry stone . . ." (760). Being "sentient," rocks per-ceive reality much as humans do, as film frames, but in slowed time. When Squalidozzi and his Argentine U-boat cohorts begin filming *Martin Fierro* under the direction of von Göll, one of the crew, Felipe, worships a rock:

> But Felipe's rock enbodies also an intellectual system, for he believes (as do M. F. Beal and others) in a form of mineral consciousness not too much different from that of plants and animals, except for the time scale. Rock's time scale is a lot more stretched out. "We're talking frames per century," Felipe like every-body else here lately has been using a bit of movie lan-guage, "per millennium!" Colossal. But Felipe has come to see, as those who are not Sentient Rocksters seldom do, that history as it's been laid on the world is only a fraction, an outward-and-visible fraction. . . . (612-613).[5]

Lyle Bland, the front man for I. G. Farben in America, who oversaw Jamf's experiment on the infant Tyrone, after a life of service to the Firm at last dis-covers that "Earth is a living critter, after all these years of thinking about a big dumb rock" (590). Bland becomes a mystic, "to find that Gravity, taken so for granted, is really something eerie, Messianic, extrasen-sory in Earth's mindbody . . . having hugged to its holy center the wastes of dead species, gathered, packed, transmuted, realigned, and rewoven molecules . . ." (590). Gravity has two aspects. First, it is the force which bonds the earth itself, compacting the wastes of life into the organic rings which living things use again in ceaseless cycle. Second, it is, as Einstein expressed it in the Principle of Equivalence of Gravitation and Inertia, one of the properties of the space-time continuum, a way of describing the geometry of the universe. Put simply, gravitation is a form of inertia. When the Rocket rises, it is predestined to fall, since its own inertia will betray its flight; its death is but the end-product of its birth, and its life is but a continuum in space-time. In its cyclicality, the Rocket and its parabola symbolize the cyclicality of existence as Pynchon sees it. If the Rocket represents man's aspirations and his limitations, it also represents the continuum which is the fabric of the world itself.

That this fabric is all of a piece Pynchon announces in numerous ways, and characters are given an awareness bordering on the mystical. Like Whitehead, these characters reject dualisms like cause and effect, substance and quality, life and matter, thing and environment, mind and body. Such dualities, according to Whitehead, are only abstractions, the result of science's "bifurcating" the universe. Roger Mexico is one of those characters, of course; his understanding makes possible his relationship with Jessica Swanlake. Of all those who achieve understanding, Mexico is the most important, because while dualism encourages confusion on many levels, its worst effect is to separate humans from each other. Thomas Gwendhidwy, whose sympathetic nature is emphasized by the bugs—"agents of unification" (173) burrowing through interfaces—that eat his lunch, tries to tell Dr. Pointsman that men are joined by common humanity, flung outward in diaspora: "What if we're all Jews, you see? All scattered like seeds? Still flying outward from the primal fist so long ago?" (170).

Another of Pointsman's associates, Kevin Spectro, asks the Pavlovian, "When you've looked at how it really is, . . . how can we, any of us, be separate?" (142). That perception notwithstanding, humans *are* separate, only rarely capable of love and a sense of community, not so very different from the isolates in the Inamorati Anonymous of *The Crying of Lot 49*. The narrator of *Gravity's Rainbow* explains this human

230

condition in terms of his favorite metaphor on the occasion of Katje's meeting with Enzian; the worst of it is that "*we will never know each other.* . . . We're strangers at the films, condemned to separate rows, aisles, exits, homecomings" (663). The isolation is enough to make the narrator deplore the Vacuum which cuts us off from one another and wish for an Aether to "bring us back a continuity, show us a kinder universe, more easygoing . . ." (726).

Mexico can accept Whitehead's injunction to embrace a cold and analytical science and in so doing warm it with humanism, but most characters in *Gravity's Rainbow* lack his courage and comprehension and can not manage the love he offers Jessica. Prisoners of a decadent romantic sensibility which postulates rigid parameters for the self, emphasizes distinctions between "Outside and Inside" the consciousness (141), and at the same time exalts the state of being "helplessly in a condition of love" (97), they tear and scratch at the self-erected barriers between themselves —which is not to say that those interfaces are any the less impervious for being artificial, since they are built from materials wrested from the chaos around them for the purpose of establishing identity. If "film and calculus" are "both pornographies of flight" (567) where the Rocket is concerned, many of Pynchon's characters employ methods more traditionally pornographic in an attempt to love, to achieve continuity, to break through selves in bizarre or even distasteful sexual relationships.

The most repulsive scenes in the book depict the coprophilic acts of Brigadier Pudding, who plays Severin to Katje Borgesius's Venus in Furs[6] in penance for having sacrificed seventy percent of the soldiers under his command in the Battle of Ypres in World War I. In this relationship Katje is the sadist; previously she has been a masochist in a reversed relationship with Blicero, who observes that

Her masochism . . . is reassurance for her. That she can still be hurt, that she is human and can cry at pain. Because, often, she will forget. . . . So, she needs the whip. She raises her ass not in surrender, but in despair. . . . But of true submission, of letting go the self and passing into the All, there is nothing, not with Katje. She is not the victim I would have chosen to end this with. Perhaps, before the end, there will be another. Perhaps I dream. . . . I am not here, am I, to devote myself to *her* fantasies! (662).

Because Katje can not shed her self, she will live in place of the victim Blicero does find, Gottfried, who surrenders totally. Gottfried and Blicero achieve the love-death Pynchon identified in *V.* as the Tristan and Isolde theme of our culture. Paradoxically, Katje's inability to pass into the All, even to the extent of dying in love, will condemn her to isolation and separateness. Pain establishes the authenticity of her self; pain and her fantasies are all that she has. For some, like Margherita Erdmann, these things are sufficient. She fantasizes continually, wild sexual images from the films in which once she starred, all of them of a sado-masochistic nature. Margherita needs pain to live and induces even the mild Slothrop to beat her. But she also needs to inflict pain, to establish her dominance over others. The impulses tug in opposite directions; one points toward the pain she must have to validate her own identity, her separateness, the other toward annihilation. With few exceptions, the sado-masochistic relationships are homosexual, reminiscent of the narcissism Pynchon attributed to V. When Blicero tortures Gottfried, he also destroys himself in mirror-image. When Margherita torments (and perhaps kills) Bianca, her film-child, almost a literal image, she moves that much closer to death herself.

The desire for annihilation is a desire for freedom. Sexual perversions are a reaction against the belief that life is determined, beyond man's control; implicit in the acts is a recognition of the limitations of the romantic self in society. To participate in perverse sexual behavior is to join others in a mutual complicity in transgression in order to liberate one's self—if only by obliterating it. By fitting one's self into stereotyped roles of master and slave, of victimizer and victim, characters like Margherita and her husband Thanatz achieve the anonymity of those types; their simultaneous ability masochistically to accept pain or to inflict it sadistically attests to their interchangeability with one another. For this reason, as we have noted before, it is pointless to accuse Pynchon of not investing his characters with personality; most of them continually attempt to cast off their selves and rid themselves of the burden of their personalities. In trying to transcend the limitations of the self, they become abstractions.

Paradox governs the behavior of such characters. They debase themselves in order to exalt themselves; they aim for extinction *and* fulfillment. For Thanatz, the trick is to *affirm* sado-masochism, to explore its potential for joy. Thanatz is the Zone's chief proponent of "Sado-anarchism." According to him, humans learn submission from their mothers, and as a result also acquire the lust for dominance, which is but the other side of the coin. Incidentally, in *Gravity's Rainbow* mothers are "Their" agents, part of the "Mother Conspiracy" (505), a cabal which encourages guilt in human offspring. Without the guilt, Thanatz decides, sado-masochism is a viable approach to life. Thanatz tells Ludwig the lemming-chaser that "a little S and M never hurt anybody," and besides, it is a way of undermining "Their" control; his bizarre theory of sexual politics one-ups Lenin:

"But why are we taught to feel reflexive shame whenever the subject comes up? Why will the Structure allow every other kind of sexual behavior but *that* one? Because submission and dominance are resources it needs for its very survival. They cannot be wasted in private sex. In *any* kind of sex. It needs our submission so that it may remain in power. It needs our lusts after dominance so that it can co-opt us into its own power game. There is no joy in it, only power. I tell you, if S and M could be established universally, at the family level, the State would wither away" (737).

Mad as the idea appears, Thanatz has something. Sado-masochism can make inroads against control, because it establishes a community of pain and allows participants to share fantasies. No longer "strangers at the films," they are part of the film—the same film, the same fantasies. Sado-masochists stand midway between the behaviorist Dr. Pointsman, who can see only the "outside" of the human consciousness, and the mystic Mondaugen, who sees opposites as necessary to one another; theirs is a philosophical approach to life which makes use of the most powerful force within humans—their sexuality, which is to say their affinity for one another. Or, to couch their vision in other terms, their total servitude and total dominance are religious acts, sacred rites; each perversion is a test of faith. Moreover, sado-masochism permits them to inhabit an erotic universe of understandable proportions: a total, connected world. Pirate Prentice, for example, can get "inside the fantasies of others: being able, actually, to take over the burden of *managing* them" (12), a talent which at first The Firm exploits, but which eventually makes it possible for him to join The Counterforce. In a surrealistic sequence Prentice and Katje exchange fantasies until they blur into a common, anonymous, bisexual lust aimed at sexual congress with every human in the world. Theirs is a dream of Whiteheadian-scaled sex:

> All these [fantasies] and many more pass for our young couple here, enough to make them understand that horny Anonymous's intentions are nothing less than a megalomaniac master plan of sexual love with every individual one of the People in the *World*—and that when every one, somewhat miraculously, is accounted for at last, *that* will be a rough definition of "loving the People" (547).

In short, the sado-masochist, like the paranoid, seeks coherence, continuity, and community.

Given a world in which cause and effect can not be said to operate, in which randomness and surprise—expressed throughout the novel as Gödel's Theorem and Murphy's Law—are inherent, is there a philosophical justification for believing that humans are "all one"? How are they connected? It is one thing to re-

234

treat into mysticism, as some of the characters do, and quite another to explore continuity and congruence in rational terms. Fortunately, balancing what might otherwise become a mushy sort of mysticism in *Gravity's Rainbow* is a novel theory of psychology, although one must pay close attention to Pynchon's seemingly casual references to it.

Human fantasies—even mindless pleasures—are composed of common elements: archetypes. Archetypes recur over and over again for everybody, and the narrator worries about the coincidences which on the one hand attest to a common consciousness among humans and on the other seem too pat to be trusted. He speculates:

It was nice of Jung to give us the idea of an ancestral pool in which everybody shares the same dream material. But how is it we are each visited as individuals, each by exactly and only what he needs? Doesn't that imply a switching path of some kind? a bureaucracy? (410).

To the paranoid, there is always that possibility, but the answer to the question is—not necessarily. Other things, like narcotics, can encourage the appearance of archetypes. For example, Oneirine, in addition to its property of "time-modulation" (389), which slows the flickering frames of consciousness to an apprehensible speed, also produces "mantic archetypes" (702); the hallucinations that derive from the drug may thus be accurate visions of reality. Narcotics were invented to relieve suffering, Wimpe the drug salesman explains to Tchitcherine, and the idea has been to "find something that can kill pain without causing addiction." The problem is that chemical drugs grip humans in much the same way that sado-masochistic urges do, and the dilemma may be explained by another analogy also. According to Wimpe:

Results have not been encouraging. . . . There is nearly complete parallelism between analgesia and addiction. The more pain it takes away, the more we desire it. It appears we can't have one property without the other, any more than a particle physicist can specify position without suffering an uncertainty as to the particle's velocity (348).

Once again Pynchon returns to the central paradox of modern micro-physics. When a physicist knows the velocity of an electron, he cannot know its location or position; when he knows the electron's position, he cannot know its velocity, because the electron seems to be both particle and wave. The phenomenon has been explained by Niels Bohr and Werner Heisenberg in the Principle of Complementarity, which holds that both aspects are accurate. Heisenberg has put the Principle in language that Pynchon can appreciate:

> The concept of complementarity is meant to describe a situation in which we can look at one and the same event through two different frames of reference. These two frames mutually exclude each other, but they also complement each other, and only the juxtaposition of these contradictory frames provides an exhaustive view of the appearance of the phenomena.[7]

The psychologist Carl Jung and the physicist Wolfgang Pauli some years ago attempted to formulate a corresponding theory to explain the recurrence of phenomena like archetypes in the human consciousness. That is, how can so general a symbol become so particular an event for the individual, the problem which disturbs the narrator of *Gravity's Rainbow*. To their theory Jung and Pauli gave the name "Synchronicity." In his application of micro-physics to psychology Jung defined synchronicity as "the simultaneous occurrence of two meaningfully but not causally related events" and also as "a coincidence in time of two or more casually unrelated events which have the same or similar meaning . . . equal in rank to causality as a principle of explanation."[8]

As Arthur Koestler points out, Jung leaned heavily on another theorist, the biologist Paul Kammerer, who explained coincidence and recurrence by an acausal principle he called seriality which tended toward unity. Koestler discusses Kammerer's "seriality" in terms particularly germane to *Gravity's Rainbow:*

> In some respects it is comparable to universal gravity —which, to the physicist, is also still a mystery; but unlike gravity which acts on all *mass* indiscriminately, this force acts selectively on *form* and *function* to bring similar configurations together in space and time; it correlates by *affinity*. . . .
>
> Kammerer was particularly interested in temporal Series of recurrent events; these he regarded as cyclic processes which propagate themselves like waves along the time-axis of the time-space continuum. But we are aware only of the crests of the waves, which appear to us as isolated coincidences, while the troughs remain unnoticed.[9]

The language and the conceptions are also those of Pynchon in *Gravity's Rainbow,* and they help to explain how he could have originally titled his work *Mindless Pleasures,* for the fantasies—and the consciousnesses—of humans are linked by a process similar to gravity itself. That linkage is our legacy, just as the wastes of life compacted by gravity are our heritage as well. The ideas of Kammerer and Jung help to explain Tyrone Slothrop's peculiar gift too; Jung's synchronicity specifically allows for precognition.[10]

Slothrop of course does not have the resources of his creator. His alternatives are a world of chance or a world of paranoia. Unlike his hero, the comic book character Plasticman, who can flow and slip through the grids of forces that Slothrop can hardly perceive, Tyrone is lost, an Orpheus similar to Rilke's in the twenty-sixth *Sonnet,* who must

> Cry chance. Into interstices/of this world-space, (into which the unbroken/bird-cry passes, as people do into dreams—) they/drive their wedges, wedges of shrieking.[11]

Slothrop has not even the consolation of knowing that his dreams—and his cries—are shared by others.

Paranoia, the belief that all things are connected, is "a Puritan reflex" (188), the successor to Weberian rationalization in our century.[12] It is the perception of "Kute Korrespondences" (590), like those which structure *Gravity's Rainbow,* synchronous events acausally connected. It is a design which defends us against chaos. Call it by whatever name, without that perception we have no existence; we dissolve, like Slothrop. That, finally, is what Preterition means: to be powerless, to have no rational scheme by which to appraise the universe. Better to be paranoids than what Weber called "specialists without spirit, sensualists without heart."[13] And if in our paranoia we fear control, suspect that our lives are determined, our fears and suspicions are also the source of our freedom. Besides, as Murphy's Law reminds us, there is always surprise. To recognize the possibilities of control is to open the way to escape, particularly since those who would control are hampered by their faith in cause and effect and cannot accept surprise.

If "They" would destroy and dehumanize others with the Rocket, we must remember that those others created it for the same reason that they love. For those others, the disinherited, it is the Angel of the Morning, the Wishing-Star. It is difficult to overstate the ambivalence of technology as Pynchon assesses it in *Gravity's Rainbow*: It represents the worst and the best in man, his limitations and his potential for perfection, entropy and entelechy. Pynchon is cautious. While he specifically attacks thinkers like B. F. Skinner who advocate using technology to control man, at the other extreme he gets in some licks against optimistic technologists like Teilhard de Chardin (539). Where de Chardin would say, "Everything that rises must converge,"[14] Pynchon would say not so—or not yet. We still belong to Earth, and to her Gravity.

CONCLUSION:

Garbage Dumps and Genius

To date, *Gravity's Rainbow* is Pynchon's principal hostage to Fortune. It is a perplexing work, not least because of its mixture of profundity and levity—and the hostile critic would add silliness to the brew. A reader at one moment convinced that he has encountered a masterpiece will at the next stumble over what looks like a cheap joke. A Goethe in greasepaint, Pynchon at times seems determined to sabotage what otherwise would be cosmic laughter with a snigger. Even as the parabola of the V-2 arcs glitteringly over the novel's characters, another image, almost as prevalent, squats prosaically at various junctures of their lives. Dr. Pointsman gets his foot stuck in one toilet bowl, Slothrop swims down a second, a bomb explodes in a third, and so on, until the device has been exaggerated into a whole Toiletship, a marvel of German specialization. Within the context of the novel, the toilet *belongs,* as a counterpart to the Rocket and its heavenly flight. Like the Rocket, the toilet is a thing that dominates human life; if we wish to embrace sacred things, we must also accept the profane. The toilet is associated with the underworld, with the wastes that layer the earth, with our deepest sexual and racial fears. Besides, it is funny, for we also laugh at toilets, probably as a defense against our fears, and Pynchon is certainly not above latrine humor. But while these associations are valid and obvious and the humor genuine, it is also true that Pynchon pushes whimsy to improbable limits, a habit that can disturb. Confronting a similar habit in another masterly work, Leslie Fiedler asserts that James Joyce's *Ulysses* "straddles and crosses a border which maybe never existed at all . . . the line between belles lettres and schlock."[1] Writers like Joyce and Pynchon force reconsideration of criteria; both take risks in the interest of their art.

Some critics have reproached Pynchon for cavalierly manipulating images, motifs, and themes in order to establish whimsical connections. The complaint has some justification in the case of *V.* There the crush of metaphors and the proliferation of allusions ensure superficial coherence while failing to guarantee real unity. Leaving aside the meticulous craftsmanship Pynchon has demonstrated since his first novel, it surely can be argued that the overburdened architecture of *V.* provokes an intended humor, if only because it implies that the narrator is as mad as Herbert Stencil and that Pynchon is parodying his own artistry. In this light, design complements theme; the amusing recurrence of figures and events becomes picture and frame. In the brilliantly conceived, consummately executed *The Crying of Lot 49,* it is hardly possible to imagine a more convincing amalgam of form and content. The same holds true of *Gravity's Rainbow.* Even when Pynchon appears to falter toward the end of his immense narrative, he is suiting form to theory: When Slothrop slips into "anti-paranoia," the narrative itself begins to dissolve. It is a calculated risk.

At the same time, the risks Pynchon takes can be overstated. In spite of his continual innovations, he is a remarkably conventional writer, as evidenced by his preference for the omniscient narrator, the skillfully orchestrated leitmotif, the archetype, the picaresque plot, and the epic sweep of narrative. Beyond the techniques of the traditionalist, however, are cultural interests which inform Pynchon's wholly modern awareness.

The effect of his work is to achieve continuity with the past, to advance the old until it explicates the new, to add another layer to historical understanding. Pop cultural on the one hand, academic on the other, the scope of his literature is matched in this century only by Joyce's.

Like Oedipa Maas of *The Crying of Lot 49*, Pynchon has an enormous respect for the Word, and like Enzian of *Gravity's Rainbow*, he seems to believe that "somewhere, among the wastes of the World, is the key that will bring us back, restore us to our Earth and to our freedom" (525). Pynchon has identified the search for the Word as a Puritan impulse similar to that which causes men to create designs and build labyrinths across the face of Nothing, for while Nature may not abhor a vacuum, Puritans do. According to George Santayana, the Puritan is "an idealist working in matter.'" Pynchon is an idealist working in language, or, to use a metaphor from *The Crying of Lot 49*, he is a spinner of tapestries for the void outside his tower. Writing for Pynchon is analogous to the human propensity for weaving tapestries and fabricating design.

Unique as his patterns are, Pynchon is not without rivals in his methods. John Barth has explored a trend in modern letters he calls "the Literature of Exhaustion," a term by which he does not mean decadence of the type employed by the phony artists in the Whole Sick Crew of *V.* Barth has in mind fiction based on the writer's resolve to leave no stone unturned to uncover meaning. One aspect involves the use of techniques from other media like films to refurbish literary modes which no longer compel, something Pynchon does in *Gravity's Rainbow*. Because such techniques have limited applicability to fiction, however, what the literature of exhaustion means in practice is the thorough exploration of older literary conventions, even to the point of parodying them. In manner, it is a deliberate repetition, a form of annotation, in spirit not so much like Eliot's generally serious footnotes to *The Waste Land* as like Pynchon's mocking, ostentatious revival of archetypes which overlap and blur into humor. Having decided that the chances for novelty are

241

slim, such a writer achieves originality through playful combinations of the old. As Barth construes it, the literature of exhaustion thus represents a highly intellectualized maze-making, the more arcane the better, for the purpose of exhausting possibilities for meaning. Barth singles out Jorge Luis Borges, the librarian-author, who devises intricate fictional labyrinths out of the storehouse of accumulated cultural and historical artifacts. In *Gravity's Rainbow* Pynchon mentions Borges as a builder of labyrinths and implies that his constructions are Calvinist in origin. Pynchon's own fictions, of course, are highly wrought labyrinths, networks, and conspiracies, built to be exhaustive, and laid out to exhaust the abilities of those characters trapped in them. They are fictions of encyclopedic metaphor.

The concept of exhaustion is helpful in understanding Pynchon because it explains his fondness for working variations on traditional and pop cultural themes, for activating allusions, and for concocting designs of immense complexity out of materials so extensive that they include trash. Thomas Mann somewhere remarked that only the exhaustive is the truly interesting; Pynchon would certainly subscribe to that precept, and for him the approach is even more central. Pynchon attempts to exhaust precisely to demonstrate that possibilities have not been exhausted and that the Word is still viable because it has not yet been revealed. In being exhaustive, Pynchon takes his materials where he finds them, in hallowed tradition or crassest schlock—which is what all humans do. Human consciousness, the perception of reality, is formed by accretion; it is the product of accumulated layers of human history given shape by the inroads of the present. Depending on how we look at Pynchon then, he is either a Schliemann unearthing ancient Troys, or a rag-picker on top of Bolingbroke's city dump, raking through the debris of past and present. Doubtless Pynchon would prefer the second view.

Humans create designs because they can not tolerate voids. Once they have constructed labyrinths, however, they become lost in them. The process is as paradoxical

242

as Max Weber envisaged it. If fear and confusion are the mothers of invention, they are also invention's progeny. The more intricately we build our structures of meaning, the more apt we are to lose our way in them. The intricacy has been magnified in our time by science and technology. Scientific advances and technological invention have transformed mazes into networks and grids, between whose interstices humans crouch in bewilderment. In addition, the complexities of science and technology have hastened destruction of the earth, adding more debris to that cast off by earlier designs and systems. Worse, the new developments have stimulated a false nostalgia for the past by exacerbating a perverse desire in some men to return to the void. The desire can take several forms. It can be outright death-wish such as that which seizes the Empty Ones among the Hereros, who wish to lose themselves in Nothing as a protest against the systems that have enslaved them. In characters like V. and Blicero, the desire is strong enough to be called sexual, especially if sex be regarded as an attempt to escape the parameters of the self—that self which is the seat of the rationalization by which we create designs and of the responsibility through which we must undertake to understand them. At a less dangerous extreme is the longing for anarchic purity and innocence which affects Squalidozzi, Tyrone Slothrop, and Dennis Flange, who want somehow to recapture the virgin void, before design was laid upon it, to start all over again, fresh and unfettered. The first two forms lead to death, inanimation, and inhumanity to others. The third is scarcely more productive. Either one sells out, like Squalidozzi, is cut to pieces by power grids, like Slothrop, or dreams that he is trapped on top of a garbage heap rising like an elevator to apocalypse, like Flange. The search for the key among the wastes is urgent, lest we too become waste.

This sense of crisis has resulted in Pynchon's work being called apocalyptic by several critics, most notably R. W. B. Lewis, who places it in a distinctly American chiliastic tradition rooted in Calvinism and manifested in prophecies of world's end in bang or whimper.[4] The apocalyptic strain is distinct and prominent from Pynchon's first short story to his latest novel, but between them the sense of crisis has been muted. Although *Gravity's Rainbow* ends with the Rocket poised over the planet, it is the Rocket's parabola which receives the most attention. The parabola seems to be Pynchon's mature symbol, displacing the earlier images of inevitable destruction. If one insists on a precedent in American literature, Hart Crane's Bridge will serve nicely: It foretells hope as well as doom. As far as Pynchon is concerned, the hope is slight but still significant. The Word is out there somewhere, under the trash or around the next turning in the labyrinth or up in the sky.

While all humans create their own patterns of meaning, the ones which trouble us most are those of collective construction, those labyrinths, networks, and grids which permit so little freedom for the individual. As have all major authors of our time, Pynchon addresses himself to the question of man's place in a mass society. Few understand the question better. Dogging most men today is a sense of powerlessness aggravated by the rapid growth of systems. They suspect that they have been conditioned, that they possess no autonomy over their lives, that unseen and incomprehensible forces control their actions and perhaps penetrate their thoughts. Worse, as Benjamin DeMott has said, modern men suffer from the belief "that events and individuals are unreal, and that power to alter the course of the age, of my life and your life, is actually vested nowhere."[5] That is the meaning of what Pynchon calls Preterition, the lack of means to change the status quo.

The inability to discover the locus of power is the starting point for Oedipa Maas's quest in *The Crying of Lot 49*. Besides her initial confusion, her paranoia at the end of the novel, if paranoia it is, is decidedly preferable. As Pynchon uses the concept, paranoia is a sort of holding action for the self, a means by which the individual traces the paths of force in the grids and systems that surround him. Implicit in paranoia is the constant possibility that the paranoiac may be wrong, that the conspiracy he perceives may not exist or that it may have an entirely different shape, but without it he may become a Slothrop, his self helpless in the present. Paranoia is a way of structuring, or restructuring, the world along comprehensible lines, and if it does not reveal the Word, it may suffice until the Word does manifest itself. In the modern world, Pynchon's universe, paranoia is rightful heir to rationalization.

The universe of *Gravity's Rainbow* is the one known, if that is the proper term, to modern science, with galaxies wheeling out to an edge eighteen billion light-years from us, where gravity gives dimension to space and holds us in thrall by reminding us of its power. Blicero feels the power: "gravity rules all the way out to the cold sphere, *there is always the danger of falling*" (723); fright makes the knowledge of unity cold comfort indeed. Even without the reminders of interstellar vastness, however, it is apparent that man's place in the cosmos is quite small. Against his insignificance man can not even advance the certitudes of his own self, for they have been melted away with the deliquescence of his romantic sensibilities. Pynchon shares with other contemporary novelists an assumption that the romantic idea of the self as an independent entity is virtually impossible to sustain, although among Pynchon's most attractive characters are those like V. and Blicero, who do cling to romantic postures and rage against their limitations. Too many factors militate against the self and erode it into anonymity at one extreme and solipsism at the other. Indeed, the pressures and energies of our era make the romantic self painful, so that the most decadent do everything possible to escape it—the gratefully anonymous soldier in von Trotha's army, who tries to penetrate the skin of others and achieve Nothingness, or the dissolving Tyrone Slothrop, for whom the self becomes an "albatross." Only the strong characters, Oedipa Maas for one, know that "the self is only incidental." Nevertheless, once the lineaments of romanticism are stripped away, something of the self remains, enough to make the individual aware of his separateness.

Within that separateness may be nothing, merely void under the skin. Not all Pynchon's characters are as hollow as Cleanth Siegel or Benny Profane, but many come perilously close, and having so little inside, they can scarcely cope with the world outside, not to mention other people. Theirs is the modern human condition. Wylie Sypher asks:

> Is it possible, while the individual is vanishing behind the functionary throughout the technological world, to have any sort of humanism that does not depend upon the older notions of the self, the independent self that is outdated or at least victimized by the operations of power on its present scale? Any such humanism must come to terms with our sense of the anonymity of the self, must therefore get beyond any romantic notion of selfhood.[6]

Pynchon himself would probably say that his intent is to illuminate the condition rather than to found a new humanism, yet it is clear that he is offering some guidelines.

The foremost is that individuals should not exclude middles, should try instead to occupy the domain of Oedipa Maas and Roger Mexico, the realm between one and zero: between absolute freedom and total control, between the void and the labyrinth, between anonymity and solipsism; and once there, "to keep cool but care." The idea is to keep choices open, to be receptive to surprise, to grasp what limited freedom is available to us, and to be as vulnerable to others as we dare. The science which afflicts us with our own sense of insignificance can also teach us to live in the world it has redefined—and his ability to explicate scientific metaphors in humanistic terms marks Pynchon's greatest innovation in modern letters—by reminding us of the possibilities of freedom and insisting that we affirm the paradoxes of existence. Just as a phenomenon can be both particle *and* wave, so can we be individual and group, and to the extent that uncertainty undermines determinism, so can we be free. Unless we are content always to remain adversaries of the systems which our ingenuity has devised, we must make a place in our humanism for science and its technological offspring.

Until we realize that the systems are interconnected—and we have the scientific model of an interconnected universe to help us—and that our selves, whatever they are, are part now of those systems, we will never achieve control over them. If we do not launch a Counterforce, "They" will keep that control. Naturally Pynchon does not use my tone. Even supposing him to don professorial robes for a few minutes, his elbow would be out and into the reader's ribs inside of three sentences. But he would agree that any such humanism is hard work and that it must be earned. If that last recommendation is not new, no one would gainsay its truth. In the meantime, until we all manage that new humanism, we should do as the narrator of *Gravity's Rainbow* suggests, and "get the Texts straight" (729).

Calibrated on scales large or small, Pynchon's texts are superlative. That he can construct a beautiful 760-page epic like *Gravity's Rainbow* is remarkable; that he can lavish a lapidary skill on each page is stunning. Having begun a sentence of great fragility, Pynchon will cheerfully clamber out upon it to hammer in the last word, and allow the reader to see him do it. It is an astonishing talent of powerful range, best demonstrated in *The Crying of Lot 49*. There he shifts from vulgar American to blank verse, from the raucous to the elegiac, from the breezy to the precise; it is language styled by a master.

That Pynchon is a genius goes without saying. Although I am wary of overpraising a writer who has a long career yet before him, in the magnitude of his themes, the breadth of his learning, and the facility of his prose, he is I think the peer of any novelist writing today. That judgment is perhaps too hyperbolic and too dependent on my own taste. Besides, his international scope notwithstanding, his Puritan instincts are wholly American, and I am on safer ground when it comes to American literature, where it seems to me that Pynchon has no equal. Barth and Vonnegut come readily to mind as possible comparisons, but Barth himself has said that he and Pynchon are not doing the same things.[7] Moreover, Barth has not Pynchon's stature, and Vonnegut, for all his interest in technology, is comparatively a lightweight. If Pynchon must be judged against others, Norman Mailer, since he claims the distinction of being America's champ, is the obvious candidate. Mailer is a worthy contender, although to judge by his latest efforts, he has passed his peak. One of Mailer's amusements is to invite competitive writers to "get into the ring" with him. Were Pynchon interested enough, the referee would find a favorite phrase of the narrator of *Gravity's Rainbow* useful: Pynchon would "hand his ass to" Mailer, and to anybody else too.

NOTES

PREFACE

[1] According to Roger B. Henkle, "Pynchon's Tapestries on the Western Wall," *Modern Fiction Studies*, 17 (1971), 208 n. 2.

[2] Pynchon's book jacket blurb for Fariña's novel; see *Been Down so Long It Looks Like Up to Me* (New York: Dell, 1970).

[3] Peter Kihss, "Pulitzer Jurors Dismayed on Pynchon," *The New York Times* (8 May, 1974), p. 38.

CHAPTER ONE:
ENTROPY AND OTHER CALAMITIES

[1] Joseph Conrad, *Heart of Darkness and the Secret Sharer* (New York: Signet, 1962), p. 143.

[3] Ibid., p. 133.

[2] Bruce Jay Friedman, Foreword to *Black Humor*, ed. Bruce Jay Friedman (New York: Bantam, 1965), p. x.

[4] Richard Poirier, *The Performing Self* (New York: Oxford University Press, 1971), p. 24.

[5] Burton Feldman, "Anatomy of Black Humor," *The American Novel Since World War II*, ed. Marcus Klein (Greenwich, Conn.: Fawcett, 1969), p. 227.

[6] Sir William Dampier, *A History of Science* (Cambridge, England: Cambridge University Press, 1961), pp. 299-300.

CHAPTER TWO:
THE TRACK OF THE ENERGY

[1]Thomas Pynchon, *V.* (New York: Bantam Books, 1968). All textual references are to this edition.

[2]Henry Adams, *The Education of Henry Adams* (Boston: Houghton Mifflin, 1961). Because we will refer to this edition several times, textual notes are given for it also.

[3]Edward Mendelson, "The Sacred, the Profane, and *The Crying of Lot 49*," unpublished essay to appear soon in a *Festschrift* for Charles R. Anderson (Duke University Press).

[4]John A. Meixner, "The All-Purpose Quest," *Kenyon Review*, 25 (Autumn 1963), 731.

[5]See Roger B. Henkle, "Pynchon's Tapestries on the Western Wall," *Modern Fiction Studies*, 17 (1971), 207-220, for an extended comparison of Graves and Pynchon. According to Henkle, *V.* "is, as Graves' Goddess becomes, a symbol of the European humanist tradition."

[6]Robert Graves, *The White Goddess* (New York: Noonday Press, 1969), p. 395.

[7]Lionel Rubinoff, *The Pornography of Power* (New York: Ballantine Books, 1968), pp. 167-168.

[8]Ibid., p. 170.

[9]One who does see the theme as all-pervasive is Joseph Campbell. See *The Masks of God: Creative Mythology* (New York: Viking, 1968).

[10]Stanley Edgar Hyman, "The Goddess and the Schlemihl," *On Contemporary Literature*, ed. Richard Kostelanetz (New York: Avon, 1964), p. 510. The phrase, of course, is William Butler Yeats's.

[11]Wylie Sypher, *Loss of the Self in Modern Literature and Art* (New York: Vintage, 1962), pp. 75-76.

[12]Most of the events in this episode are based on fact. The airplane bombardment, for instance, actually took place. See Faye Carroll, *South West Africa and the United Nations* (Lexington, Kentucky: University of Kentucky Press, 1967), pp. 31-32.

[13]Robert E. Golden, "Mass Man and Modernism: Violence in Pynchon's *V.*," *Critique*, 14 (1972), 14.

CHAPTER THREE:
THE STREET OF THE 20TH CENTURY

[1]According to Roger B. Henkle, "Pynchon's Tapestries on the Western Wall," *Modern Fiction Studies,* 17 (1971), 208N.

[2]R. W. B. Lewis, *Trials of the Word* (New Haven: Yale University Press, 1965), p. 204.

[3]The word Mixolydian Pynchon may have lifted from James Joyce, who uses it in *Ulysses.* It is the name of a Greek musical mode and is associated with the Renaissance conception of the "Music of the Spheres." Perhaps the name suggests the kind of thinking that leads Pynchon to call a musician McClintic Sphere.

[4]Probably Mafia is intended as broad parody of Ayn Rand.

[5]According to Stanley Edgar Hyman, Sphere is modelled on Ornette Coleman. See "The Goddess and the Schlemihl," *On Contemporary Literature,* ed. Richard Kostelanetz (New York: Avon, 1964), p. 509.

[6]Quoted by H. G. Schenk, *The Mind of the European Romantics* (Garden City, Doubleday Anchor Books, 1969), p. 94.

[7]César Graña, *Fact and Symbol* (New York: Oxford University Press, 1971), p. ix.

[8]The reader will discover that among the various fetishes covered in Pynchon's novels, the one the narrators seem to prefer is the ass.

[9]This sequence, which begins in a bar with a bartender saying "Time, gentlemen," and ends in the waste land of Central Park with homosexual love being proffered and rejected, seems to be inspired by free association with Section II of *The Waste Land.* The teeth would appear to clinch the association.

CHAPTER FOUR:
EXCLUDED MIDDLES AND BAD SHIT

[1]Alfred Kazin, *Bright Book of Life: American Novelists From Hemingway to Mailer* (Boston: Little, Brown, 1973), p. 277.

[2]Thomas Pynchon, *The Crying of Lot 49* (Toronto:

Bantam Books, 1967). All textual references are to this edition.

[3]Mircea Eliade, *The Sacred and the Profane: The Nature of Religion* (New York: Harper Torchbooks, 1961), p. 202.

[4]Norbert Wiener, *The Human Use of Human Beings: Cybernetics and Society* (New York: Avon Books, 1967), pp. 20-21.

[5]Ervin Laszlo, *The Systems View of the World: The Natural Philosophy of the New Developments in the Sciences* (New York: Braziller, 1972), pp. 105-106.

[6]Victor C. Ferkiss, *Technological Man: The Myth and the Reality* (New York: New American Library, 1969), p. 75.

[7]Sir William Dampier, *A History of Science* (Cambridge, England: Cambridge University Press, 1961), p. 487.

[8]Wiener, p. 31. Wiener also discusses another facet of the theory, probability—"the more probable the message, the less information it gives"—which Pynchon will make use of to bedevil Oedipa's search, but which is not really relevant here. Nevertheless it would be interesting to apply probability theory to some of Oedipa's clues to determine whether Pynchon has actually encoded a message. A starting point might be to analyze the names of Inverarity's holdings in terms of the frequency with which letters occur. Something significant might emerge from such an "ordering" of the estate, and Pynchon is certainly capable of encoding it. (Paranoia grips us all.)

[9]Warren Weaver, "The Mathematics of Communication," *Science and Literature: New Lenses for Criticism,* ed. Edward M. Jennings (Garden City: Doubleday and Co., 1970), pp. 20-21.

[10]Gregory Bateson, "Information and Codification: A Philosophical Approach," in Jurgen Ruesch and Gregory Bateson, *Communication: The Social Matrix of Psychiatry* (New York: Norton, 1968), pp. 176-178.

[11]Joseph Conrad, *Heart of Darkness and The Secret Sharer* (New York: New American Library, 1962), p. 68.

[12]Edward Mendelson, "The Sacred, the Profane, and *The Crying of Lot 49,*" unpublished essay to appear

soon in a *Festschrift* for Charles Anderson. Professor Mendelson develops the religious aspects of the novel in considerably more detail and in different directions than I do here.

[13]Robert Sklar, "The New Novel, USA: Thomas Pynchon," *The Nation,* 205 (September 25, 1967), 278.

CHAPTER FIVE:
LIVING ON THE INTERFACE

[1]Thomas Pynchon, *Gravity's Rainbow* (New York: Viking, 1973). All textual references are to this paperback edition.

[2]W. T. Lhamon, "The Most Irresponsible Bastard," *The New Republic,* 168 (14 April 1973), 27.

[3]Anthony Sampson, *The Sovereign State of ITT* (New York: Stein and Day, 1973), p. 40.

[4]J. B. Leishman and Stephen Spender, trans., *Duino Elegies* (New York: Norton, 1967), pp. 87-88.

[5]Rainer Maria Rilke, *Duino Elegies,* p. 21.

[6]Ibid., p. 31.

[7]Quoted by Leishman and Spender, p. 93.

[8]See *Bullfinch's Mythology* (New York: Crowell, n. d.), p. 333.

CHAPTER SIX:
THE PHYSICS OF HEAVEN

[1]Rainer Maria Rilke to Marie von Thurn und Taxis, September 12, 1912, *The Letters of Rainer Maria Rilke and Princess Marie von Thurn und Taxis,* trans. Nora Wydenbruck (London: Hogarth Press, 1958), p. 77. The reader will remember the important role of the Thurn und Taxis family in *The Crying of Lot 49.*

[2]Andrew Hacker, *The End of the American Era* (New York: Atheneum, 1973), p. 57.

[3]It is possible that Pynchon is playing here with the five-dimensional universe of three spatial and two temporal dimensions postulated by the physicist Adrian Dobbs.

[4]They are omitted in the Bantam paperback edition.

[5]M. F. Beal is a California writer and teacher at whose home Pynchon discussed the material in this

passage. She is married to David Shetzline, who is also mentioned in *Gravity's Rainbow*. The two met Pynchon originally through Richard Fariña. W. T. Lhamon to the author, 27 November 1973.

[6]The allusion of course is to Leopold Sacher-Masoch's *Venus in Furs*.

[7]Werner Heisenberg, quoted in Arthur Koestler, *The Roots of Coincidence* (New York: Vintage, 1973), pp. 54-55. This book, on which I have relied extensively, is of great help in understanding Pynchon.

[8]Carl Jung, quoted by Koestler, pp. 94-95.

[9]Koestler, pp. 86-87.

[10]Koestler, p. 95. See also M. L. von Franz, "Science and the Unconscious," *Man and His Symbols*, ed. Carl G. Jung et al. (New York: Dell, 1968), pp. 377-387; and C. J. Jung, "On Synchronicity," *Man and Time: Papers From the Eranos Yearbooks*, ed. Joseph Campbell (New York: Pantheon, 1957), pp. 201-211.

[11]Rainer Maria Rilke, *Sonnets to Orpheus*, trans. M. D. Herter Norton (New York: Norton, 1942), p. 121.

[12]See Henrdrick Hertzberg and David C. K. McClelland, "Paranoia," *Harper's*, 248 (June 1974), p. 52.

[13]Max Weber, *The Protestant Ethic and the Spirit of Capitalism*, trans. Talcott Parsons (New York: Scribner's, 1958), p. 182.

[14]Teilhard de Chardin, *The Future of Man* (London: Fontana Books, 1964), p. 137.

CONCLUSION:
GARBAGE DUMPS AND GENIUS

[1]Leslie Fiedler, quoted by William Kennedy, "The Quest for Heliotrope," *Atlantic* (May, 1968), p. 58.

[2]George Santayana, *Character and Opinion in the United States; With Reminiscences of William James and Josiah Royce and Academic Life in America* (New York: Scribner's, 1921), p. 175.

[3]John Barth, "The Literature of Exhaustion," *The American Novel Since World War II*, ed. Marcus Klein (Greenwich, Conn.: Fawcett, 1969), pp. 267-279.

[4]R. W. B. Lewis, *Trials of the Word* (New Haven: Yale University Press, 1965).

[5]Benjamin DeMott, quoted by Philip Roth, "Writing American Fiction," *The American Novel Since World War II*, p. 145.

[6]Wylie Sypher, *Loss of the Self in Modern Literature and Art* (New York: Vintage, 1962), p. 14.

[7]John J. Enck, "John Barth: An Interview," *Wisconsin Studies in Contemporary Literature*, 6 (1965), 14.

SELECTED BIBLIOGRAPHY

In the Preface I have suggested several texts as background reading to Pynchon's works. Below are a few sources directly relevant to Pynchon that I think readers will find helpful.

Hausdorff, Don. "Thomas Pynchon's Multiple Absurdities." *Wisconsin Studies in Contemporary Literature,* 7 (1966), 258-269.

Henkle, Roger B. "Pynchon's Tapestries on the Western Wall." *Modern Fiction Studies,* 17 (1971), 207-220.

Lhamon, W. T. "The Most Irresponsible Bastard." *The New Republic,* 168 (14 April 1973), 24-28.

Mendelson, Edward. "Pynchon's Gravity." *The Yale Review,* 62 (Summer 1973), 624-631.

Piorier, Richard. "Rocket Power." *Saturday Review of the Arts,* 1 (March 1973), 59-64.

Sklar, Robert. "The New Novel, USA: Thomas Pynchon." *The Nation,* 205 (25 September 1967), 277-280.

Tanner, Tony. "Caries and Cabals," *City of Words: American Fiction 1950-1970.* New York: Harper & Row, 1971, pp. 153-180.

Weixlmann, Joseph. "Thomas Pynchon: A Bibliography." *Critique,* 14 (1972), 34-43.